Shipping Lords and C

Shipping Lords and Coolie Stokers

Class, Race, and Maritime Capitalism in the Early Twentieth Century

Ravi Ahuja

VERSO
London • New York

First published by Verso 2024

1 3 5 7 9 10 8 6 4 2

Verso
UK: 6 Meard Street, London W1F 0EG
US: 388 Atlantic Avenue, Brooklyn, NY 11217
versobooks.com

Verso is the imprint of New Left Books

ISBN-13: 978-1-80429-351-5
ISBN-13: 978-1-80429-352-2 (UK EBK)
ISBN-13: 978-1-80429-353-9 (US EBK)

British Library Cataloguing in Publication Data
A catalogue record for this book is available from the British Library

Library of Congress Cataloging-in-Publication Data

Names: Ahuja, Ravi, author.
Title: Shipping lords and coolie stokers : class, race, and maritime capitalism in the early twentieth century / Ravi Ahuja.
Description: London ; New York : Verso, 2024. | Includes bibliographical references and index.
Identifiers: LCCN 2024021581 (print) | LCCN 2024021582 (ebook) | ISBN 9781804293515 (trade paperback) | ISBN 9781804293539 (ebook)
Subjects: LCSH: Shipping—History—20th century. | Shipping—Social aspects. | Occupations and race. | Merchant mariners. | Seafaring life.
Classification: LCC HE571 .A37 2024 (print) | LCC HE571 (ebook) | DDC 331.7/61387509041—dc23/eng/20240603
LC record available at https://lccn.loc.gov/2024021581
LC ebook record available at https://lccn.loc.gov/2024021582

Typeset in Minion by Biblichor Ltd, Scotland

Contents

Introduction: 'Lascar' Seamen and 'Racial Management' under Steamship Capitalism 1

1. Collision Course: British Merchant Shipping and the Loss of a Mail Steamer 16
2. Good Copy: The Savagery of Panic-Stricken 'Natives' 28
3. Spelling Disaster: Class and Race When a Ship Goes Down 41
4. Indian Outrage: Who Speaks for the 'Lascar'? 58
5. Lines of Defence: 'Natives, Properly Led' 71
6. Discomforting Testimonies: Eight 'Native Seamen' in Court 90
7. Communication Collapse: The Steamship and 'Naval Hindustani' 105
8. Fireroom Hierarchy: Stoking, Skill, and Status 122
9. Stoker's Stigma: The Two Lives of the 'Hairy Ape' 140
10. Gains of 'Racial Management': Manning Scales and Liner Schedules 159
11. The Break-Up: Findings, Rulings, and the Limits of 'Racial Management' 182
12. Course Adjustment: The Names of the 'Native' 204

Acknowledgements 233
Index 237

Introduction: 'Lascar' Seamen and 'Racial Management' under Steamship Capitalism

'True stories' of shipwrecks were sure to find a ready market in 1930 and Robert L. Hadfield, a prolific commercial writer churning out a diverse range of pulp fiction, was clearly aware of this when he launched, in that year, a popular history of 'maritime disasters' in the first three decades of the twentieth century – a narrative professedly 'drawn from authentic sources'. The book included a brief account of the shipwreck of the Royal Mail Ship *Egypt* in 1922, which Hadfield introduced with the following words:

> An unsatisfactory business, this sinking of the liner *Egypt*. Seamanship was not lacking, nor was vigilance against the enemy fog, but good order and discipline fled in the face of peril. A lascar crew, child-like in its respect for authority well exerted, but also child-like in its incontrollable fears during danger if the guiding hand be absent, failed in its duty and brought death to many of its members and to the passengers in its care.[1]

A 'lascar' was, in the jargon of British imperialism, a South Asian seafarer – an ambiguous term that carried, however, legal meaning as it denoted

1 Robert L. Hadfield, *Sea-Toll of Our Time: A Chronicle of Maritime Disaster during the Last Thirty Years Drawn from Authentic Sources*, London: H. F. & G. Witherby, 1930, p. 180.

an inferior contractual status than that stipulated in the 'articles of agreement' for 'European seamen'. The denomination 'lascar' was the maritime equivalent for the inland 'coolie': it indicated not only lower levels of compensation for wage labour but also inferior racial status and a high degree of unfreedom. In the interwar period, the real wages of 'lascars' could amount to as little as a fifth of those of British seamen, while other contractual and non-contractual working conditions were likewise worse, ranging from reduced shipboard accommodation and cheaper provisions via less regulated work time and unenforceable accident compensations to a severely constricted right to terminate contract. British shipowners clearly considered this racially subordinated colonial segment of their maritime workforce a competitive advantage and pushed forward with its expansion: if 8 per cent of Britain's merchant seafarers had been categorized as 'lascars' in 1886, this share had trebled to almost a quarter by 1930, when Hadfield published his book.[2]

Hadfield's account of the *Egypt* disaster had only the loosest of connections to 'authentic sources', as we shall see. But, to ensure the commercial success of his book, it was surely more essential to satisfy his readers' expectations and to evoke resonance with what they may have considered 'common sense'. The opening paragraph thus latched on to a timeworn theme of colonial ideology that had been immortalized in Rudyard Kipling's infamous 1899 poem: the 'white man' had to carry the 'burden' of directing the 'new-caught' childlike (as well as devilish) 'sullen peoples' of the colonies and put them to good, rational use.[3]

How 'authority [be] well exerted' by the 'guiding hand' on board ship was seldom formulated in explicit terms, was unlikely to be recorded, and very rarely reported from a critical perspective. Even among unionized British workers, few disowned publicly the imperial ideology of colonial labour discipline, but George Hardy, a former militant of the

2 The literature of 'lascars' is extensive as will be discussed below. For a brief overview of the main features of 'lascar' employment on British steamers see Ravi Ahuja, 'The Age of the Lascar: South Asian Seafarers in the Times of Imperial Steam Shipping', in Joya Chatterji and David Washbrook (eds), *Routledge Handbook of the South Asian Diaspora*, London: Routledge, 2013, pp. 110–22.

3 Rudyard Kipling, 'The White Man's Burden', in *The Writings in Prose and Verse of Rudyard Kipling*, vol. 13, New York: Charles Scribner's Sons, 1899, pp. 479–80.

syndicalist Industrial Workers of the World in North America and, subsequently, in Britain a leading figure of the communist seamen's Minority Movement, was one of them. In 1915, he joined the crew of a Belgian freight ship sailing to Congo with a predominantly African crew. 'One day,' he recalled in his memoirs,

> the Africans on my four to eight morning watch . . . failed to scrub out chalk marks from the passengers' deck games. The boatswain's mate rushed at the nearest African sailor and kicked him hard, again and again. 'That's the only way to make the savage work,' he told me. 'You must make them work.'[4]

And he would hear this very sentence – 'they must be made to work' – reiterated time and again by 'white' officials, missionaries, and settlers in Congo.[5] This was, he observed, the central dogma and perpetual mantra of a violent labour regime he associated not only with Belgian colonialism but with imperialism in general. Habitual – even structurally embedded – physical violence, as encountered by Hardy, was certainly a regular trait of many racialized labour regimes including those, as we shall see, in imperial shipping. Yet the methods of 'racial management', of employing racial subordination to fulfil the imperative of 'making them work' were not reducible to boot, stick, and whip.[6] They were being perpetually elaborated and refined on various sites of capitalist production dispersed over large parts of the globe that included the slave societies of the Americas as much as colonial territories in Africa and Asia. While theories and practices of 'racial management' remained deeply inconsistent and varied according to their field of application, they also bore common characteristics as all of them were premised, as I shall argue, on notions of commodified labour.

This book approaches these common characteristics by scrutinizing one such field of 'racial management': the imperial labour regime that

---

4 George Hardy, *Those Stormy Years: Memories of the Fight for Freedom on Five Continents*, London: Lawrence & Wishart, 1956, p. 61.

5 Ibid., pp. 64–6.

6 The concept has been introduced into the debate in a seminal article to which we shall return severally: Elizabeth Esch and David R. Roediger, '"One Symptom of Originality": Race and Management of Labor in US History', in D. R. Roediger, *Class, Race, and Marxism*, London: Verso, 2017, pp. 115–56.

regulated the work process on board British steamers. It does so by excavating the microhistory of the same shipwreck that Hadfield dealt with in a few prejudiced sentences: the sinking of the S.S. *Egypt* in 1922. For the extensive documentation generated around this fatal event gives us a close-up view of a racialized labour regime at work: daily routines that remained unrecorded under normal circumstances were fleetingly visible, as if illuminated by lightning, at the very moment when they broke down on a sinking ship. But, before we move up close, we need to step back: shipwreck accounts are far from straightforward. They follow, almost unconsciously, long-established moral, legal, and narrative conventions, which need to be unpacked and fractured to allow for a critical analysis. If Robert Hadfield and many subsequent writers submitted to established expectations to sell their shipwreck stories, we cannot afford to do so for our own purposes. Instead, we must find a vantage point that allows us to break free from such conventions and read the documents in unexpected ways that were neither intended nor even perceivable by their authors. We must, therefore, first lay out the historical contexts of our analysis, disclose the theoretical propositions from which we proceed and consider to what extent existing research can help us in our undertaking. These, too, are conventions, of course, namely the commonly tedious ones of academic scholarship, and readers may be tempted to flip over the rest of this introduction to get to the 'meat of the story'. Yet, as the aim of this book is explicitly *not* to conjure up contemplative empathy with people of another age but to facilitate critical engagement with enduring structures of social power and exploitation, it will help if the premises of the narrative are open on the table.[7]

The ship has figured throughout history as the most dramatic materialization of human engagement with the forces of nature and of the limitations of that engagement. The urge to exchange goods along coastlines and across the seas provoked maritime risk-taking and

7 The point that the empathetic approach to history was ultimately conservative and irreconcilable with an emancipatory 'concept of history' was emphasized by Walter Benjamin. If we are to overcome the intellectual and political vacuity of the identitarian neo-romanticism of our own time, this remains, I believe, a fundamental issue to address. Cf. Walter Benjamin, *Selected Writings*, vol. 4, *1938–1940*, ed. Howard Eiland and Michael W. Jennings, Cambridge, MA: Belknap Press, 2003, pp. 391, 401, 405f.

technological ingenuity in diverse societies, though the expanding commodity circuits in the long history of capitalism have reshaped the ship as a social institution and as a technical artifact in an accelerating rhythm.[8] More specifically, the exponential growth of maritime trade, the fundamental changes in the political economy and social organization of shipping, and the repeated technological transformations since the second half of the nineteenth century are historically without precedent.

The rise of the steamship as a bulk carrier permitted (in combination with expanding railway and telegraph networks) not only explosive growth of the volume of maritime trade, but also accelerated and regularized rhythms of commodity exchange. This increased, in turn, the ability to coordinate and distribute commodity production across far-flung geographical regions and generated an incessant diversification of goods and of labour forces to be exchanged and moved profitably between the continents. As maritime logistics became more fully integrated with a progressively generalized process of capitalist production, shipping was transformed from an activity controlled by merchant capitalists or, since the seventeenth century, by joint stock trading companies, into an industry in its own right. When steamers turned into ever more giant, technologically complex, and costly machines requiring an equally capital-intensive and fundamentally transformed port infrastructure, this new shipping industry came into its own. Highly capitalized as well as specialized shipping businesses emerged that were, in turn, confronted with an unrelenting drive towards a centralization of shipping capital by way of cartels and mergers. They stood a chance to withstand this vortex of centralization only if they could gain privileged access to (preferably imperial) state power to secure subsidies, infrastructural support, and market control. The age of steam shipping drew to a close in the interwar decades with a shift from coal- to diesel-fuelled shipping, and container shipping eventually emerged as the dominant form of bulk carriage after the Second World War. As a result, maritime transport became even more capital intensive, and shipping capital was driven to further centralization, while dramatic new changes in business

8 For a recent analytical overview of the interconnected histories of capitalism and of shipping see Liam Campling and Alejandro Colás, *Capitalism and the Sea: The Maritime Factor in the Modern World*, London: Verso, 2021.

organization, maritime technology, and port infrastructure signified yet another distinct period in shipping history.

It is less well appreciated, however, that the age of steam shipping, lasting from about the 1860s to the mid-twentieth century, also brought about historically specific labour regimes as well as a thoroughly transformed and distinctly organized set of labour processes. If skill profiles and shipboard hierarchies on a steamer diverged fundamentally from those of the sailing ship, the need for massive inputs of labour power remained. As steamers required sizeable crews (that included firemen laboriously working the coal and stewards catering to increasing numbers of passengers), seafaring continued to be a large, politically indispensable, and highly visible occupational sector in many parts of the world. When the International Labour Organization was created in the wake of the First World War and against the backdrop of a global revolutionary crisis, it was, therefore, no coincidence that the establishment of international labour standards in maritime transport was high on their agenda.[9]

The shift from coal to oil and diesel had already reduced the labour intensity of ship propulsion in the final decades of the age of the steamship, but, from the mid-century onwards, container shipping permitted a mechanization of cargo handling and a more dramatic reduction of the maritime workforce, which was further sharpened as overseas passengers came to prefer aircrafts to liners. Maritime social space was now transformed beyond recognition as harbour facilities were removed from lively and often politically unruly urban waterfronts to sparsely populated and socially invisible suburban port zones.

If we can thus trace at least two major transformations of the maritime world of labour within the space of little more than a century, maritime labour historians have nevertheless tended to emphasize continuities rather than changes in this world. As most of them have been mainly concerned with the history of labour relations (rather than work processes) this perspective has been plausible on many counts. In international maritime labour law, for instance, changes appear to have been gradual rather than radical in the past two centuries and a pronounced

9 Leon Fink, *Sweatshops at Sea: Merchant Seamen in the World's First Globalized Industry, from 1812 to the Present*, Chapel Hill: University of North Carolina Press, 2011, pp. 149–52.

transnational mobility and multilingual composition persists as a defining feature of the maritime workforce across the ages. Ports like Liverpool, Marseille, Hamburg, Bombay, or New York, on which much of the archival evidence for maritime labour relations is focused, thus did not present themselves as less cosmopolitan in the age of steam than they had in the age of sail. Seen from the outside, furthermore, the very work site of the ship, characterized simultaneously by its movement between jurisdictions and by its extreme insularity (that some scholars have even perceived as the perfect precondition for the emergence of a 'total institution') has suggested a long continuity or even a trans-historical nature of shipboard hierarchies and forms of conflict.[10]

Finally, certain ethnic patterns of maritime recruitment survived the age of sail and did so, at first sight, without much alteration. The predominantly South Asian maritime labour force known to Europeans as 'lascars' (derived from the Farsi word *lashkar* for military labour) appears to be a prominent case in point.[11] If 'lascars' replenished as early as in the sixteenth-century crews on Portuguese (and subsequently on Dutch, French, and British) trading vessels in the Indian Ocean, seafarers of the same designation continued to be hired for British and German steamship liners 400 years later. Such 'lascar' workforces have been the subject of extensive research over several decades and a sizeable corpus of writings has emerged that covers a wide array of relevant themes. Much of the research has been concerned with the presence of 'lascars' in British and other North Atlantic port cities and with attempts of such seafarers to opt out of the maritime labour market and find a foothold as immigrants. Rozina Visram's pioneering work placed the 'lascar' in a long-term history of South Asian immigration;[12] Michael Fisher examined the highly visible 'lascar' presence in London in the

10 Cf. Heide Gerstenberger, 'Men Apart: The Concept of "Total Institution" and the Analysis of Seafaring', *International Journal of Maritime History* 8, no. 1 (1996), pp. 173–82.

11 Henry Yule and A. C. Burnell, *Hobson-Jobson: A Glossary of Colloquial Anglo-Indian Words and Phrases . . .*, new 4th ed., New Delhi: Munshiram Manoharlal, 1984 (1st ed. 1903), pp. 507–9.

12 Rozina Visram, *Ayahs, Lascars and Princes: The Story of Indians in Britain 1700–1947*, London: Pluto Press, 1986; Rozina Visram, *Asians in Britain: 400 Years of History*, London: Pluto Press, 2002. As for more recent publications see for instance Shompa Lahiri, 'Patterns of Resistance: Indian Seamen in Imperial Britain', in A. J. Kershen (ed.), *Language, Labour and Migration*, Aldershot: Ashgate, 2000, pp. 155–78.

early nineteenth century and particularly during the Napoleonic Wars;[13] Laura Tabili's work stands out in particular from a more extensive literature on racist policies in early twentieth-century Britain targeting the immigration and employment of 'coloured seamen';[14] and community activists, anthropologists, and historians documented and analysed the experiences of South Asian immigrants with a seafaring background in the interwar and middle decades of the twentieth century.[15]

Conrad Dixon initiated another line of inquiry focusing on the employment relations of South Asian seafarers and their racialized legal regulation in the British Empire, assuming, once again, a long-term perspective that covered crews of sailing vessels as much as those of steamers a century later.[16] Gopalan Balachandran's wide-ranging studies took account of many aspects of South Asian maritime labour history but were particularly thorough in their analysis of conflicts over the regulation of 'lascar' mobility and employment relationships in the early decades of the twentieth century[17] – a field of intensive research, which

---

13 Michael H. Fisher, *Counterflows to Colonialism: Indian Travellers and Settlers in Britain 1600–1857*, Delhi: Permanent Black, 2004.

14 Laura Tabili, *'We Ask for British Justice': Workers and Racial Difference in Late Imperial Britain*, Ithaca, NY: Cornell University Press, 1994. Earlier, groundbreaking research in this area was conducted by Marika Sherwood. See for instance her 'Race, Nationality and Employment among Lascar Seamen, 1660 to 1945', *Journal of Ethnic and Migration Studies* 17, no. 2 (1991), pp. 233f (229–44).

15 Caroline Adams (ed.), *Across Seven Seas and Thirteen Rivers: Life Histories of Pioneer Sylheti Settlers in Britain*, London: Eastside Books, 1994 (1987); Yousuf Choudhury, *The Roots and Tales of Bangladeshi Settlers*, Birmingham: Sylheti Social History Group, 1993; Yousuf Choudhury, *Sons of the Empire: Oral History from the Bangladeshi Seamen Who Served on British Ships during the 1939–45 War*, Birmingham: Sylheti Social History Group, 1995; Katy Gardner, 'Keeping Connected: Security, Place, and Social Capital in a "Londoni" Village in Sylhet', *Journal of the Royal Anthropological Institute* 14, no. 3 (2008), pp. 477–95; David Holland, 'Toffee Men, Travelling Drapers and Black-Market Perfumers: South Asian Networks of Petty Trade in Early Twentieth Century Britain', *Twentieth Century British History* 30, no. 2 (2019), pp. 145–73; Ceri-Anne Fidler, 'The Impact of Migration upon Family Life and Gender Relations: The Case of South Asian Seafarers, c.1900–50', *Women's History Review* 24, no. 3 (2015), pp. 410–28.

16 Conrad H. Dixon, 'Seamen and the Law: An Examination of the Impact of Legislation on the British Merchant Seaman's Lot, 1588–1918', doctoral thesis, University College London, 1981.

17 Balachandran's important research, much of it previously published in numerous articles, is conveniently compiled in Gopalan Balachandran, *Globalizing Labour? Indian Seafaring and World Shipping, c. 1870–1945*, New Delhi: Oxford University Press, 2012.

others, including the present author, cultivated as well.[18] Yet other researchers examined the history of 'lascar' employment in the context of an Indian Ocean maritime economy and culture,[19] and some shifted the temporal scope of this research back into the seventeenth and eighteenth centuries.[20] A diverse body of writings has been concerned with unearthing forms of labour militancy among a South Asian maritime workforce that was regularly represented, in colonial imaginations, as particularly 'docile'. Some authors focused, in this regard, on modalities of shipboard conflict both on sailing vessels and on steamers[21] with a recent intervention emphasizing the continuity of behavioural patterns.[22] Others, taking

18 See, e.g., Ravi Ahuja, 'Mobility and Containment: The Voyages of South Asian Seamen, c. 1900–1960', *International Review of Social History* 51 (2006, supplement), pp. 111–41; Ravi Ahuja, 'Networks of Subordination – Networks of the Subordinated: The Case of South Asian Maritime Labour under British Imperialism (c. 1890–1947)', in Harald Fischer-Tiné and Ashwini Tambe (eds), *Spaces of Disorder: The Limits of British Colonial Control in South Asia and the Indian Ocean*, London: Routledge, 2008, pp. 13–48.

19 See for instance Janet Ewald, 'Crossers of the Sea: Slaves, Freedmen, and Other Migrants in the Northwestern Indian Ocean, c. 1750–1914', *American Historical Review* 105, no. 1 (2000), pp. 69–91; Jonathan Hyslop, 'Steamship Empire: Asian, African and British Sailors in the Merchant Marine c.1880–1945', *Journal of Asian and African Studies* 44, no. 1 (2009), pp. 49–67; Heather Goodall, Deevlana Ghosh, and Lindi R. Todd, 'Jumping Ship – Skirting Empire: Indians, Aborigines and Australians across the Indian Ocean', *Transforming Cultures eJournal* 3, no. 1 (2008), pp. 44–74.

20 Matthias van Rossum, 'The Rise of the Asian Sailor? Inter-Asiatic Shipping, the Dutch East India Company and Maritime Labour Markets (1500–1800)', in Sabyasachi Bhattacharya (ed.), *Towards a New History of Work*, New Delhi: Tulika, 2014, pp. 180–213; Ghulam Nadri, 'Sailors, Zielverkopers, and the Dutch East India Company: The Maritime Labour Market in Eighteenth-Century Surat', *Modern Asian Studies* 49, no. 2 (2015), pp. 336–64; James W. Frey, 'Getting Away with Murder: The Wrongful Deaths of Lascars Aboard the *Union* in 1802', special issue, *International Review of Social History* 59 (2014), pp. 45–68.

21 Aaron Jaffer, *Lascars and Indian Ocean Seafaring, 1780–1860: Shipboard Life, Unrest and Mutiny*, Suffolk: Boydell & Brewer, 2015; Michael H. Fisher, 'Finding Lascar "Wilful Incendiarism": British Ship-Burning Panic and Indian Maritime Labour in the Indian Ocean', *South Asia: Journal of South Asian Studies* 35, no. 3 (2012), pp. 596–623; Ravi Ahuja, 'A Freedom Still Enmeshed in Servitude: The Unruly "Lascars" of the S.S. City of Manila or, a Micro-History of the "Free Labour" Problem', in Ravi Ahuja (ed.), *Working Lives and Worker Militancy: The Politics of Labour in Colonial India*, Delhi: Tulika, 2013, pp. 97–133.

22 Naina Manjrekar, 'Violent and Not Quite Modern? Lascars and Everyday Resistance Across the Sail-Steam Divide', Special Issue on Maritime History, *Labour History* 116 (2019), pp. 29–55.

a cue from Frank Broeze's pathbreaking work,[23] have been more concerned with forms of unionization, large-scale industrial action, and labour movement internationalism that became feasible and increasingly organized among South Asian seafarers only after the First World War and particularly during the Second.[24]

The level of interest that 'lascars' have attracted among researchers in recent decades may come as a surprise, even if we consider that one out of four crew members of the British merchant marine, by far the largest commercial fleet internationally, was hired in the 'lascar' recruitment ports of Calcutta and Bombay in the interwar period. In addition to these roughly 50,000 men, almost as many were registered in some years as having been recruited for other steamers, and an unknown but unquestionably sizeable number of South Asian seafarers found work on the subcontinent's numerous coastal sailing vessels. If this was indeed a very sizable workforce, the main reason for the growing interest in its history may still have to be located for the main part in the ideological context of our own time, and, specifically, the two decades between the fall of European state socialism and the global financial crisis of 2008. This was a time when deafening neoliberal 'globalization' narratives were ubiquitous, when the 'prehistory of globalization' was a career-building and commercially promising sector of historiographical manufacture, and when even those who dared to dissent often believed that a mere inversion of the hegemonic discourse – counter-histories of a 'globalization from below' – offered a radical alternative. For the latter, a seemingly uninterrupted cosmopolitan tradition of plebeian oceanic culture and of maritime work, a longue durée history of the 'motley

23 Frank Broeze, 'The Muscles of Empire: Indian Seamen and the Raj, 1919–1939', *Indian Economic and Social History Review* 18, no. 1 (1981), pp. 43–67; Frank Broeze, 'Militancy and Pragmatism: An International Perspective on Maritime Labour, 1870–1914', *International Review of Social History* 36, no. 2 (1991), pp. 165–200.

24 See in particular Gopalan Balachandran, 'Conflicts in the International Maritime Labour Market: British and Indian Seamen, Employers, and the State, 1890–1939', *Indian Economic and Social History Review* 39, no. 1 (2002), pp. 71–100; David Featherstone, 'Maritime Labour, Circulations of Struggle, and Constructions of Transnational Subaltern Agency: The Spatial Politics of the 1939 Indian Seafarers' Strikes', *Antipode* 55, no. 5 (2022), pp. 1411–32; Diane Kirkby and Lee-Ann Monk, 'Indian Seamen and Australian Unions Fighting for Labour Rights: "The Real Facts of the Lascars' Case" of 1939', *Labour History* 113 (2017), pp. 209–39; Heather Goodall, 'Port Politics: Indian Seamen, Australian Unions and Indonesian Independence, 1945–47', *Labour History* 94 (2008), pp. 43–68.

crew' seemed a promising addition to a proliferating literature on 'subaltern agency'. If Peter Linebaugh and Marcus Rediker's riveting history of a 'revolutionary Atlantic' had made a highly suggestive (if perhaps not always compelling) case for a diverse yet coherent radical, emancipatory, and anti-capitalist tradition that had been forged by often maritime plebeians as they crossed oceans in the seventeenth to early nineteenth centuries, might it be possible that 'the lascar's' contributions to this tradition just needed to be recovered from the condescending ignorance of posterity?[25]

Yet the implicit presupposition of an unbroken transhistorical identity of 'the lascar' reveals itself as implausible as soon as we think it through in concrete terms: Can we really assume that South Asian seafarers remained involved in largely the same social relations irrespective of whether they worked the sails on a moderately sized vessel owned by an eighteenth-century British 'country trader' in the Indian Ocean or whether they toiled in the engine room of an infinitely more capital-intensive twentieth-century passenger liner run by a globally operating and state-subsidized shipping conglomerate? If such questions have rarely been asked in historical writings, this is due to two limitations of the otherwise rich research into the history of maritime labour and particularly of steamship labour.

The first limitation, alluded to already, is that labour historians (of South Asia as well as of other regions) have tended to approach the history of seafarers in the nineteenth and twentieth centuries from firm ground rather than from heaving decks on the ocean: vantage points of their examination have been largely the 'sailortowns' of port cities or the inland regions from which ship workers were recruited, and much less their – admittedly less abundantly documented – floating work sites. The second – and connected – limitation derives from the unfortunate parting of ways of labour history with economic and business history, which has been almost pervasive in recent decades. Historians of British shipping in the nineteenth and twentieth century thus analysed changing business models and technologies as well as the inextricable entanglements of the shipping industry with the imperial state, but have rarely stooped to consider the implications of their findings for the

25 Peter Linebaugh and Marcus Rediker, *The Many-Headed Hydra: The Hidden History of the Revolutionary Atlantic*, London: Verso, 2002.

management of labour. Labour historians, in turn, have closely studied the colonial dimensions of maritime labour recruitment, but most of them appear to have lost the inclination to examine the place of labour in business strategies. While the relations of workers to the state have been highlighted, the relations between labour and capital remained largely in the shadows. The consequences of both limitations are much the same: while land-based vantage points and a focus on the state permitted analyses of the regulation of recruitment, international mobility, and contractual labour relations, historians' avoidance of the work site and their reluctance to engage with shipping capital and its changing and diverse accumulation strategies meant that labour management on board ship – the work process, the moment when maritime labour power was utilized and set into value – was given short shrift. This shortcoming is, as we shall see, particularly pronounced for ship-work after the age of sail though it is not unique to this field of labour history. Studies of labour processes on board steamers are rare, accordingly, and the only systematic investigation I have been able to trace is an excellent German-language monograph that owes much of its acuity, perhaps, to having been jointly authored by a historical sociologist (Heide Gerstenberger) and a ship's-engineer-turned-historian (Ulrich Welke).[26]

To anticipate one of the arguments of the present book, close attention to the labour process allows to perceive and explain momentous shifts in the composition of the maritime workforce and a heightened importance of 'race' in the management of ship-work in the age of steam. For the proverbial 'motley crew' that was multilingual, ethnically diverse, and had joined the ship from ports all over the globe became much less frequent in the age of steam than it had been in the age of sail (or would be in the age of the container). Instead, steamship crews were more likely to be ethnically segmented than 'cosmopolitan': the departmental structure of the ship's hierarchy that emerged with the spread of the new propulsion technology and the expansion of maritime passenger traffic, i.e., the compartmentalization into deck, engine room, and cabin crews, each with their own chain of command, could be mirrored by an ethnic compartmentalization along these organizational divisions.

26 Heide Gerstenberger and Ulrich Welke, *Vom Wind zum Dampf. Sozialgeschichte der deutschen Handelsschiffahrt im Zeitalter der Industrialisierung*, Münster: Westfälisches Dampfboot, 1996.

The point is certainly not that the pervasiveness of racist stereotypes in the age of imperialism has been overlooked in the existing historiography. It has been well known that the attributes of 'docility', inferior physical strength, lack of skill, and 'unmanliness' were regularly attached in British discourses to 'lascars', other 'coloured seamen', and even more generously to all seafarers who did not happen to be 'white' and British. It has also been pointed out that specific work capacities (to bear with extreme heat or cold, for instance) were believed to be inherent qualities of particular 'races'. At issue is, however, whether it is sufficient to study merely the most overtly abusive linguistic expressions of maritime racism and expose their evident irrationality. I argue that racist ideology must be examined in the context of social relations of power shaped by the (il)logic of capital accumulation. This presupposes that the racism of the most powerful classes in society, the structurally dominating form of racist ideology and social practice, needs to be examined with the greatest care even if the linguistic forms in which this hegemonic racism has been expressed may appear less violent. This presupposes conversely that white working-class racism can be examined in isolation from the study of boardroom racism only at the risk of concealing the roots of modern racism in structures of social power under capitalism.

At the level of language, this implies that the politics of 'polite' ethnic renaming should be regarded as a common practice of racist subordination and do not possess the quasi-magic quality of disarming racism that contemporary liberal identitarians seem to ascribe to them. The racist content of publicly and officially used categories like 'lascar', 'coloured seaman', or 'native seafarer' becomes fully perceivable only if we make explicit that they were used as publishable and recordable equivalents for the deliberately offensive 'nigger' that was commonly used to refer to South Asian as much as to African seafarers on British and other Euro-American ships at least until the mid-twentieth century. Joseph Conrad's infamous choice of the title *The Nigger of the 'Narcissus'* for his first commercially successful novel was no inadvertent slip-up, as I will show.[27] The title did not merely reflect contemporary linguistic usage but condensed the gist of a novel that naturalized racialized social hierarchy. No obfuscation on the part of liberal or radical literary

27 Joseph Conrad, *The Nigger of the 'Narcissus'*, ed. Cedric Watts, London: Penguin, 1989 (1st ed. 1897).

scholars, no mannerly asterisk, nor retroactive retitling (as in a recent German retranslation) will make this go away.[28] Crucially, and for all practical purposes, the usually restrained language employed to regulate the working conditions and residential entitlements of 'coloured seamen' *defined* a social position that implied, reinforced, and enabled violently abusive everyday racism.

The key issue, I argue, is not *how* ethnic categories of workers were denominated but the fact of ethnic categorization itself. For these categories, whether they were articulated in overtly insulting or politely disguised racist terms in the interwar period or, as is more likely a century later, in a seemingly less offensive 'culturalist' idiom, have had very practical implications for the management and for the experience of labour.[29] Modern racism is deeply informed by the logic of commodification (and so is postmodern culturalism): if commodities are qualitatively distinguished according to their useability, modern essentialist ideologues assign specific features of usability and differential use values to racially (or culturally) defined sections of the global workforce. This can be observed historically for all forms of commodified labour ranging from slavery to presumably 'free' waged work.

While studies on racially segmented labour markets have been undertaken frequently and for many decades, the role of 'racial management' in capitalist labour processes is still insufficiently understood. I argue that the blatant irrationality of theories of racially defined labour value – we will have to engage with some more hair-raising outpourings in this book – does not preclude their practical utility for capital. And this utility is only revealed if racialized practices of managing labour processes are closely investigated. If pioneering studies of this kind have been undertaken for the post-slavery USA, I propose that connected and similar practices unfolded in the British Empire and, in all likeliness, elsewhere.[30]

28 This refers in particular to the interpretations of this novel offered by Edward Said; see below, p. 51. The novel was republished in German in 2020 under a misleading title that translates as 'The Nobody of the "Narcissus"': Joseph Conrad, *Der Niemand von der 'Narcissus'*, transl. Mirko Bonné, Hamburg: Mare Verlag, 2020.

29 For a contemporary application of cultural essentialism to the management of 'human resources' see Geert Hofstede, *Culture's Consequences: Comparing Values, Behaviors, Institutions, and Organizations across Nations*, 2nd ed., Thousand Oaks, CA: Sage, 2001.

30 See especially the work of David Roediger and Elizabeth Esch as discussed in more detail in subsequent chapters.

In this book I argue, more specifically, that 'racial management' provided the imperial British shipping industry with a feasible alternative to regularized and more expensive forms of employment and with a means to avoid or delay heavy investment in technologically more advanced fixed capital.

I had promised transparency at the beginning of this introduction – the analytical instruments and my main contentions are now on the table. What they are worth remains to be seen, as we move on from abstract concepts and theories to a concrete historical field of forces where numerous social actors engaged with each other in complex ways, all in pursuit of their respective interests and motivations. For 'racial management', a modality of class relations buttressed by racist status ascription, assumed historical reality only through multiple and contradictory practices of numerous social actors: practices of coercion and of consent, of adaptation and of resistance. Such constellations of social practices can be grasped by historians most distinctly whenever they assume a relatively stable form: when they 'crystallize', as it were, if only for a (historically) brief moment. Such fleetingly stable constellations can emerge in various forms – they can converge, for instance, on a certain event or also in the life history of a particular individual.

In this book, we will mainly reconstruct an *event* comprising a shipping disaster and its judicial and political aftermath – an event during which the practices of a racialized labour regime became discernible as if seen through a magnifying glass. But, as we proceed through the stages of this event, we will find that its very nature and the ways in which it was recorded tinged the emerging picture in a specific colour: the efficacy of power structures is highlighted more than their limitations. The final chapter, therefore, shifts the perspective and probes the unusual life history of a rebellious South Asian fireman to assess the scope for challenging the racialized labour regime of British imperial shipping in the early twentieth century. But, to reach this more hopeful vista, we must first descend from the airy heights of abstraction to the stifling workplaces of a steamer's stokehold.

1

Collision Course: British Merchant Shipping and the Loss of a Mail Steamer

If British colonial imperialism had survived the 'Great War' and the global revolutionary upheaval in its wake, the interwar years appear, in hindsight, as a period of *Götterdämmerung*: a period when cracks appeared and deepened in the political and economic foundations of imperial power. The twilight extended to the British shipping industry, which had served as a key infrastructure for imperial expansion in the latter half of the nineteenth century and had risen to unrivalled global pre-eminence in the bargain.[1] Between the world wars of the twentieth century, this position began to slip. British merchant shipping suffered from the decline of British exports and continued to rely, more than its competitors, on a coal-based and increasingly outdated steam technology, while the state subsidies it had been enjoying for almost a century were no longer sufficient to fend off US, Japanese, and European rivals. The British share of the world shipping tonnage plummeted from 51.5

1 Key studies of the intimate connection between British imperial expansion and the rise of large steam shipping concerns include Freda Harcourt, *Flagships of Imperialism: The P&O Company and the Politics of Empire from Its Origins to 1867*, Manchester: Manchester University Press, 2006; J. Forbes Munro, *Maritime Enterprise and Empire: Sir William Mackinnon and His Business Network, 1823–93*, Woodbridge: Boydell, 2003. For a recent theoretical exposition of the link between capitalism, imperialism, and the shipping industry see Liam Campling and Alejandro Colás, *Capitalism and the Sea: The Maritime Factor in the Modern World*, London: Verso, 2021, especially chapter 5.

per cent in 1900 to 29.9 per cent in 1930, while the US share rose from 3.9 to 15.6 per cent in the same period.[2]

Even so, Britain's shipping imperialists did not appear to be a spent force in those years: the Great War had offered excellent business opportunities and splendid profits to British liner companies and other shipowners who were able, therefore, to quickly rebuild the severely decimated merchant fleet.[3] Privileged access to a vast colonial empire, to its seemingly inexhaustible resources – including cheap labour power – and to its expansive trade networks continued to serve as a cushion for losses British shipping concerns sustained in their core business of maritime logistics.[4] Moreover, the tendency towards oligopolistic mergers continued from the 1910s onwards to create ever more expansive shipping conglomerates. The most powerful of the British 'big five' was the Peninsular and Oriental Steam Navigation Company (P&O) after its merger, in 1914, with the equally large British India Steam Navigation Company (BISN). In 1919, this concern accounted for more than 10 per cent of the carrying capacity of the British merchant marine or a quarter of the tonnage held by the eight largest UK shipping conglomerates. The liner business – large passenger or cargo ships running on schedule that also provided the heavily subsidized mail services – was by then exclusively conducted by these eight shipping concerns.[5]

2 Robert Gardiner and Ambrose Greenway (eds), *The Golden Age of Shipping: The Classic Merchant Ship, 1900–1960*, London: Conway Maritime Press, 1994, p. 170.

3 Dividends paid out by liner companies in 1917 were double those distributed in 1913. S. G. Sturmey, *British Shipping and World Competition*, London: Athlone Press, 1962, p. 36f, 46–53.

4 While British ships accounted for 30 per cent of all sea-borne trade between territories outside the British Empire in 1912, this proportion had shrunk to 12 per cent by 1936. In the same period, the British share of sea-borne trade within the British Empire remained at about 95 per cent. Sea-borne trade within the British Empire made up between 12 and 16 per cent of world maritime trade in that period and hence a significant proportion. The intra-imperial trade nexus thus absorbed to some extent the shock of the heavy losses sustained in other segments of world trade. Cf. Sturmey, *British Shipping*, p. 89.

5 Mail subsidies received by the P&O, which held the most valuable mail contract for guaranteeing communication between Britain and India, accounted for 22 per cent of the company's operating cost between 1840 and 1914; Freda Harcourt, 'British Oceanic Mail Contracts in the Age of Steam, 1838–1914', *Journal of Transport History* 9, no. 1 (1988), p. 6 [1–18]. Gordon H. Boyce, *Information, Mediation and Institutional Development: The Rise of Large-Scale Enterprise in British Shipping, 1870–1919*, Manchester: Manchester University Press, 1995, pp. 128f.

The P&O group's fortunes were most directly connected to Britain's colonial empire as Euro-Asian shipping constituted its main business: from the beginning of the First to the outbreak of the Second World War the conglomerate appears to have accounted alone for between a quarter and a third of the total steamer tonnage calling at Indian ports.[6] Not only government mail, but also troops and colonial officials (who made up two-thirds of the company's passengers to India) were carried by the P&O making it 'in a large degree . . . an unofficial arm of the Raj, deriving much of its income from the public purse'.[7] This role was embraced, at least in official correspondence, by the company, when it referred to its effective status as that of 'an external Department of the Government'.[8]

The chairman of the P&O group since its merger with the BISN, James Lyle Mackay, embodied British shipping imperialism like no other in this twilight period.[9] Beginning his career in 1874 as a shipping clerk in India, he served and eventually succeeded the leading shipping imperialist of the latter half of the nineteenth century, William Mackinnon, who had linked the fortunes of the BISN to British policies of aggressive colonial expansion in East Africa and West Asia.[10] From the 1890s onwards, Mackay served as a member of the Governor-General's Legislative Council (of India) and the (British) Secretary of State's Council of India, and on numerous government committees both in India and Britain. In 1909, he was in the race for the succession of the viceroy of India – an office he was denied eventually. At a time when bankers and ministers played musical chairs even more freely than at present and when British prime ministers were likely to be business tycoons, the viceroyalty of India continued to be a preserve of a largely

6 Cf. Stephanie Jones, *Two Centuries of Overseas Trading: The Origins and Growth of the Inchcape Group*, Houndmills: Macmillan, 1986, pp. 54, 59.

7 Ronald Hope, *A New History of British Shipping*, London: John Murray, 1990, p. 341.

8 Letter to General Post Office, 31 March 1886 (NMM, Caird Library, P&O/30/1), quoted in Harcourt, 'British Oceanic Mail Contracts', p. 14.

9 The following paragraph is based on the officially sanctioned, but informative biography of Lord Inchcape: Stephanie Jones, *Trade and Shipping: Lord Inchcape, 1952–1932*, Manchester: Manchester University Press, 1989, especially chapters 1, 3, and 5.

10 For a detailed study see: J. Forbes Munro, *Maritime Enterprise and Empire: Sir William Mackinnon and His Business Network, 1823–93*, Woodbridge: Boydell, 2003.

aristocratic service gentry, however.[11] Mackay was passed over and compensated with a baronetcy in 1911, after which he styled himself 'Lord Inchcape'.

The intricacies of imperial office-hunting notwithstanding, in everyday governance no need was felt whatsoever to mark off the pursuit of British business interests from 'public service' for the empire. Mackay/Inchcape archetypically embodied the personal union between corporate and state imperialism: representing a business nexus that combined imperial shipping with a wide range of commercial and industrial operations in colonial India, he was also a powerful player over more than four decades in shaping the Raj's (as well as Britain's) economic policies on fundamental issues like currency, state expenditure, or railways – issues where the interests of British agency houses were at odds with those, among others, of rising Indian business concerns.[12]

The personal union of political and economic power also meant that shipping lords like Inchcape could maintain within their businesses an air of godlike managerial omnipotence in this period of self-conscious imperial pompousness. Inchcape ruled the P&O group like an autocrat who held court at the largely ceremonial annual meetings of proprietors. When closing the shipping giant's Eighty-First General Meeting in December 1921, he proclaimed: 'You may rely upon it that, despite all the difficulties ahead of us, we shall do our very best to maintain the reputation, and also the dividend, of the P. and O. Company.'[13] The proprietors responded readily with cheers to their chairman's assurances and refrained from raising overly inquisitive questions regarding the deliberately uninformative business reports. They had little reason to do otherwise, as they could indeed depend throughout the 1920s on handsome dividends, with that on deferred stock ranging between 10 and 12 per cent.[14]

It was only during the Great Depression and after Inchcape's death in 1932 that the strained financial situation of the conglomerate came out into the open: 'creative accounting' had concealed the diminished

11 Cf. David Edgerton, *The Rise and Fall of the British Nation: A Twentieth-Century History*, London: Penguin, 2019, pp. 116f.

12 Cf. Jones, *Trade and Shipping*.

13 'Peninsular and Oriental Steam Navigation Company', *The Times*, 8 December 1921, p. 18.

14 Jones, *Trade and Shipping*, p. 202.

profitability of the company's liner business, declining liquidity, depleted depreciation funds, and a growing tendency to defer investments.[15] Increasingly opaque business practices and strained liquidity were not confined to the P&O group, however, which ultimately fared rather well: the other mammoth of British shipping, the Royal Mail Steam Navigation Company that controlled large chunks of the Latin America trade as well as a wide-ranging network of commercial undertakings, collapsed in a major business scandal in 1930.[16] Such liquidity crises, concealed better in some cases than in others, clearly played a role when British shipping companies, including Inchcape's P&O, were more reluctant in the 1920s than their American, Japanese, or Scandinavian competitors to replace steam propulsion with diesel motors: oil-fuelled motor ships required higher initial investment than conventional coal-burning steamers and their lower operation costs paid off only in due time.[17] As a result, British shipping – both owners and builders – lost the leadership in maritime technology they had possessed around the turn of the century.[18]

That Britain's dominance over world shipping was fraying at the edges thus became more clearly discernible over the 1920s. Inchcape, doyen of the shipping lords, complained about hard times, unreasonably high labour costs and – even as he accepted ever more powerful government assignments – undue state interference.[19] This did not prevent him, however, from claiming for the P&O conglomerate a position of leadership and primacy allowing them to set standards for the shipping industry at large. At the proprietors' meeting in December of 1921, he smugly quoted from a letter from Lord Northcliffe, whose powerful press conglomerate included, among other newspapers, the *Daily Mail* and *The Times*. The media mogul thanked the shipping nabob for the professionalism of the P&O's passenger services, which he had

15 Ibid., pp. 121–8, 202.

16 Cf. Edwin Green and Michael Moss, *A Business of National Importance: The Royal Mail Shipping Group, 1902–1937*, London: Methuen, 1982.

17 Between 1923 and 1937 the percentage of British tonnage moved by diesel engines was consistently lower than the world average – this despite the large-scale reconstruction of the British merchant fleet after the World War. Sturmey, *British Shipping*, p. 84.

18 Cf. Max E. Fletcher, 'From Coal to Oil in British Shipping', *Journal of Transport History* 3, no. 1 (1975), pp. 1–19.

19 Jones, *Trade and Shipping*, pp. 128–30.

used extensively on his recent world tour and attested that 'so far I have found nothing but efficiency in the handling of the ships of your combine'.[20] This was more than complacent indulgence in the prevailing British self-celebration of superiority in all matters maritime. Significantly, Inchcape had assured the proprietors that management would continue to protect, apart from their dividend, the company's public reputation as a key parameter of sustained business success and stock market value. A few months later, however, a shipping disaster left a dent in the reputational armour of the Peninsular and Oriental Steam Navigation Company.

On 20 May 1922, the Royal Mail Ship *Egypt*, on its way from London to Bombay, was about to leave the English Channel for the Bay of Biscay when it ran into a series of fog banks. The S.S. *Egypt*'s third officer had the fog whistle sounded every two minutes and tried to pick up signals of other vessels on this busy shipping lane, though the fog would distort sound and hamper an exact localization of approaching ships. Built in 1897 for the P&O, the *Egypt* was a comparatively old middle-sized steel-hulled and coal-fuelled passenger liner, about 150 metres long, with an internal volume of almost 8,000 tons and a depth of ten metres between the upper deck and the bottom of the hold. The ship had been refitted a few months earlier and was held to be in excellent condition. Shortly before seven in the evening and about twenty-five miles from Ouessant – an island off the coast of Brittany known to the British as 'Ushant' – the fog thickened. The commanding officer reduced the ship's speed on hearing a faint whistle, when a smaller French steamer, the S.S. *Seine*, emerged from a fog bank and hit the *Egypt* at right angles, tearing into its hull midships on the port side. The impact was all the greater as the *Seine*'s bows had been reinforced to break ice on its winter voyages to northern shores. After the collision, the vessel pulled back into the fog immediately: the *Seine* was damaged but manoeuvrable and could even assist in the rescue operations shortly after. On the *Egypt*, the jolt caused by the collision felt relatively benign and even Captain Collyer, an experienced shipmaster, needed a few minutes to grasp that the impact had been devastating in fact. The sturdy steel hull had ripped open like a tin can and the forward holds and the fireroom were flooded almost at

20 'Peninsular and Oriental Steam Navigation Company', p. 18.

once, leaving the steamer bereft of its power plant. The P&O Company's seasoned passenger liner rapidly went into a heavy list and sank within as little as twenty minutes.[21]

The *Egypt*'s passenger certificate permitted it to carry 807 persons – passengers and crew – whose safety was provided for with 953 life jackets and 18 lifeboats capable of carrying 860 persons. The workforce required to operate a coal-fuelled passenger liner like the *Egypt* was very large indeed: when the ship went down on 20 May 1922, its predominantly male crew consisted of 294 persons – more than a third of the certified passenger load. There were 95 men employed in the engine and boiler rooms alone, most as coal passers ('trimmers') and firemen; 128 persons worked in the purser's department, mainly as stewards and stewardesses; 74 or only a quarter of the crew were 'seamen' in the conventional sense of the word and assigned to the 'deck department'. The number of passengers on board was very small at the time of the accident: 14 first-class and 30 second-class passengers only due to the season and since a larger number intended, for reasons of convenience, to board the ship later in Marseille for their voyage to Bombay. Thus, there should have been an overabundance of safety gear to protect the 338 persons on board from drowning.

Yet eighty-seven persons did not in fact survive the shipwreck: seventy-one (or nearly a quarter) of the *Egypt*'s crew and sixteen (or more than a third) of the passengers, mainly of the second class. This heavy death toll as well as the loss of 1 million British pounds' worth of gold and silver bullion for the use of the Government of India directed at once considerable public attention to this shipping accident. Almost exactly a decade after the much more deadly shipwreck of that much more famous Royal Mail Ship, the *Titanic,* the *Egypt* disaster was clearly the stuff of newspaper headlines. It also led to a detailed Board of Trade inquiry into the reasons for the high loss of human lives, which was closely monitored by the press. The wreck commissioner's final report concluded, as we shall see, with a severe censure of both the ship's officers and the P&O Company making the latter, as the British Indian

21 If not stated otherwise, the information contained in this and the following two paragraphs is drawn from: BL: OIOC, IOR/L/E/7/1123, F. 1989, Commerce and Revenue Department, Loss of the S.S. Egypt (Report of Court on the Loss of the S.S. Egypt, 4 September 1922, with Annex); TNA, TS 34/9 'R.M.S. Egypt. Exhibits' (crew lists and casualty lists).

trade commissioner put it, 'distinctly uneasy' and eager to bury the incident in oblivion.[22]

The proceedings of the *Egypt* inquiry filled hundreds of pages, even though the cause of the accident could not be examined comprehensively as the French owners of the *Seine* were beyond the jurisdiction of the court and did not voluntarily submit to it.[23] The inquiry thus focused on whether safety regulations had been complied with on the *Egypt* and on how rescue operations had been executed by the ship's officers and crew. UK wreck commissioner Butler Cole Aspinall presided over the court as the sole judge with four senior British shipping experts acting as assessors. Aspinall was a well-versed maritime lawyer who had represented the Board of Trade in various shipping inquiries, including that into the *Titanic* disaster.[24] He had also served the P&O concern as legal counsel in other cases of shipwreck, which evidently did not disqualify him from chairing an inquiry concerning the same company.[25] Board of Trade and India Office officials, along with P&O and British trade union representatives, assisted the court in questioning a long line-up of witnesses to draw divergent conclusions from their testimonies.[26]

When I leafed through this voluminous material almost a century after the event and found myself returning to it over and over again, it was not to establish the 'ultimate truth' on the causes of the *Egypt* disaster or of its high death toll – a task I was neither sufficiently equipped for nor much interested in. As a social historian, I understood that this terrible accident had generated an unusually thick description and dense documentation of labour relations and processes on board a passenger steamer in late imperial Britain. It had thrown a spotlight, as it were, on everyday social practices that did not require and induce textual recording under less dramatic circumstances. Together with the

22 NAI, Commerce Department, Lascar Seamen, October 1922, F.Nos. 48–70, f. 31 (F. Noyce, Indian trade commissioner, to H.A.F. Lindsay, secretary to the Government of India, Commerce Department, 24 August 1922, f. 31).

23 TNA, TS 34/8 '"R.M.S. Egypt": Various Proofs and Documents' ('The British Steamship "Egypt" of Greenock, Official No. 105581. Formal Investigation Ordered by the Board of Trade . . .', n. d.), detailed brief for the legal counsel of the Board of Trade, p. 6.

24 *Daily Mail* (Hull), 16 November 1935, p. 1.

25 He had represented the P&O Company for instance at the *Oceana* inquiry in 1912, when 'lascars' were likewise accused of panicking. *Daily Mail*, 4 May 1912, p. 8.

26 Cf. TNA, TS 34/10 'R.M.S. Egypt. Transcript of Court Proceedings'.

P&O's internal correspondence, with India Office files and the extensive international press coverage of that shipping accident, the detailed court proceedings could thus be used to gain new insights into the history of a labour regime emerging from the age of imperialism – a racist labour regime, I argue, the fundamental structures of which are still observable in our own time. This book thus uses the dense documentation of a shipping accident to study the steamer as the central work site of shipping imperialism in two connected ways: first, it investigates the 'common sense' that had been established socially in the British Empire about the norms and realities of shipboard order, which involved notions of an imperial hierarchy of race as much as those of class. Second, it uses the detailed materials of the *Egypt* inquiry to reconstruct racialized power relations in the organization of labour on a steamer in late imperial Britain, power relations that remained undocumented for as long as they remained embedded in everyday routine procedures, and that gain visibility for the historian only in brief moments of breakdown.

The organic link between colonial imperialism and the British shipping industry was mirrored in the composition of the merchant marine's crews. In the interwar period, about a quarter of the workforce employed on British merchant ships were recruited from the Indian subcontinent while West Africa, Yemen, and China also provided substantial numbers of non-European ship workers.[27] If the loss of the S.S. *Egypt* did not remain a domestic British news item and provoked both international and intra-imperial public debate, this was even more due to the composition of its crew than to the occurrence of the accident in French waters or to the P&O Company's prominence in the shipping world. More than two-thirds of the *Egypt*'s crew, 208 of 294 persons, all of them male, originated from the subcontinent, of which 49 did not survive the ship's sinking – almost one out of four men, or the same proportion of fatalities as among the 'white' crew. Most of the men employed in the deck and engine departments were Indian Muslims, mainly from the west coast and the north-western regions respectively, while Indian Christians from the Portuguese colony of Goa made up the majority of the workforce in the purser's department. Deep down in the ship's steel hull,

27 Ravi Ahuja, 'Mobility and Containment: The Voyages of South Asian Seamen, c. 1900–1960', *International Review of Social History* 51 (2006, supplement), p. 111.

below the waterline, the proportion of Indian ship workers was highest: 83 of the 95 men tending to the ship's four triple-expansion steam engines, namely the coal passers and firemen, were South Asians while only the engineers and a few workers (with skills required for specific technical tasks) had been recruited from Britain.[28]

If coal-burning steamships had revolutionized shipping and facilitated an unprecedented growth of world trade in the latter half of the nineteenth century, even the most technologically advanced steamers continued to depend on large inputs of labour power: on labour processes that demanded the ravenous consumption of enormous amounts of human muscle energy harnessed to simple tools and a limited scope of repetitive operations.[29] While ship architecture and steam-plant development pushed towards the limits of the technologically possible, fuel supply on coal-burning steamers was no focus of technological innovation and even available labour-saving solutions were rarely applied. We shall see in more detail that the curious combination of sophisticated capital-intensive technologies with labour-intensive labour processes seemed preferable to British shipping managers to a consistent application of the most advanced technologies. To keep up the steam, vast and renewable resources of labour were needed, marked out more than anything else by youth, physical resilience and replaceability, for which India's often precarious smallholding peasantry provided a seemingly boundless supply base. Shipowners in Britain and elsewhere had valued Indian ship workers for decades as a much cheaper workforce in terms of wages, food, ship accommodation, and compensation entitlements. Perhaps even more importantly, they were also appreciated as a workforce that could be subjected more easily than the increasingly rights-conscious (and rights-owning) British 'Jack tar' to an uninterrupted labour process – demanded both by the technology and the capital-intensive economy of steamers in general and of liners in particular.[30]

---

28 TNA, TS 34/9 'R.M.S. Egypt. Exhibits' (crew lists).

29 The *Mauretania*, a turbine-driven, technologically advanced liner built almost a decade after the *Egypt*, required a crew of 812 – more than a quarter of its certified passenger load. Ronald Hope, *A New History of British Shipping*, London: John Murray, 1990, pp. 339f.

30 For a systematic discussion of the labour processes and their development on British coal-burning steamers see chapters 8–10, below.

The proportion of Indian ship workers on British ships had thus grown continuously since the 1890s, prompting leaders of British seamen's unions time and again – whether motivated by genuine jingoism, untroubled opportunism or, most likely, a combination of the two – to demand restrictions on their employment or even their total exclusion from the labour market.[31] The post-war shipping crisis and consequently high levels of maritime unemployment had charged this debate with a new urgency. Campaigners for a 'white' prerogative to maritime employment appealed to a hegemonic, seemingly self-evident anthropological worldview – to a racist common sense. This common sense was shared, on the one hand, in varying degrees across most political persuasions and class divisions not merely in Britain but all along the North Atlantic rim. It was, on the other hand, never uncontested, always rife with tensions and far from homogeneous as racist assumptions were intertwined with ideologies of class and gender in various ways. We shall return to these tensions at a later stage of our discussion.

At this point, we confine ourselves to one aspect only of this multiform racist common sense, namely, that it crystallized in a corpus of lurid and long-lived modern myths. One of these myths (and one of the numerous 'invented traditions' of the nineteenth century) proclaimed a purportedly 'eternal law of the sea' according to which women and children were to be rescued first in the event of shipwreck – a 'law' more honoured in the breach than in observance even at times when it was declared most categorically. Initially, in the British context, this 'chivalric code' was claimed by the 'respectable' classes as a behavioural norm that distinguished 'civilized' masculinity from the 'animality' of the working class. But, as the nineteenth century wore on, this distinction was increasingly nationalized and racialized. By the time of the *Egypt* shipwreck, the assertion that 'oriental' (as well as other 'coloured' or Southern European) seafarers lacked the 'manliness' of British crews

31 Cf. Marika Sherwood, 'Race, Nationality and Employment among Lascar Seamen, 1660 to 1945', *Journal of Ethnic and Migration Studies* 17, no. 2 (1991), pp. 233f; Laura Tabili, *'We Ask for British Justice': Workers and Racial Difference in Late Imperial Britain*, Ithaca, NY: Cornell University Press, 1994, pp. 81–112. Laura Tabili, in particular, has emphasized the opportunist and inconsistent nature of the racism displayed by British seamen's unions: while her argument that racist tropes were used tactically in the context of employer policies is important and well taken, the mere inconsistency of trade union leaders concerning racial exclusion does not rule out ideological investment.

and were unable to cope with situations of emergency had been repeated ad nauseam over decades until it assumed the appearance of self-evidence.[32] When the news of the *Egypt* disaster spread, when the death count came to include nine women and children, and when a public hunt for culprits began, the surviving Indian crew were thus high up on the list of plausible culprits.[33]

32 Lucy Delap, '"Thus Does Man Prove His Fitness to Be the Master of Things": Shipwrecks, Chivalry and Masculinities in Nineteenth- and Twentieth-Century Britain', *Cultural and Social History* 3, no. 1 (2006), pp. 45–74; Laura Tabili, '"A Maritime Race": Masculinity and the Racial Division of Labor in British Merchant Ships, 1900–1939', in Margaret S. Creighton and Lisa Norling (eds), *Iron Men, Wooden Women: Gender and Seafaring in the Atlantic World, 1700–1920*, Baltimore, MD: Johns Hopkins Press, 1996, pp. 169–88.

33 TNA, TS 34/9 'R.M.S. Egypt. Exhibits' (casualty lists).

2

Good Copy: The Savagery of Panic-Stricken 'Natives'

Shipping disasters promise to boost newspaper sales even today and did even more so at a time when steamers, perpetually growing in passenger capacity and sheer size, were the predominant means of overseas travel, including the most glamorous 'liner' segment. On 21 May, after long hours of searching for survivors, the *Egypt*'s rescued passengers and crew reached Brest on board the damaged *Seine*.[1] Telegrams circulated first reports of the collision almost immediately and internationally. By 22 May, the *Egypt* disaster was big news not only in France and Britain, but filled a column, too, on the front page of the *New York Times*.[2] The editors of *Le Petit Journal*, the veteran of the French tabloid press, were quick to grasp the story's potential and sent a special correspondent to Brest to interview the survivors of the *Egypt* disaster. On 23 May, the daily carried on its front page a garish report that would receive immediate international attention and frame the media coverage of the event over the next few days.[3] While its main French competitor, *Le Petit Parisien*, published a long account comparing the *Egypt* disaster with earlier similar accidents to conclude, reasonably enough before the invention of the marine radar, that 'signals, manoeuvres and laws are

1 *The Times*, 22 May 1922, p. 10.

2 *Daily Mail*, 22 May 1922, pp. 8f; *The Times*, 22 May 1922, p. 10; *Le Petit Journal*, 22 May 1922, p. 1; *New York Times*, 22 May 1922, p. 1.

3 'Le tragique abordage', *Le Petit Journal*, 23 May 1922, p. 1.

powerless against fogs', *Le Petit Journal* reserved its space for a simpler and more rousing tale of heroism and villainy.[4] The special correspondent claimed to derive his story from interviews with various eyewitnesses, including Capitaine Le Barzic, the commander of the French vessel *Seine* ('the perfect type of a Breton mariner') and various unnamed members of his crew. He further quoted a Swiss ship's cook, Jean Wintsch, who had served on the *Egypt*, and Admiral Schwerer, the maritime prefect of Brest.[5] Wintsch and Schwerer later both denied the authenticity of what was represented in the article as their statements. Yet the story sold well, spread far, and caused some concern in the P&O's company headquarters.[6]

Le Petit Journal's report commenced with an opening sequence playing up to the nationalist sentiments of its readers by celebrating the bravery of the French crew of the *Seine*. 'My men', Capitaine Le Barzic was quoted, 'did the impossible to save as many as they could', while the same could not be said for all of the *Egypt*'s crew. Le Barzic was reported to have declined further comment, since there were things a mariner was bound not to talk about. The special correspondent claimed, however, to have extracted damning detail from less dignified members of both crews as well as from some passengers. Asserting, incorrectly, that all officers of the *Egypt* had saved themselves, he referred to enraged French sailors who alleged that the sunken liner's shipmaster, Captain Collyer, had reached the *Seine* without even a drop of water on his attire. Collyer, the report proclaimed, had seemed barely concerned about the accident when he retired to the cabin with an air of insouciance. Admiral Schwerer was quoted with the speculation that the officers of the *Egypt* must have misjudged the severity of the damage and held off salvage operations for too long to prevent a heavy death toll that should have been perfectly avoidable under the circumstances. The correspondent allowed for exceptions, however: for heartrending examples of self-sacrifice on the part of British crew and passengers – the ship doctor who refused to enter a life boat in place of a passenger and went down

4 'Signaux, manoeuvres et lois sont impuissants contre les bouillards.' 'Le naufrage de l' "Egypt" a fait cent deux victimes', *Le Petit Parisien*, 23 May 1922, p. 1.

5 'Le tragique abordage', *Le Petit Journal*, 23 May 1922, p. 1.

6 NMM, Caird Library, P&O Collections, 65/2, f. 111 (letter by Admiral Schwerer, prefect of marine, Brest, to the British Consul at Brest, 5 June 1922); TNA, TS 34/8 'R.M.S. Egypt' (statement of Jean Wintsch, p. 3, n.d.).

with the vessel; the ship's printer, a non-swimmer, who surrendered his lifebelt to a lady thus embracing imminent death; the junior officer who would not give up the search for survivors.[7] Further instances of heroism were published for the edification of readers both in France and Britain, where the *Daily Mail* took the lead in providing 'human interest stories'. Another celebrated case of self-abandonment was that of 'Hardwick of the *Egypt*', the senior telegrapher who persisted in sending SOS messages from the sinking ship until the last moment and was eventually picked up from the water only to die of exhaustion. The worship of hands-on manliness was complemented with the praise for an American nun's womanly resignation to God's will: she was reported to have declined rescue while others waited for help and immersed herself in deep prayer until she was drowned in the sea.[8]

While *Le Petit Journal* commended the chivalrous French mariners on their impeccable conduct, the British sailors were presented to have stood the test of the sea with more mixed results. *L'Éclaireur de Nice*, on 24 May, recycled much of the material published by *Le Petit Journal* a day earlier on its front page under a remarkably verbose headline: 'Si l'équipage de l'"Egypt" avait tout son devoir le nombre des noyés eût eté insignificant' ('Had the crew of the *Egypt* done their full duty, the number of victims of drowning would have been insignificant').[9] Yet, in *Le Petit Journal's* version of the story, narrative tension was provided, in the main, not by staging a European gallantry contest, but by foregrounding a contrast between the selflessness (*dévouement*) and heroism that European maritime men were capable of and the presumably innate savagery (*sauvagerie*) of the Indian majority of the *Egypt*'s crew.[10] The racist binary trumped the rivalry of nationalisms, as it were: the former storyline may have promised even higher newspaper sales than the latter (except perhaps on the Promenade des Anglais in Nice) and was taken up instantly by *Le Petit Journal*'s competitors. On the front page of *Le Radical*'s 23 May edition, for instance, one subheading 'Scènes d'heroisme . . .' was completed by the next: 'et scènes de sauvagerie'.[11]

7 'Le tragique abordage', *Le Petit Journal*, 23 May 1922, p. 1.

8 *Daily Mail*, 23 May 1922, pp. 9f; see also *Le Petit Parisien*, 23 May 1922, p. 1.

9 *L'Éclaireur de Nice*, 24 May 1922, p. 1.

10 'Le tragique abordage', *Le Petit Journal*, 23 May 1922, p. 2.

11 'L'"Egypt" a coulé dans le Raz des Sein par un Fond de 119 mètres', *Le Radical*, 23 May 1922, p. 1.

The 'savagery' of the Indian seafarers was depicted most graphically: an 'indescribable panic' had seized the English ship, *Le Petit Journal* claimed. The '*Hindou matelots*' ('Hindu seamen'), they reported, had forcibly occupied the lifeboats and did not even stop at driving off women and children with kicks and punches. One witness was quoted to have observed how a passenger attempted to make space for his wife in one of the lifeboats, when one of the '*Hindous*' drew a revolver from his pocket and shot the passenger in the head before vanishing into the anonymity of the turmoil. Other '*Hindous*', the witness presumably claimed, jumped into a lifeboat already occupied by passengers, particularly women and children, in such great number that the boat overturned, broke away from its mooring, and killed those who struggled to stay afloat. According to the correspondent, Admiral Schwerer had confirmed that a terrible panic, grisly scenes, and savage brawls had occurred on board the *Egypt* as knives were wielded and revolvers fired. Several of the recovered corpses, he was quoted, had their skulls battered in by blows from clubs.[12] This narrative was repeated, amended, and embellished in the French press for several days until, at last, the story grew cold.

When the reporters had spilled their ink, the illustrators began to apply their most garish colours.[13] The weekly illustrated issue of *Le Petit Journal* presented a full-page cover image foregrounding 'white' manly chivalry and womanly piety on the backdrop of a violent scramble for a lifeboat with an armed shipmaster struggling to assert his authority – 'the best and the worst human instincts', the legend explained, were released at the same time. The weekly supplement of the *Lyon Republicain* used images that folded anxieties of class into those of race and of gender. Turbaned men wearing sailor suits raised handguns against well-clad European passengers of all ages: men, women, and children. The passengers, the caption insisted, had initially kept their cool, while the '*Hindous*' displayed 'an attitude so far unknown among seafarers'.

Once framed, the narrative spilled across borders easily with Reuters spreading *Le Petit Journal*'s version internationally and telegraphic news

12 'Le tragique abordage', *Le Petit Journal*, 23 May 1922, p. 1.

13 The following illustrations were traced and pointed out to me by my colleague Radhika Singha.

Le Fauteuil Hanté par Gaston Leroux.

Le Petit Journal illustré

HEBDOMADAIRE
61, rue Lafayette, Paris

PRIX : 0 fr. 30
4 Juin 1922

Scènes d'horreur et d'héroïsme

Dans la brume opaque le paquebot *Egypt* est éperonné par un steamer français. Une effroyable panique fait surgir sur le pont équipage et passagers. Et, dans ces circonstances dramatiques, les meilleurs et les pires instincts humains se donnent libre cours.

Figure 2.1. 'Scenes of horror and heroism', front page of *Le Petit Journal Illustré*, 4 June 1922

N° 20 - 11 Juin 1922

30 c

LYON RÉPUBLICAIN

SUPPLÉMENT HEBDOMADAIRE ILLUSTRÉ

Films et Ciné-Romans, Caricatures, Nouvelles, Actualités, etc.

ADMINISTRATION
6, rue Childebert
LYON

ABONNEMENTS (France)
Un an. . . . : 14 fr.
Six mois. . . : 7 50
Trois mois. . : 4

Le naufrage du paquebot "Egypt"

Le paquebot anglais « Egypt », courrier des Indes, naviguait dans le raz de l'Ile de Sein, dangereux parage de la côte bretonne, au milieu d'une brume épaisse qui couvrait la région depuis plusieurs jours, quand un choc formidable se produisit. Le cargo français « Seine » venait d'aborder la malle des Indes, dans laquelle la collision ouvrait une large voie d'eau. Vingt minutes après, l'« Egypt » disparaissait pour toujours. Si les passagers conservèrent tout d'abord leur sang-froid, les Hindous, qui formaient la plus grande partie de l'équipage, eurent une attitude inconnue jusqu'ici par les marins. Ils se ruèrent sur les chaloupes, menaçant de leur revolver ceux qui voulaient également s'y réfugier. Pendant ce temps, officiers et matelots français rivalisaient de courage et d'abnégation dans les travaux de sauvetage. Malgré les nombreux rescapés recueillis par le cargo, on déplore la disparition d'une centaine de victimes

Figure 2.2. 'The loss of the liner "Egypt"', front page of *Lyon Republicain* (weekly illustrated supplement), 4 June 1922

bouncing back and forth on a transcontinental scale:[14] within a couple of days Turin's *La Stampa* and Milan's *Corriere de la Sera*, the *Berliner Volkszeitung* and the *Hamburger Anzeiger*, the *Chicago Daily Tribune* and the *Washington Post* all hawked reports proclaiming that fear-crazed Indian sailors, armed with revolvers, knives, or clubs, had prevented passengers from entering the lifeboats and had not even stopped at pushing them overboard.[15] The *Egypt* disaster was of course front page news in the British press, too, even though their reporting varied to some extent from that of their French counterparts and was also more diverse. Here, French heroism was obviously celebrated less than British valour and the damning prejudgment of the Indian seafarer was less unisonous, too.

The Times, giving much space to the accident over several days, referred to accounts by British passengers in suggesting that the 'lascars' panic' had been controlled efficiently by the British officers and that French reports of knives and revolvers in the hands of Indian seafarers were mere sensationalism.[16] On 29 May, this newspaper published a short piece by their Calcutta correspondent who reported that 'stories about the behaviour of the lascars on board the P. and O. Egypt are received with incredulity in Bengal' since Indian seafarers had 'won a great reputation' during the war. While 'Chittagong lascars are descended from pirates and retain the best traditions of seamanship', he conceded, however, that not the same could be said of the 'Pathan' (Pashtun) firemen and the Goan stewards recruited in Bombay.[17] We shall see that a similar line of defence was chosen by the representatives of the P&O Company and of the India Office during the official inquiry over the following months: the notion that Indian seafarers were 'built' of racially inferior 'stuff'[18] was held to be too self-evident to be contested, but the racial binary was replaced by a graded racial hierarchy that would render certain purportedly 'maritime races' eligible nevertheless for employment on British steamers.

---

14 Cf. *Daily Herald*, 24 May 1922, p. 3.

15 *La Stampa*, 23 May 1922, p. 3; *Corriere de la Sera*, 23 May 1922, p. 3; ibid., 24 May 1922, p. 3; *Berliner Volkszeitung*, 23 May 1922, p. 3; *Hamburger Anzeiger*, 22 May 1922, p. 2; *Chicago Daily Tribune*, 22 May 1922, p. 2; *Washington Post*, 23 May 1922, p. 3.

16 *The Times*, 23 May, p. 10; ibid., 25 May 1922, p. 9.

17 *The Times*, 29 May 1922, p. 9.

18 This phrase was offered by the trade unionist Joseph Cotter: TNA, TS 34/10 'R.M.S. Egypt. Transcript of Court Proceedings', Second Day: 25 July 1922, p. 16.

Other British newspapers showed less consideration for the nuances of 'scientific' racism. This included numerous regional newspapers as well as the *Daily Mail* and the *Evening News*, leaders of the British yellow press, and, like *The Times*, parts of Lord Northcliffe's newspaper empire.[19] 'If it had not been for the Lascars and natives rushing for the boats, all the women would have been saved', a Scottish passenger of the *Egypt*, Joseph Duff, was reported to have declared to the *Evening News* – a statement that was promptly replicated by other newspapers, including the *New York Times*, the *Washington Post* and the *Los Angeles Times*.[20] The *Daily Mail* covered the shipwreck initially in a restrained voice – evoking the P&O Company's 'fine record of service', calling solemnly for an application of all scientific means against fog as 'the direst foe of safety at sea', and reminiscing mournfully that the paper's owner, Lord Northcliffe, had concluded his world tour on board the *Egypt* only in the previous year.[21] Within a couple of days, however, the paper had joined the race for the hottest story: 'white' female passengers, their Paris correspondent claimed, had provided him with shocking accounts. A Mrs Hansen purportedly stated that she had been beaten back by 'lascars' on attempting to enter a lifeboat while a Mrs Taylor was quoted with the words that 'the natives ran shrieking about the ship, pushing women aside and struggling with each other to get into the boats'.[22] The *New York Times* readily reproduced these accounts the following day.[23]

The P&O Company's management immediately took particular notice of 'various sensational telegrams', which the *Daily Mail*'s correspondent in France had 'produced'. Relations with the paper were apparently friendly, however: the editor sent the telegrams for perusal to the P&O's headquarters in Leadenhall Street and leading figures of the company then summoned the correspondent, 'Mr Curnock, who agreed to treat the interview as private'.[24] The editor had taken care, already, that

19 Searches in the British Newspaper Archive (britishnewspaperarchive.co.uk) show that the *Petit Journal*'s stories were spread and further embellished by numerous regional newspapers across Britain.

20 *New York Times*, 23 May 1922, p. 2; *Washington Post*, 23 May 1922, p. 3; *Los Angeles Times*, 23 May 1922, p. 17.

21 *Daily Mail*, 22 May 1922, pp. 8f.

22 *Daily Mail*, 24 May 1922, p. 9.

23 *New York Times*, 25 May 1922, p. 17.

24 NMM, P&O/65/1, f. 210 ('Memorandum for Mr Shaw', 23 May 1922, and 'Postscriptum', 24 May 1922.

the allegations of the female passengers were printed together with a kind of disclaimer: quoting the liberal MP Sir Robert Thomas's question in Parliament to the president of the Board of Trade about whether he had any information of armed 'lascars' preventing women from entering the life boats and whether any steps would be taken 'to prevent Lascars in passenger ships from carrying firearms', the report ended with the following statement: 'French correspondents at Brest write in severe terms of the conduct of the Lascars in the Egypt, but it is obviously impossible for any judgment to be formed until the Board of Trade inquiry into the collision is held.'[25] And, indeed, the *Daily Mail* let the issue drop for the time being.

Other sections of the British conservative press would not be discouraged so easily from gainful scandalmongering. The *Pall Mall Gazette* was among several newspapers that printed the 'graphic account' that two moderately prominent survivors of the *Egypt* disaster, Prof. H. G. D. Turnbull of the Indian Educational Service and his wife, Eleanor Lucia, a prolific author of edifying children's books, were reported to have made on returning to London. Mrs Turnbull was quoted to have said that the 'lascars' 'were perfectly dreadful', 'rushed about like madmen', and 'pushed women into the water', while the officers were 'occupied in trying to force the Lascars under control'.[26] Before the Court of Inquiry, her husband later confirmed that a 'struggle or scrum was going on near the davits and I saw a deck Officer trying to prevent lascars forcing themselves in front of passengers'.[27] Mrs Turnbull stated similarly that Indian firemen had created some 'trouble' while the 'Goanese and Lascars behaved well', though only the behaviour of the 'white Officers' qualified for the epithet 'beyond praise'.[28]

However, Lucia Turnbull appears to have been somewhat unhappy about her moment of yellow-press fame. In a letter to the P&O Company she wrote:

---

25 *Daily Mail*, 24 May 1922, p. 9. See also Hansard, vol. 154 (24 May 1922), col. 1200–1.

26 'Liner's Survivors Reach London', *Pall Mall Gazette*, 25 May 1922, p. 12.

27 TNA, TS 34/8 '"R.M.S. Egypt": Various Proofs and Documents' (depositions by passengers and crew: Harold George Dalway Turnbull, p. 6).

28 NMM, Caird Library, P&O 64/4 ('Memorandum for Mr Ritchie: statement of Mrs Turnbull', 25 May 1922).

> I sent to the Times, Morning Post & Daily Mail a disclaimer of the extravagant statements attributed to me in some of the papers, re my experience of the Egypt. I only saw one reporter for about two seconds at Victoria to speak to, and the others catching my name wrote down what they wanted me to say I suppose.[29]

Whatever they may have perceived or felt about the South Asian crew on board the sinking ship, the Turnbulls' professional lives as colonial educationists in India made them ill at ease with wholesale condemnations of 'natives'. Three years later, the couple jointly published a book entitled *Golden Deeds of India*, which they dedicated 'to the Girls and Boys' of that country: it contained thirteen morally uplifting tales of 'courage' and 'heroism', beginning with the benignity of emperor Ashoka and the self-immolation of the Rajput princess Padmini. It concluded, however, with an account of 'lascar' valour and loyalty in times of distress at sea – in a British imperial setting, both before and during the Great War.[30]

Liberal British newspapers at first showed even less concern for imperial harmony and fewer qualms than the conservative yellow press about flogging the racist rumours surrounding the *Egypt*'s wreck: the *Manchester Guardian*, flagship of the liberal press, fully relied on *Le Petit Journal's* report, even rehashed the fabricated tale of a passenger gunned down by a 'lascar'.[31] The tendency in liberalism to conceive of social inequality as a *natural condition* opened, not only at this historical juncture, the floodgates for a social-Darwinistic and racist radicalization of the 'moderate' political mainstream.[32] If the decades enfolding the turn of the century proved, accordingly, the reconcilability of liberal reform with politics of racist exclusion in various parts of the world, the most prominent spokesmen of a xenophobic brand of trade unionism was perhaps Joseph Havelock Wilson, founder of Britain's largest

29 Ibid. (Letter from Eleanor Lucia Turnbull, 4 June 1922).

30 Eleanor Lucia Turnbull and Harold George Dalway Turnbull, *Golden Deeds of India: Book I*, London: Oxford University Press, 1925 (numerous reprints until at least 1951).

31 *Manchester Guardian*, 24 May 1922, p. 7.

32 In the context of slavery, this argument has been powerfully proposed in Thomas Holt, *The Problem of Freedom: Race, Labor, and Politics in Jamaica and Britain, 1832–1938*, Baltimore, MD: John Hopkins University Press, 1992, pp. xixf. For a more comprehensive critique of ideology see Domenico Losurdo, *Liberalism: A Counter-History*, London: Verso, 2011, p. 231 and *passim*.

seamen's union and Liberal Party MP for Middlesbrough.[33] But even the more left-leaning *Daily Herald* with their large working-class and trade union readership published at first, when the *Egypt* foundered, a narrative very similar to the one disseminated by the *Manchester Guardian.*[34] Certainly, the hegemony of racist 'common sense' did not remain uncontested among the readers of liberal and labourite papers – we shall see that in subsequent months both would give more space than conservative tabloids to counter-narratives even of Indian crew members.[35] And, only a few days after the accident, Labour politician Ernest Thurtle sharply expressed his unease with the *Daily Herald*'s reporting in a letter to the editors:

> There appears to be a deplorable tendency on the part of the Press and the public to condemn off-hand the conduct of the Lascars on the ill-fated Egypt after the manner of the gallant Americans who lynch the 'nigger' first and inquire into the facts of his crime afterwards.

He pointed out that 'panic is no respecter of skin colour . . . The Lascars were good enough to do the hard and unpleasant work of the Egypt. They ought to be good enough to be accorded the elementary right of trial before conviction.'[36]

Despite such objections and regardless of mounting evidence to the contrary, the *Daily Herald*'s reporting on the *Egypt* disaster continued to argue that the employment of 'lascars for cheapness' was responsible for the high death toll on the *Egypt* – an allegation the most influential trade union spokesmen of US seamen, Andrew Furuseth, had also made to strengthen the case for excluding Chinese and Filipino seafarers from employment in the US merchant marine.[37] Even journalistic writings on

---

33 David Montgomery, 'Empire, Race and Working-Class Mobilization', in Peter Alexander and Rick Halpern (eds), *Racializing Class, Classifying Race: Labour and Difference in Britain, the USA and Africa*, Basingstoke: Macmillan, 2000, pp. 5–7. For a detailed account of Havelock Wilson's political career and his role in seamen's unionism see Arthur Marsh and Victoria Ryan, *The Seamen: A History of the National Union of Seamen*, Oxford: Malthouse Press, 1989.

34 *Daily Herald*, 24 May 1922, p. 3.

35 *Daily Herald*, 24 June 1922, pp. 1, 4; *Manchester Guardian*, 29 July 1922, p. 13

36 *Daily Herald*, 30 May 1922, p. 7.

37 'Lascars for Cheapness', *Daily Herald*, 6 September 1922, p. 5; 'Furuseth Warns Americans of Sea Danger from Cheap Labor', *Labor World*, 3 June 1922, p. 2.

the far left of the British political spectrum could be deeply ambivalent. In the *Communist*, the syndicalist seafarer Gunnar Soderberg thus speculated, not implausibly, that 'lascars' knew 'perfectly well that if they do not make a fight to save themselves, no one else would care a hang what became of them', while effectively endorsing the view of Havelock Wilson's seaman's union that Indian seafarers were on the whole incompetent and if the *Egypt* had 'carried a white crew only . . . no lives had been lost'.[38]

A few weeks later, however, the socialist suffragette Sylvia Pankhurst quipped in the *Workers' Dreadnought* that the 'Lascar panic aboard the Egypt appears now to have been a figment of the panic-stricken brains of some of the British passengers'.[39] Doubts about the racist storyline were raised, too, from other, politically less dissident quarters: the P&O's directors received various letters of sympathy after the *Egypt* disaster, one of which drew attention, for instance, to panic-related losses of life in ship accidents involving all-white crews. The letter concluded: 'Panic is not confined to any nationality or colour, and will remain so, until the human being is built on other lines.'[40] Such views appear to have made limited impact, however, on the overall public appraisal of the S.S. *Egypt*'s losses. A racist 'common sense' on matters maritime showed few cracks around and beyond the North Atlantic rim – a 'common sense' that was summed up in a *New York Times* editorial confidently and in a suitable tone of bourgeois decorum:

> Examples of heroism, indeed, were not lacking. Not a few of the officers died at their posts, and there is no hint that any of them – that any of the white men on board, for that matter – failed to equal the highest demands that duty makes on their class and nation . . .
>
> The trouble, such as there was, came from the Lascar crew – men useful at sea except in the great emergencies, but then likely to peril their own lives as well as those of others by panic rushes. This is not the first time that the economy of employing at sea these 'men of the lesser breeds' has proved expensive in the end. That it continues only

38 'The Shipowners or the Lascars?', *Communist*, 3 June 1922, p. 10.

39 *Workers' Dreadnought*, 29 July 1922, p. 5. This paper was, like the *Communist*, associated with the early Communist Party of Great Britain.

40 Matt B. Walker to Managing Directors, P&O, 11 September 1922: NMM, P&O/65/2, f. 134.

> shows that some shipowners value profits above their own and their country's good name.[41]

The editor's judgment, made when little was known about the circumstances of the *Egypt*'s shipwreck, was purely based on precedent: 'This is not the first time', he insisted. The notion that Asian seafarers panicked and came up wanting in times of crisis, particularly in the North Atlantic had, in fact, been circulated for decades – usually derived from the assertion of a general racial inferiority, at times backed up with the claim that they were biologically unsuited for ship-work in northern climates. The *New York Times*' editors recycled and endorsed this racist pattern of reasoning while keeping a distance from any unseemly coarseness: invoking Nobel laureate Rudyard Kipling, they placed the 'lesser breeds' within the most civilized inverted commas.[42]

41 *New York Times*, 24 May 1922, p. 15.

42 The 'lesser breeds without the law' was a familiar phrase since Kipling had coined it in his 1897 poem 'Recessional': Rudyard Kipling, *Sixty Poems*, London: Hodder and Stoughton, 1939, pp. 59f.

3

Spelling Disaster: Class and Race When a Ship Goes Down

By the early 1920s, maritime racism had postured for decades as embarrassed truth-speaking dressing up, at times, as salty but profound popular wisdom. 'Them Niggers', again within inverted commas, was the title of a 'humorous' piece published in London's gentlemanly *Pall Mall Gazette* in 1896. The author, presenting himself as a 'Mariner of England', narrated an encounter with an old sailor, the conversation shifting quickly to the question of why British shipping companies employed 'darkies' or 'lascars'. After displaying his own mannerly and polished eloquence, he put the following words into the sailor's mouth:

> 'Why!' with huge contempt, 'becos half-a-dozen of 'em sign on for less money than on'y one of us 'ud sail for. And wot's the result?' – taking his pipe out of his mouth to give expression to his sentiment – 'why, there's more passenger boats lost on account of these coolies than what you'd think for. It's only about two years ago, mister, that a big liner was lost off the Portuguese coast through about five-score of these fellers bein' benumbed, an' in a holy funk, in a gale that any boat could 'ave weathered if she'd been properly manned. Ye see, mister, in their own climit they work like 'osses; so why not keep 'em there?'[1]

1 *Pall Mall Gazette*, 7 September 1896, p. 3.

The 'common sense' of imperialist societies thus had thrown up a repertoire of replicable racist images that was readily available when journalists strove to convert ship accidents into good copy. In 1898, the *New York Times* covered the foundering of the *Clan Drummond* suggesting that the 'details have also served as a warning of the danger which has been frequently pointed out of having large proportions of Lascars in the crews of British vessels'. The paper admitted that 'great reticence is maintained on the subject' by their (white) interviewees – indicating perhaps that some effort had to be made to extract the desired juicy details. Yet they stated that 'it appears that the Lascars became panic-stricken and fought like demons. A survivor relates that several Europeans were drowned by being dragged down by frantic Lascar coolies, who lost all discipline.'[2] Reporting on the sinking of the *Oceana*, another P&O steamer, in the English Channel almost exactly ten years before the *Egypt* disaster, the *Manchester Guardian*, too, gave a standard account of the crew's behaviour: 'Discipline among officers and the European crew was exemplary, but the Lascars behaved "like frightened chicken".'[3] The *Daily Mail* quoted a rescued passenger, an army captain, who opined that the 'lascars did not behave badly for lascars, but they were simply petrified with "blue funk"' – a statement that was echoed by one of the *Oceana*'s officers who agreed that 'the lascars did not act so badly for black men'.[4]

The repetition and invariability of certain representational features served to corroborate the argument that deviant behaviour in times of crisis was not ascribable to individual decisions but to racial essence: 'lascars' did not shout, for instance, when trying to save themselves from a sinking ship – they uttered 'unnerving . . . howls' and 'weird, ear-piercing screams' or 'shrieked' effetely.[5] Not only did they forgo any claim to manliness and chivalry, they did not seem to possess any human individuality at all: unless shepherded strictly they strayed about as a

2 *New York Times*, 18 December 1898, p. 1.

3 *Manchester Guardian*, 18 March 1912, p. 7. The phrase 'like frightened chicken' was apparently quoted from the statement of a German ship's officer who had been a passenger on the *Oceana*; the statement was quoted at length in a report of the *Observer*, 17 March 1912, p. 9.

4 *Daily Mail*, 18 March 1912, p. 8.

5 *Daily Mail*, 18 March 1912, p. 7; *Observer*, 17 March 1912, p. 9; *New York Times*, 25 May 1922, p. 17.

headless, nameless flock, from which neither culprits nor victims could be identified.[6] And, of course, it was assumed that the 'panic-stricken native' could not speak comprehensibly and sensibly, that he had no individual voice to be taken account of. No need was felt accordingly to record their versions of the respective incident.[7]

The consistently racializing but otherwise variable terminology used in British imperial and American contexts for referring to Indian seafarers facilitated this imputation of an unchanging and homogeneous collective identity: 'lascar' was used, by the early twentieth century, as a term of British maritime law and public discourse that distinguished seafarers originating either from 'British India' or South Asia at large from European and other non-European seamen.[8] However, we shall see that the term 'lascar' could also be interpreted to apply to Indian deckhands only in contrast to equally South Asian firemen and stewards. While its exact meaning shifted and was never conclusively defined, it was commonly understood that the word 'lascar' signified a more comprehensively subordinated, sub-standard employment relationship and was thus combined or used interchangeably with the term 'coolie'.[9] Indian deckhands, on their part, did not usually refer to themselves as 'lascars', but as *khalasis* – a long-established

6 See also Lucy Delap, '"Thus Does Man Prove His Fitness to Be the Master of Things": Shipwrecks, Chivalry and Masculinities in Nineteenth- and Twentieth-Century Britain', *Cultural and Social History* 3, no. 1 (2006), pp. 71–3.

7 I have not come across a single newspaper report identifying an Indian seafarer by name as a perpetrator of acts of violence on a sinking ship or as a witness of a ship accident. The names of drowned Indian crew were recorded and publicly mentioned only rarely except during the World Wars, when compensation claims came to be recognized and forms of commemoration like the erection of the Lascar War Memorial in Calcutta became conceivable. Cf. p. 79. For an exceptional case, in which Indian seafarers received a medal for their contribution to saving passengers and crew of the foundering German steamer *Hammonia*, see chapter 11 below.

8 For a summary of various reinterpretations of the legal term 'lascar' from 1888 to 1920 see OIOC, Bombay Marine Proceedings P/10793, A345–46: Government of Bombay, Marine Department, Order 1900, 20 November 1920. See also Frank Broeze, 'Underdevelopment and Dependency: Maritime India during the Raj', *Modern Asian Studies* 18, no. 3 (1984), p. 435; Marika Sherwood, 'Race, Nationality and Employment among Lascar Seamen, 1660 to 1945', *Journal of Ethnic and Migration Studies* 17, no. 2 (1991), p. 230.

9 See for instance House of Commons Papers, *Report of the Mercantile Marine Committee* [hereafter: *MMC*], vol. 2, Minutes of Evidence, London: His Majesty's Stationary Office, 1903, pp. 233, 289, 295, 315, 348.

expression in Indian Ocean seafaring signifying the 'free' sailor or a 'labourer of a superior order, employed chiefly about ships or in the army'.[10] Even the first 'English and Hindoostanee Naval Dictionary', compiled by Thomas Roebuck in 1811, introduced 'lascar' as a term of naval *English*, for which *khulasee* and *kharwa* were given as the Hindustani equivalents.[11]

A century later, the Anglo-Saxon press appeared to opt for the designation 'native' even more frequently than for 'lascar', however, when referring to Indian seafarers. Much like the label 'migrant' in our own time, the term 'native' abstracted altogether from the employment relationship and redirected focus solely to ethnicity. After the *Egypt* inquiry, a correspondent from Manchester to the Indian nationalist paper *Bombay Chronicle*, Dr A. D. Jilla, noted the curious shift in the meaning of the word: the 'ordinary Britisher', he wrote, 'dubs the Indian twice "native", in other words the Indian is native not only in India – mainly at the hands of the arrogant, impetuous and snobby Anglo-Indians – but he is also "native" in England, France, America etc. wherever they happen to labour under the idea that the Indian is not his own master.'[12] Yet the notion of the 'native' had not merely conquered the British public sphere, but also entered the nomenclature of maritime management. 'In the P. and O. service,' noted Liversidge's manual for ship engineers, 'these greasers and firemen are called "natives".'[13] Shipping

10 Horace Hayman Wilson, *A Glossary of the Judicial and Revenue Terms, and of Useful Words Occurring in Official Documents Relating to the Administration of the Government of British India*, London: W. H. Allen & Co., 1855, pp. 272–5; G. Small, *A Laskari Dictionary or Anglo–Indian Vocabulary of Nautical Terms and Phrases in English and Hindustani. Chiefly in the Corrupt Jargon in Use among Laskars or Indian Sailors* (originally compiled by Capt. Thomas Roebuck, revised and corrected by William Carmichael Smyth), London: W. H. Allen & Co., 1882. See also Ravi Ahuja, 'Networks of Subordination – Networks of the Subordinated: The Case of South Asian Maritime Labour under British Imperialism (c. 1890–1947)', in Harald Fischer-Tiné and Ashwini Tambe (eds), *Spaces of Disorder: The Limits of British Colonial Control in South Asia and the Indian Ocean*, London: Routledge, 2008, p. 14.

11 Thomas Roebuck, *An English and Hindoostanee Naval Dictionary of Technical Terms and Sea Phrases . . .*, London: Black, Parry & Co., 1813 (London reprint of the original Calcutta edition), p. 60. *Kharwa* is the designation of a Gujarati caste conventionally associated with seafaring.

12 *Bombay Chronicle*, 11 October 1922, p. 9. 'Anglo-Indian' was the term used for members of the British colonial establishment in India.

13 John G. Liversidge, *Engine-Room Practice: A Handbook for the Royal Navy and Mercantile Marine*, London: Charles Griffin & Co., 1923 (11th ed.), p. 32.

officials occasionally even considered the designation 'non-European' as a politer alternative, but whichever of these '*n*-words' were used, it was understood that they signified racial subordination and a reduced entitlement to 'freedom'.[14] The epithet 'native' appears to have been considered a better-mannered, publicly utterable and recordable paraphrase for the earlier designations 'lascar' and 'coolie' as well as for the unabashedly racist invective 'nigger'. The latter term of racist abuse with its implication of slave status was routinely used by British officers and crew for Indian seafarers, so much so that some of the latter would refer to themselves, and, as we shall see, even in court, as *kala admi* or 'black man'.[15] Conversely, racial status or relative 'whiteness' appears to have served as a metaphorical gauge for the maritime quality even of – invariably 'white' – masters of early twentieth-century British merchant vessels. James Dalziel, in one of his 'engine-room stories', thus claimed that shipmasters were assessed by their (British) crews within the first six months of service and kept this 'label' 'till the act of God, or the will of the owners, removes him to another sphere'. Being categorized as 'a real white man', wrote the former mariner Dalziel, was the ultimate praise a master could hope for while being called a 'pukka pariah' indicated the highest degree of 'badness'.[16]

Racism was a hegemonic ideology of the age of imperialism, and its hegemonic power, its status as an ideology that reached out from the ruling strata to large sections of the labouring classes, reveals itself only in full measure if we take close account of its 'politer' forms: it was the racism of the boardrooms, hiding between quotation marks while flaunting gentlemanly decorum, that had the greatest political and regulatory impact, not the uncouth racism of the dockyards and the forecastles. Harsh structures of racial segmentation were laid out and justified, as we shall see, in a deliberately bland and sanitized business language. But the hegemonic status of racism also implied that it *had* an important place in British working-class life and politics, even though, as Laura Tabili rightly insists, racial exclusion and closure were never

---

14 TNA, TS 34/10 'R.M.S. Egypt. Transcript of Court Proceedings', Eighth Day: 2 August 1922, p. 114: A. D. Bateson, legal counsel for the P&O Company at the *Egypt* inquiry, thus spoke of 'natives, or non-Europeans as they are now called'.

15 See p. 98.

16 James Dalziel, *The First Watch and Other Engine-Room Stories*, London: Fisher Unwin, 1907, p. 1.

complete and uncontested.[17] When the American journalist Whiting Williams took a tour of post–First World War Britain to explore the 'worker's mind', he met impoverished, underemployed men in London's port district who felt aggrieved by Asian labour market competitors: 'See them Lascars? . . . The law's been letting them things [*sic*] and the Chinks get the places on the boats that should belong to us. 'Taint right.'[18]

British seamen's unions had campaigned unsuccessfully against growing foreign, and especially Indian, labour market competition since the 1890s (and would continue to do so well into the 1930s). In this they had sought to mobilize public support, reverting at times more or less openly to jingoistic and racist rhetoric.[19] Edward Tupper, one of the most well-known organisers of the dominant National Union of Seamen thus recalled in his memoirs that the union's founder, autocratic leader and liberal politician Joseph Havelock Wilson, had declared 'that over 25 per cent of the men in the mercantile marine, Asiatics of all kind, were not fit for the job, and should never have been employed in the British service'. As for himself, Tupper believed that 'conditions have got to be bettered, unless Great Britain wants to find itself with no Merchant Navy at all, or with a Merchant Navy run entirely by untrustworthy Asiatics'.[20] That British sailors were more difficult to control, but superior in terms of courage in an emergency, had already been asserted strongly by various witnesses heard in 1902 by the Mercantile Marine Committee.[21] Yet positive evidence seemed hard to come by and the spokesmen of colonial and shipping interests could always counter such assertions with examples of 'lascar' sacrifice and heroism.[22] Lead by the

17 Cf. Laura Tabili, *Global Migrants, Local Culture: Natives and Newcomers in Provincial England, 1841–1939*, Basingstoke: Palgrave Macmillan, 2011.

18 Whiting Williams, *Full Up and Fed Up: The Worker's Mind in Crowded Britain*, New York: Charles Scribner's Sons, 1921, p. 20.

19 Cf. Sherwood, 'Race, Nationality and Employment', pp. 229–44; Laura Tabili, *'We Ask for British Justice': Workers and Racial Difference in Late Imperial Britain*, Ithaca, NY: Cornell University Press, 1994, pp. 81–112.

20 Edward Tupper, *Seamen's Torch: The Life Story of Captain Edward Tupper, National Union of Seamen*, London: Hutchinson, 1938, pp. 62, 309.

21 *MMC*, vol. 2, Evidence, pp. 36, 48, 223, 356, 494, 525, 644, 660.

22 See, e.g., a 'Newspaper Extract Illustrating the Courage of Lascar Seamen' published in the *Liverpool Journal of Commerce*, 14 June 1902, submitted as evidence to the Mercantile Marine Committee by John Hughes, spokesman of the Liverpool Steamship Owners' Association and reproduced as Appendix N, No. 4, in *MMC*, vol. 3, Appendices to Evidence, Analysis of Evidence and Subject Index, p. 164. See also *MMC*, vol. 2, Evidence, pp. 301, 532.

P&O and the BISN companies, the shipping industry eventually succeeded in thwarting restrictions on the employment of 'lascars', even though the committee stated that it was 'satisfactory to find that no competent authority alleges that the foreigner is a better seaman than the British subject, especially at times of danger'.[23]

Seamen's unions continued to mobilize widespread anti-Asian resentment – for instance, in May 1912, when they called for a national strike in the wake of the above-mentioned foundering of the *Oceana* in March and the much more deadly *Titanic* disaster a few weeks later. The *Daily Herald*, presenting itself as the voice of the British trade union movement, published a rousing leader supporting the call for a 'national seamen's strike'. The leader condemned the 'slaughter of the steerage', namely the carelessly inadequate safety facilities of the *Titanic*, and demanded to enforce adequate working and safety conditions on board the ever more sizeable liners. At the same time, however, it dealt side blows against disreputable and socially or racially inferior labour market competitors. The latter, it was argued, unfairly underbid and drove out British sailors thereby violating the latter's moral entitlement to a respectable place within the nation:

> Portsmouth and Plymouth drifters, loafers and criminals fresh from prison cells, Chinese and Lascars, the filthy and diseased wrecks of the five continents are recruited to man British boats, whilst British sailors are left to tramp or starve or rot on land because they demand a reasonable wage.[24]

A week later, strike action concentrated on the P&O Company, that was presented with a long list of demands for the improvement of employment conditions on board ship. The list combined, similarly, matters of safety equipment, payment, shore leave, and other working conditions with demands for racial segregation and employment restrictions: the unions insisted that 'the accommodation for European stewards be provided apart from the Goanese' and raised as their first and key claim that 'two European seamen for each [life]boat [be] carried'.[25] Tom Chambers, presenting the case to the *Daily Herald*, defended this demand as being 'extremely moderate':

23 *MMC*, vol. 1, Report, pp. vi–vii, ix.
24 *Daily Herald*, 2 May 1912, p. 1.
25 *Manchester Guardian*, 9 May 1912, p. 6.

> We asked that there shall be two efficient seamen for each lifeboat carried on every ship; and this the general public, as well as ourselves, were entitled to expect would have been conceded. I should have thought that the loss of life in the 'Oceana' collision would have been a sufficient lesson to the P. and O., considering the evidence of the passengers as to the conduct of the India crew in such difficult circumstances.

He repeated that the 'safety of the general public' demanded reform and added, as further proof for the need of 'two efficient men for each lifeboat', that it was 'not unusual for Lascars to go to sleep while on lookout duty'. The union's general secretary, Edmund Cathery, was quoted to have drawn the same connection between 'efficiency' and 'Europeanness' when commenting on 'lascars': 'Whatever these men might be in ordinary circumstances, there was no doubt that when there was danger they were too frightened to be of any use in life-saving.' [26]

The emphasis on the 'safety of the general public' allowed the union to represent their struggle not as a 'mere' issue of class conflict that would not be met with much sympathy in a wider social arena, but as an issue of great importance to society as a whole: as a matter of nation, empire, and race. Trade union tactics were, in other words, adapted to the dominant ideologies of the time, which appear to have been both internalized and used 'pragmatically' to achieve inclusion and recognition at any cost. Keepers of hegemonic opinion conceded, at times, that the unions' objectives could be deemed worth consideration. Referring explicitly to the 'threatened strike in the transport trade', the conservative *Daily Mail* thus argued that 'a larger quota of white seamen' was a matter of 'deep national importance' since subsidized mail steamers 'should be able to provide a reserve of British seamen for the Navy'.[27] The *Manchester Guardian*, when commenting on impending seamen's strike, made clear that the tactical edge of this particular demand was well understood:

> Amongst various other demands which appear to have been forwarded more or less under the wing of a favourable opportunity that

26 *Daily Herald*, 8 May 1912, p. 1.

27 'The Lascar in the Liner', *Daily Mail*, 10 May 1912, p. 6.

> relating to the manning of all lifeboats by two European seamen has attracted, and was no doubt meant to attract, attention and sympathy in quarters not usually well disposed to the proposals of trade unions.

The mouthpiece of liberal opinion yet proposed to deal with the unions' initiative by setting up a 'Parliamentary inquiry into the whole question of manning from the point of view of the safety of life in passenger ships' since the decision on whether 'Indian seamen . . . should be discriminated against on account of any *natural disability*' could not be left to 'local branches of trade unions'.[28] The dilemma of a 'pragmatic', tactical racism came out in the open immediately: when the possibility was admitted that trade union demands were in the 'public' interest and for the 'greater good', these demands were not only raised to a higher, more 'respectable' political level, but also removed from the sphere where trade unions could exert direct influence. At the end of the day, no major political force chose to meddle seriously with the recruitment policy of the empire's most powerful shipping concern: between 1910 and 1925 the number of Indian seafarers employed in British merchant ships *grew*, in fact, from 44,000 (or 17.5 per cent) to 55,000 (or 24 per cent), while the total number of employed seafarers declined from 250,000 to 230,000.[29]

Attempts by liberal trade unionists to trump class with race failed because both categories of social dominance continued to be folded into each other in the discourses and practices of the middling and upper classes. The extensive evidence presented to the Mercantile Marine Committee in 1902 provides ample material to demonstrate this point. Shipping officials and representatives of shipping companies sometimes agreed with opponents of 'lascar' employment that British sailors were more muscular and more 'efficient', especially in situations of emergency, on warships and under cold climatic conditions.[30] Yet issues of class were of even greater concern to them: the deterioration of discipline among increasingly rights-conscious British sailors, the 'blight of insubordination' as it was put by a campaigner for the reinforcement of the shipmaster's authority, was identified as the problem overshadowing all

28 *Manchester Guardian*, 9 May 1912, p. 8. Emphasis added.

29 Tabili, '*We Ask for British Justice*', p. 47.

30 *MMC*, vol. 2, Evidence, pp. 30f, 48, 133, 135, 327f, 356f.

other labour issues.[31] The 'sea lawyer' – the sailor who incited the crew to indiscipline, proclaimed demands on board ship, and questioned the absolute power of the shipmaster – was the demon that tortured many of the witnesses: Captain Henry Henderson, superintendent of Liverpool's Mercantile Marine Office, defined the 'sea lawyer' as 'a man who is constantly bringing about irritation between the master and the crew on little points of things . . . He has a little knowledge, and it is dangerous.'[32] Henderson believed that the spread of education in Britain among the 'lower ranks of society' had resulted in a 'little unhinging' by reducing, both on shore and at sea, the inclination 'to take orders quietly'.[33] While referring to instances of 'sea lawyers' even among Indian crews, he, like many other representatives of the shipping industry, assured the committee that greater amenability to both discipline and excessive heat were the ultimate reasons for the 'lascar's' increasing employment.[34]

The spectre of the 'sea lawyer' had emerged in the latter decades of the nineteenth century, when shipping legislation proliferated and trade unionism struck roots among British seafarers.[35] Not just shipowners, sea captains, and port officials were haunted by it; the 'sea lawyer' also made appearances as a literary figure in narratives widely read among the British middle classes. One such narrative was Joseph Conrad's *The Nigger of the 'Narcissus'* – published in 1897, immediately celebrated by contemporaries as a major contribution to modern literature and characterized, more recently, by Cedric Watts as 'a distinctly successful new departure for Conrad' and 'the first novel in his decade of brilliance'.[36] Watts does not conceal that this novel also sported a 'militant Toryism', that it reflected 'the mood of imperialistic enthusiasm' and 'came close' to recommending a '"feudal" pattern of society: a corporate, hierarchic

31 W. H. Hood, *The Blight of Insubordination: The Lascar Question and Rights and Wrongs of the British Shipmaster*, London: Spottiswoode & Co., 1903.

32 *MMC*, vol. 2, Evidence, p. 41. See also p. 78.

33 Ibid., p. 27.

34 Ibid., pp. 32, 35; see also pp. 9, 21, 48, 61f, 73, 77, 98, 137, 199f, 302, 475, 531f, 538, 543, 546, 553, 563f, 582, 586.

35 Arthur Marsh and Victoria Ryan, *The Seamen: A History of the National Union of Seamen*, Oxford: Malthouse Press, 1989, pp. 17–58; Conrad H. Dixon, 'Seamen and the Law: An Examination of the Impact of Legislation on the British Merchant Seaman's Lot, 1588–1918', doctoral thesis, University College London, 1981, pp. 108–259.

36 Cedric Watts, *Joseph Conrad: A Literary Life*, London: Macmillan, 1989, pp. 66, 72f.

and authoritarian community'.[37] Moreover, he feels it presents 'difficulties to readers who admire Conrad and dislike racism'.[38] The latter may be the main reason why even radical literary scholars like Edward Said, when engaging with Conrad's oeuvre, have tended to eschew a critical analysis of this novel the title of which, playing 'crudely on black and white', had created some unease already when it was first published.[39] For our purposes, Conrad's first sea-tale is highly relevant, however: the author, holding a shipmaster's certificate, was intensely familiar with the shipping circles of the time and had even stood witness before the Board of Trade's 'Manning of Merchant Ships Committee' only a few years before the publication of the novel.[40] *The Nigger of the 'Narcissus'* was written when Conrad was still making his transition from mariner to novelist and chose to reflect on the interplay of race and class in an imperial world of seafaring. The book merits, therefore, a closer look.

The plot traces the making of a crisis of authority and discipline on board the *Narcissus*, a sailing vessel on its voyage from Bombay to London, and the resolution of that crisis, which restores the presumably 'natural' community of the ship. Conrad presents the reader with two sources of disorder: one is Jim Wait, a 'black' sailor who is signed on in Bombay to join an otherwise all-'white' crew but turns out to be fatally diseased and unfit for work soon after the anchor is lifted: he is the 'nigger' whose presence defiles the pristinely white *Narcissus*. The other is 'a man with shifty eyes and a yellow hatchet face' called Donkin who

---

37 Ibid., p. 48.

38 Cedric Watts, 'Introduction', in Joseph Conrad, *The Nigger of the 'Narcissus'*, ed. Cedric Watts, London: Penguin, 1989, p. xxiv.

39 A case in point is Edward Said's first monograph, based on his doctoral dissertation and solely focused on Joseph Conrad's oeuvre, where he summarized the *Nigger of the 'Narcissus'* in a strikingly depoliticized manner: 'The crew's conflict between service to the ship and service to Wait [the diseased black sailor, see below] dramatizes the human vacillation between social well-being and personal individuality.' Edward W. Said, *Joseph Conrad and the Fiction of Autobiography,* New York: Columbia University Press, 2008 (1st ed. 1966), pp. 144f. A very recent monograph on Conrad 'in a global world' mentions the endorsement of union-bashing and the identification of seafaring with whiteness in *The Nigger of the 'Narcissus'*, without exploring, however, the global context in which these ideological propositions became intertwined. Maya Jasanoff, *The Dawn Watch: Joseph Conrad in a Global World*, New York: Penguin, 2017, pp. 112–14.

40 *Report of the Committee Appointed by the Board of Trade to Inquire into the Manning of British Merchant Ships* (hereafter: *Manning Committee*), vol. 1, Report, London: Eyre and Spottiswood, 1896, pp. 147ff.

has also joined the ship in Bombay.[41] He is the 'sea lawyer', introduced by Conrad as an abominable Cockney-speaking, Thersites-like figure:

> The man who can't do most things and won't do the rest. The pet of philanthropists and self-seeking land-lubbers. The sympathetic and deserving creature that knows all about his rights, but knows nothing of courage, of endurance, and of the unexpressed faith, of the unspoken loyalty that knits together a ship's company. The independent offspring of the ignoble freedom of the slums full of disdain and hate for the austere servitude of the sea.[42]

Hence Donkin's introduction on the novel's opening pages comes with a programmatic refutation of enlightenment values: freedom and rights of labour are contrasted with servitude and duty – the former indicative of a degenerate, softened urban civilization, the latter of a harsh but vigorous natural order. This order, called into question by Donkin, will be restored towards the end of the sea-tale by the shipmaster's resolute assertion of absolute power: Odysseus, the aristocrat, did not stoop to reason with Thersites; he clubbed the insubordinate foot soldier into submission.[43] Captain Allistoun of the *Narcissus* likewise exacts obedience from Donkin by way of physical intimidation.

Jim Wait's physical features are described in unabashedly racist terms – his face is 'pathetic and brutal: the tragic, the mysterious, the repulsive mask of a nigger's soul'.[44] Yet the black seafarer's role is not that of the stereotypically ludicrous 'Jim Crow' of contemporary racism in the US South: unlike the white crew, he speaks eloquently, even 'loftily' without any accent and his sharp intelligence is only marred by his refusal to accept imminent death. Instead, he undermines the 'ship's company' by extracting cunningly, in his diseased state, an 'unnatural' interracial solidarity and unmanly solicitude from the white crew: 'He

---

41 Conrad, *The Nigger of the 'Narcissus'*, p. 6.

42 Ibid., p. 7.

43 The confrontation of Thersites and Odysseus in the *Iliad* may well have provided a model Conrad used when constructing his sea-tale and 'Ulysses' may thus have found a reincarnation in 'Allistoun'. For a lucid analysis of this confrontation see Moses Finley, *The World of Odysseus*, New York: New York Review Books, 2002 (1st ed. 1954), pp. 112f.

44 Conrad, *The Nigger of the 'Narcissus'*, p. 12.

was demoralising. Through him we were becoming highly humanised, tender, complex, excessively decadent.'[45] An Irish sailor 'tended him, talked to him; was as gentle as a woman, as tenderly gay as an old philanthropist, as sentimentally careful of his nigger as a model slave-owner'.[46] As a result, Jim Wait's 'moribund carcass' becomes the 'fit emblem of their aspirations'[47] – it alerts the crew to their own piteous condition, to being 'oppressed by the injustice of the world', thus making them susceptible to Donkin's 'picturesque and filthy loquacity' that flows 'from a poisoned source'.[48]

The vitalist defence of hierarchy, *both of class and race*, was the core of this discourse: any indication of 'sentimentality' on the part of the 'model slave-owner', not to mention abolitionism, was a step towards the decadent, life-draining humanism of labour rights. Conrad deplored the demise of an older generation of 'men hard to manage, but easy to inspire; voiceless men – but men enough to scorn in their hearts the sentimental voices that bewailed the hardness of their fate'. The ancient sailor Singleton represented these 'inarticulate and indispensable', 'strong and mute' men in the novel: he was an old salt who found it hard to count his pay but possessed an intuitive, unthinking yet deep understanding of the sea and of an organic shipboard hierarchy that was in consonance with the unfathomable, extra-rational forces of the elements.[49] Compassion and the morbid procedures of democratic reasoning, Conrad implied, were alien in their essence to a maritime realm that belonged to the noble if brutal vitality of *nature*. Their application could only lead towards the doldrums and cause decadence, duplicity, and anarchy as demonstrated by the pernicious duo of Wait and Donkin – the disgruntled 'nigger' and the rabble-rousing proletarian lowlife who did not know their place.

Conrad was not alone with this sentiment; he expressed widespread anxieties in a bourgeois Europe facing an unnerving radicalization of the enlightenment call for equality, with workers who did not merely raise their voices, but demanded voting rights and a redistribution of riches, some even aspiring to a fundamental transformation of the social

45 Ibid., p. 103.
46 Ibid., p. 104.
47 Ibid., p. 90.
48 Ibid., pp. 74f.
49 Ibid., pp. 17f.

order.[50] Friedrich Nietzsche's *Anti-Christ*, written in 1888 though published only two years before *The Nigger of the 'Narcissus'*, had expressed the same rage against the 'Socialist rabble, the Chandala apostles who undermine the worker's instinct, his pleasure, his feeling of contentment with his little state of being – who make him envious, who teach him revengefulness'. Like Conrad, Nietzsche had denounced egalitarianism as degradation and decadence: 'Injustice never lies in unequal rights, it lies in the claim to "*equal*" rights.'[51]

If the tone of Conrad's novel is any guide to British 'public opinion' in the early twentieth century, the strategy of trade unionists to conjure up 'racial bonds' with their middle- and upper-class compatriots to exclude Asian and African competitors from the labour market was far from foolproof.[52] It was, in fact, up against strong conservative, anti-egalitarian currents that resented the abolition of British 'master and servant' law in 1875,[53] the 'tyranny' of the 'new unionism' that struck roots among seamen from the late 1880s, and the efforts of philanthropists like Samuel Plimsoll and trade union organisers like Havelock Wilson to improve safety and working conditions on board ship.[54] Conrad, giving

---

50 Cedric Watts rightly pointed out in his commentary the family resemblance between the anti-egalitarianism in Conrad's *Nigger of the 'Narcissus'* and that of Nietzsche's late writings: ibid., p. 137.

51 Friedrich Nietzsche, *Twilight of Idols and Anti-Christ*, transl. R. J. Hollingdale, Harmondsworth: Penguin, 1979 (1st ed. 1968), p. 179. Hollingdale's translation is closer to the German original than the more recent one by Judith Norman. Cf. Friedrich Nietzsche, *Der Fall Wagner, Götzen-Dämmerung, Der Antichrist, Ecce homo, Dionysos-Dithyramben, Nietzsche contra Wagner*, ed. G. Colli and M. Montinari, Munich: DTV/de Gruyter, 1988, p. 244.

52 Cedric Watts indeed suggests that this novel was written with an eye to please a conservative audience: '*The Nigger of the "Narcissus"* offers, from the whole of Conrad's output, probably the clearest instance of a text ideologically modified by the immediate circumstances of magazine publication.' Watts, *Joseph Conrad*, p. 70. Watts continues to clarify that 'Conrad repeatedly inflected his sea-tales so as to flatter a patriotic British readership': ibid., p. 73.

53 Cf. Douglas Hay, 'England, 1562–1875: The Law and Its Uses', in D. Hay and P. Craven (eds), *Masters, Servants, and Magistrates in Britain and the Empire, 1562–1955*, Chapel Hill: University of North Carolina Press, 2004, pp. 59–116. The largest number of convictions under this law was actually recorded during its last years: ibid., p. 116. For the continuation of penal sanctions after 1875 in the employment relations of British seafarers see Jonathan Hyslop, 'British Steamship Workers, c. 1875–1945: Precarious before Precarity', *Labour History* 116 (May 2019), pp. 12f [5–28].

54 Cf. Marsh and Ryan, *The Seamen*, pp. 17–58; Leon Fink, *Sweatshops at Sea: Merchant Seamen in the World's First Globalized Industry, from 1812 to the Present*, Chapel Hill: University of North Carolina Press, 2011, pp. 67–81.

voice to such middle-class resentment, had a sailor refer to a 'Plimsoll man' scornfully as an 'old weeping spunger'.[55] The Toryism of that time conceived of British seafarers not as equal citizens but as essentially unequal servants who rebelled against nature itself whenever they withdrew their silent, 'voiceless' compliance. The Shipping Federation, founded in 1890 by the P&O Company and other London-based shipowners, translated this sentiment into assertive action: it distinguished itself as the institutional embodiment of ultra-conservative policies of organized strike-breaking and union busting.[56]

To the politically liberal or labourite leaders of the embattled seamen's unions, the appeal to racial bonds may have seemed a promising and 'pragmatic' route for outflanking the shipowners' confrontational politics and binding them into a racially exclusionary cross-class alliance. But the 'wages of whiteness', the 'racial dividends' union leaders like Havelock Wilson, Edmund Cathery, or Joseph Cotter demanded for 'white' seamen – most relentlessly on occasion of shipping disasters – proved to be modest and were paid out, if at all, only reluctantly by British employers.[57] It is not as if efforts of the former 'for the elimination of Chinese, Lascars, Kroo Boys, etc. from British ships' had lacked in energy, persistence, or even government support: the Coloured Alien Seamen's Order of 1925 and the British (Tramp) Shipping Assistance Act of 1935, both of which had been strongly supported by the National Union of Seamen, reduced employment opportunities for Chinese, African, Arab, and Indian seamen residing in British ports.[58] These laws certainly contributed to sharpening racial boundaries in interwar British society as they deepened divisions within the maritime workforce along racialized lines. However, they never achieved the comprehensive exclusion of 'coloured seamen' from the maritime labour market. The NUS was, therefore, even forced to admit 'coloured seamen' to their

55 Conrad, *The Nigger of the 'Narcissus'*, p. 79.

56 Cf. Alessandro Saluppo, 'Strikebreaking and Anti-Unionism on the Waterfront: The Shipping Federation, 1890–1914', *European History Quarterly* 49, no. 4 (2019), pp. 570–96.

57 The phrase 'wages of whiteness' was introduced by David Roediger in his path-breaking *The Wages of Whiteness: Race and the Making of the American Working Class*, London: Verso, 1991. For the suggestive phrase 'racial dividends', see Harald Fischer-Tiné, *Low and Licentious Europeans: Race, Class and 'White Subalterneity' in Colonial India*, Hyderabad: Orient Blackswan, 2009, pp. 239f, 318.

58 'Orientals in British Ships', *The Seaman*, 29 November 1933, quoted in Tabili, *'We Ask for British Justice'*, p. 95.

membership and saw itself confronted, by the end of the 1920s, in Cardiff, Liverpool, and other ports with self-organized antiracist associations of 'black' and 'colonial seamen' that were encouraged, to some extent, by the communist-led militant Minority Movement.[59] Furthermore and crucially, the recruitment of Indian crews for the P&O as well as other British liner companies in India's major recruitment ports Calcutta and Bombay was beyond the remit of the two above-mentioned laws: the former applied to recruitment in British ports only, while the latter was confined to 'tramp' ships (i.e., ships carrying cargo from one port to another without the fixed schedules of 'liners'). On balance, therefore, the proportion of seafarers employed 'under Asian agreements' (i.e., as 'lascars') by the British merchant marine did *increase*, despite these political efforts, from 18 per cent in 1913 to 27 per cent in 1938.[60]

The unrecognized champions of maritime Britishness at the helm of seamen's unions, and particularly Havelock Wilson's dominant NUS, bemoaned the 'apathy of the public' and sought relief in compensatory deals with hostile shipowners and the government.[61] The main achievement of racially exclusive trade unionism appears to have been that, from 1911 onwards, employers deducted a part of the wages of all merchant seamen, including 'lascars' and other 'non-domiciled' seafarers,

---

59 Tabili, *'We Ask for British Justice'*, pp. 113–34; Gopalan Balachandran, *Globalizing Labour? Indian Seafaring and World Shipping, c. 1870–1945,* New Delhi: Oxford University Press, 2012, pp. 184–94; David Featherstone, 'Maritime Labour, Transnational Political Trajectories and Decolonization from Below: The Opposition to the 1935 British Shipping Assistance Act', *Global Networks* 19 (2019), pp. 539–62; idem, 'Seafarers' Organising in the Interwar Period', *Political Geography* 49 (2015), pp. 7–16. This is not to suggest that the radical 'white' left of the maritime trade union movement fully escaped the racist hegemony: the above studies have also revealed their tensions with the organizations of 'black' and 'colonial seafarers'. See also Marika Sherwood, 'The Comintern, the CPGB, Colonies and Black Britons, 1920–1938', *Science and Society* 60, no. 2 (1996), pp. 137–63; Hakim Adi, 'The Comintern and Black Workers in Britain and France, 1919–37', *Immigrant and Minorities* 28, nos 2–3 (2010), pp. 224–5.

60 S. G. Sturmey, *British Shipping and World Competition*, London: Athlone Press, 1962, p. 296. The proportion of West African ('Kru') seamen who were employed on regular articles of agreement declined, however, in that period. Cf. Diane Frost, 'Racisms, Work and Unemployment: West African Seamen in Liverpool, 1880s–1960', in Diane Frost (ed.), *Ethnic Labour and British Imperial Trade: A History of Ethnic Seafarers in Britain*, London: Frank Cass, 1995, pp. 22–33.

61 'Orientals in British Ships', *The Seaman,* 29 November 1933, quoted in Tabili, *'We Ask for British Justice'*, p. 95.

for contributions to the Royal Seamen's Pensions Fund while only 'domiciled' seafarers – about two-thirds of the workforce – were entitled to collect the pensions. The NUS expressed their concern in the 1940s that the payment of this subsidy to British seamen's income, the so-called 'Lascar money', might cease together with colonial rule.[62] The wages of solicitous trade union imperialism were thus limited, both in extent and duration: in the eyes of a conservative 'public', Donkin hardly rose to the status of a respectable compatriot when he turned against Wait. Nor would 'Explosive Joe' Cotter, the leader of the Amalgamated Marine Workers' Union, be rewarded for his vitriolic attacks on Indian seafarers during the *Egypt* inquiry.[63]

62 Tabili, '*We Ask for British Justice*', pp. 95f; Gopalan Balachandran, 'Making Coolies, (Un)making Workers: "Globalizing" Labour in the Late-19th and Early-20th Centuries', *Journal of Historical Sociology* 24, no. 3 (2011), p. 282; Dinkar D. Desai, *Maritime Labour in India*, Bombay: Servants of India Society, 1940, pp. 181f. Tabili and Balachandran date the beginning of this scheme to the year 1911 and appear to refer to the National Insurance Bill of that year: House of Commons Papers 1911, Bills and Acts No. 377, 'National insurance. A bill [as amended in committee and on report] to provide for insurance against loss of health and for the prevention and cure of sickness and for insurance against unemployment, and for purposes incidental thereto', p. 58. Desai refers explicitly to the National Insurance Act of 1924. Interestingly, schemes of this type appear to have existed well into the 1970s.

63 Cotter was marginalized in the trade union movement and reportedly died in poverty. Cf. Marsh and Ryan, *The Seamen*, p. 259, fn. 32.

4

Indian Outrage: Who Speaks for the 'Lascar'?

In selling the news of the *Egypt* disaster, British and other newspapers of the North Atlantic region sought to present the surviving 'white' crew and passengers as individuals with distinctive faces, names, and voices. 'Native' crew were made to appear as a different matter altogether: they seemed to lack any individuality and no 'lascar' was ever referred to by name or quoted with a personal statement. Even though South Asian seafarers accounted for more than half of the Egypt disaster's death toll – forty-nine out of eighty-seven fatalities – none of them appears to have been mentioned by name in the extensive international newspaper coverage, even as journalists made sure to season their disaster reports with as many 'white' faces and names as possible.[1] Hence the names of the forty-nine 'missing' 'native crew' are only to be found in the racially organized departmental crew lists that were filed away among other legal exhibits after the death count had been completed for the purposes of the Board of Trade inquiry.[2]

Similarly, very few photographic representations of Indian seafarers can be found between the numerous depictions of the *Egypt*'s gallant

1 BL: OIOC, IOR/L/E/7/1123, F. 1989, Commerce & Revenue Department, Loss of the S.S. Egypt (Report of Court on the loss of the S.S. Egypt, 4 September 1922, with Annex); TNA, TS 34/9 'R.M.S. Egypt. Exhibits' (crew lists).

2 For the following list of the deck department see TNA, TS 34/9 'R.M.S. Egypt. Exhibits' (crew lists).

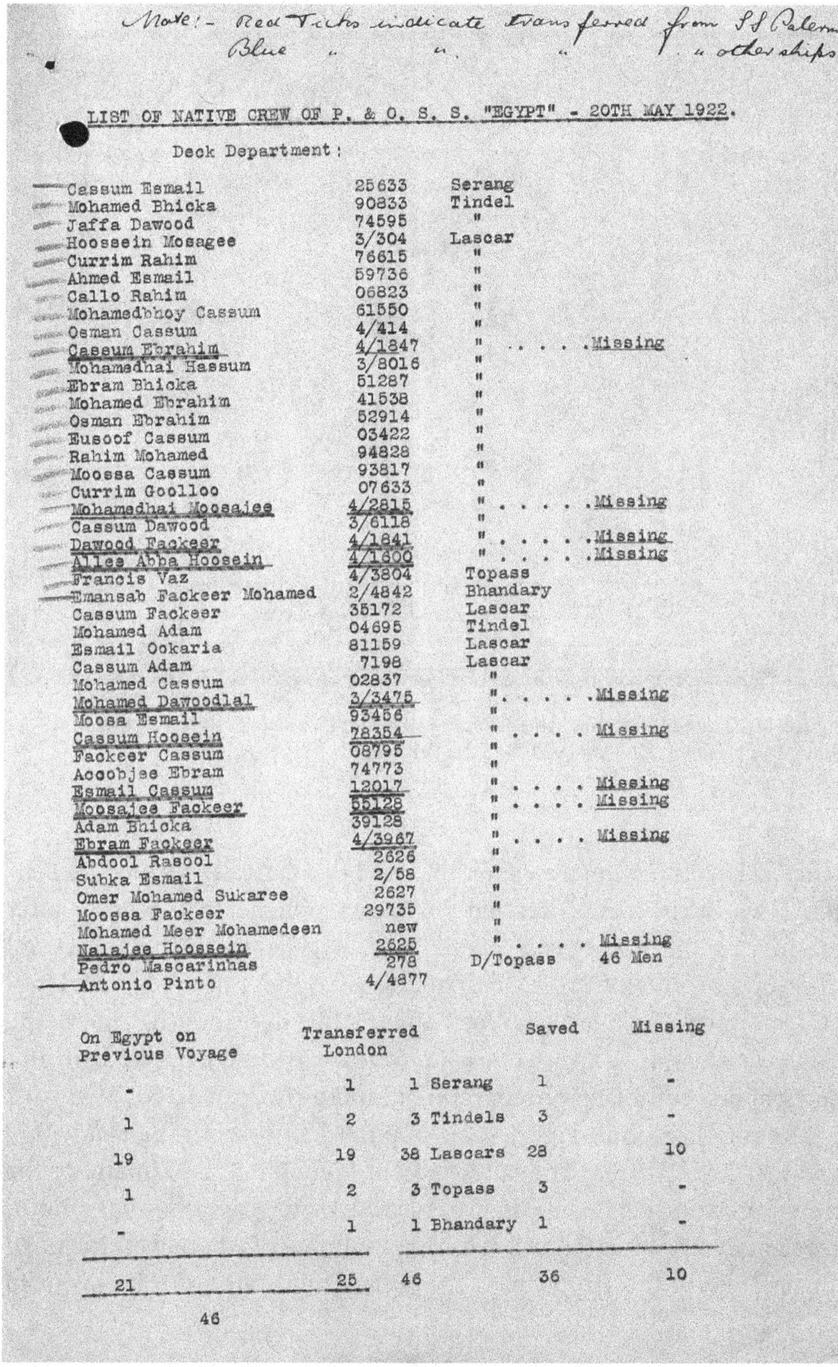

Note:- Red Ticks indicate transferred from SS Palermo
Blue " " " " other ships

LIST OF NATIVE CREW OF P. & O. S. S. "EGYPT" - 20TH MAY 1922.

Deck Department:

Cassum Esmail	25633	Serang	
Mohamed Bhicka	90833	Tindel	
Jaffa Dawood	74595	"	
Hoossein Mosagee	3/304	Lascar	
Currim Rahim	76615	"	
Ahmed Esmail	59736	"	
Callo Rahim	06823	"	
Mohamedbhoy Cassum	61550	"	
Osman Cassum	4/414	"	
Cassum Ebrahim	4/1847	"	. . . . .Missing
Mohamedhai Hassum	3/8016	"	
Ebram Bhicka	51287	"	
Mohamed Ebrahim	41538	"	
Osman Ebrahim	52914	"	
Eusoof Cassum	03422	"	
Rahim Mohamed	94828	"	
Moossa Cassum	93817	"	
Currim Goolloo	07633	"	
Mohamedhai Moosajee	4/2815	"	. . . . .Missing
Cassum Dawood	3/6118	"	
Dawood Fackeer	4/1841	"	. . . . .Missing
Allee Abba Hoosein	4/1600	"	. . . . .Missing
Francis Vaz	4/3804	Topass	
Emansab Fackeer Mohamed	2/4842	Bhandary	
Cassum Fackeer	35172	Lascar	
Mohamed Adam	04695	Tindel	
Esmail Ookaria	81159	Lascar	
Cassum Adam	7198	Lascar	
Mohamed Cassum	02837	"	
Mohamed Dawoodlal	3/3475	"	. . . . .Missing
Moosa Esmail	93456	"	
Cassum Hoosein	78354	"	. . . . Missing
Fackeer Cassum	08795	"	
Acoobjee Ebram	74773	"	
Esmail Cassum	12017	"	. . . . Missing
Moosajee Fackeer	55128	"	. . . . Missing
Adam Bhicka	39128	"	
Ebram Fackeer	4/3967	"	. . . . Missing
Abdool Rasool	2626	"	
Subka Esmail	2/58	"	
Omer Mohamed Sukaree	2627	"	
Moossa Fackeer	29735	"	
Mohamed Meer Mohamedeen	new	"	
Nalajee Hoossein	2625	"	. . . . Missing
Pedro Mascarinhas	278	D/Topass	46 Men
Antonio Pinto	4/4877		

On Egypt on Previous Voyage	Transferred London			Saved	Missing
-	1	1	Serang	1	-
1	2	3	Tindels	3	-
19	19	38	Lascars	28	10
1	2	3	Topass	3	-
-	1	1	Bhandary	1	-
21	25	46		36	10

46

Figure 4.1 List of the 'native crew' in the deck department of S.S. *Egypt*. Source: The National Archives (UK), TS 34/9 'R.M.S. Egypt. Exhibits' (crew lists).

Figure 4.2 'Four of the crew who survived the Egypt disaster walking in the streets of Brest', *Daily Mirror*, 24 May 1922. Source: British Newspaper Archives.

officers, heroic 'white' crew members and dramatically rescued passengers. Two British dailies carried pictorial supplements a few days after the loss of the S.S. *Egypt*. These 'picture galleries' included several close-up portraits of British individuals (like those of a 'Miss McDiarmid, an operatic singer' who lost, after a '20ft dive into the water', 'the trousseau she was taking to Gibraltar for her wedding'), but also, in both newspapers, one group photograph of Indian seafarers.[3]

The photograph in Figure 4.2 was published by both the *Daily Mail* and the *Daily Mirror*. The latter tabloid highlighted that 'many of the crew were Indian'.[4] A day later, the *Daily Mirror* captioned the photograph in Figure 4.3 as follows: 'Lascars, a number of whom were included in the crew of the Egypt, pass the time while waiting to be taken to

3 For references, see the following two footnotes.

4 *Daily Mirror*, 24 May 1922, p. 10. See also 'The Sunken P.&O. Liner: First Photographs from Brest', *Daily Mail*, 24 May 1922.

Figure 4.3 *Daily Mirror*, 25 May 1922, p. 10. Source: British Newspaper Archives.

England. They wear native dress.'[5] The seafarers' faces, shot from a distance and highly rasterized for publication, remain indistinct in both photographs. No close-up portraits highlighting individual facial features were deemed necessary of 'lascars', who were depicted as exchangeable specimens of a generic racial type. Their part in the events, moreover, was described, in the captions, as largely passive: they were 'included', 'rescued', then 'taken' somewhere while independent manifestations of life were reduced to 'waiting' and 'wear[ing] native dress'. The latter photograph, one suspects, may even have been entirely unrelated to the *Egypt* disaster and drawn from the *Daily Mirror*'s picture archive: in contrast to the photograph selected by the *Daily Mail*, the men here appear to wear their own clothes, having been able, the snapshot suggests, to save even turbans and sandals when the *Egypt* capsized and many could rescue themselves only by jumping into the sea. Their smiling, relaxed demeanour, moreover, gives no indication of grief about the recent drowning of shipmates and friends, of concerns about the loss of personal belongings, or of any misgivings about their treatment by the authorities after their landing in Brest: racial typecasting allowed to altogether separate their representation from the specificity of the preceding distressful events.

5 'Survivors of the Egypt Disaster Safe at Brest', *Daily Mirror*, 25 May 1922, p. 10.

Nor was the peculiarity of this selectiveness in media representation lost entirely on contemporaries. 'I find all the reports and statements, by Reuter [*sic*!] . . . and others are onesided, and it appears that nobody cared to have (if not purposely avoided) an interview, with any of the surviving Indian Seamen,' observed A. Mazarello, who had represented Indian seafarers in 1920 at the Maritime Session of the International Labour Conference in Genoa, in a letter to the nationalist *Bombay Chronicle* two weeks after the accident.[6] The common disregard of the European and American press for 'native' witness accounts in their coverage of the *Egypt* disaster indeed did not result from the unattainability of such testimonies. If conservatives considered 'voicelessness' a precious virtue in the working classes, this virtue did not come naturally to even the more fully subordinated 'coolie' seafarers of the *Egypt*: it needed to be impressed upon them; it had to be engineered socially.

James Beveridge, the P&O's representative in France who had rushed to Brest after the accident, encountered on 25 May, five days after the accident, a 'native crew' that was 'restless & troublesome'.[7] This was hardly surprising: whereas passengers and the European crew had been put up in hotels, hospitals, and boarding houses, Goan stewards reported later that the Indian crew had been 'lodged in some shed' and had not been served food or hot drinks after the accident for almost a day. They received some clothing, but no money, only three days later. No effort was made, moreover, to inform their families of their survival.[8] Beveridge 'realized the difficulty of taking 156 [*sic*!] of these men all through France to London besides the question of expense & suggested that the "Macedonia" should call here & take them direct to Bombay'. But 'when the Chief Officer informed them that witnesses would be required,' he wrote, 'they got rather out of hand [and] said they would refuse to go on board the "Macedonia" to return to Bombay'.[9] The reasons for their anger are not made explicit, but the Indian crew appears to have resisted the attempt to hand-pick only a couple of them as witnesses for the

6 'The "Egypt" Disaster' (letter by A. Mazarello), *Bombay Chronicle*, 6 June 1922.

7 NMM, Caird Library, P&O Collections, 65/1 (letter to P&O directors from James Beveridge, Brest, 25 May 1922).

8 '"Egypt" Disaster: The Lascars' Version' (letter by Joseph Baptista), *Bombay Chronicle*, 19 June 1922.

9 NMM, Caird Library, P&O Collections, 65/1 (letter to P&O directors from James Beveridge, Brest, 25 May 1922).

upcoming inquiry in London and remove the rest from the European public at the earliest occasion, while compensation issues were left unsettled.[10]

The British Consul apparently succeeded in diffusing the tension, however: the crew came to insist merely on 'fair treatment as regards the loss of their kit etc.' and agreed to proceed to India, while eight men were selected to stand as witnesses – ultimately each of the three departments of the ship was to be represented according to the Board of Trade's instructions.[11] Beveridge anticipated further trouble, however, and was much relieved when the crew boarded the *Macedonia* peacefully a couple of days later: 'I had taken, in conjunction with the Consul certain precautions, and I am glad to say, that these were not necessary.'[12] Both the references to the crew's dissatisfaction and to the anticipated need for coercion are hinted at obliquely in the records – perhaps deliberately so. Yet the perceived necessity of controlling the accounts of the Indian survivors is borne out by the fact that the carefully selected eight witnesses (four 'lascars' of the deck department, two firemen, and two stewards) were subjected to intense grooming by the company's solicitors, who prepared 'draft statements' with each of them to rehearse their upcoming examination in court.[13] Most of the Indian witnesses had been on the payroll of the P&O regularly for a decade or longer and were high up on the pay scale. Even so, their testimonies, especially those of the firemen, could not be fully smoothened out and shed an unfavourable light on the P&O's shipboard practices as we shall see later.

When the *Macedonia* reached Bombay on 16 June, a couple of journalists finally saw sufficient reason to talk at least briefly to some of the *Egypt*'s repatriated crew. The reporter sent by the *Times of India*, the central organ of imperial loyalism with close links to Bombay's

10 '"Egypt" Disaster: The Lascars' Version'.

11 NMM, Caird Library, P&O Collections, 65/1 (letter to P&O directors from James Beveridge, Brest, 25 May 1922).

12 NMM, Caird Library, P&O Collections, 65/3, f. 63 (letter to P&O directors from James Beveridge, Brest, 27 May 1922).

13 NMM, Caird Library, P&O Collections, 65/3, ff. 256-316 ('draft statements' of Mohammed Adam, Phillip Azevedo, Moossa Fackeer, Moossa Ismail, Abdool Rasched [Rasool], Sabdeen Fazuldeen, Barrum Mustaffa, Antonio Phillip de Silva). The typed statements indicate that Freshfields, Leese and Munn was the solicitors' company that had been charged with this task by the P&O.

multi-ethnic business circles, discovered that the two dozen men he interviewed personally

> were fully aware of the newspaper reports about their alleged misbehaviour and seemed to be labouring under a sense of the wrong and injustice done to them by such reports. They emphasise that the impact was immediately followed by so much uproar and confusion and the vessel inclined to the port side so quickly that there was almost an entire absence of any organised effort at rescue work on the part of the officers.

The men denied, he wrote, any wilful disobedience of orders or breach of discipline and refuted the allegations of having 'invaded any boats to the exclusion of women and children' and of having 'fought with knives and revolvers to get into the boats'. Most of them claimed they had been unable to secure a place in any of the lifeboats on board the sinking *Egypt* and had survived only because they were picked up from the sea later. They pointed out that in Brest 'they were not interviewed and questioned by any representative of the press, nor [were] their depositions taken by any officers of the Company'.[14] On the same day, the correspondent of the *Bombay Chronicle,* one of India's most vocal nationalist newspapers, gave a more guarded and rather vague account of his exchanges with the seafarers. He felt that, on account of the confusion prevailing on the ship after the accident, it was just as impossible to obtain any coherent account from the Indian crew as it had proved to be from white passengers gripped by 'panic, blinded by race prejudice, rushing forward to save themselves'. Nevertheless, he, too, reported that 'one and all the Lascars' had refuted the charges to have 'rushed to the boats, fighting their way all along'. The seafarers had pointed out to the correspondent the sheer absurdity of the accusation that they had searched for knives and revolvers on a foundering ship instead of trying to save their lives.[15]

A couple of days later a more detailed report was published by the same newspaper. In a letter to the editor, Joseph Baptista, a nationalist

14 '"Egypt's" Crew. Arrival in Bombay. Panic Stories Denied', *Times of India,* 17 June 1922.

15 '"Egypt Disaster". Lascars Arrive in Bombay. Emphatic Repudiation of Charges', *Bombay Chronicle,* 17 June 1922.

politician, one of the stalwarts of India's politically moderate post-war trade unionism and president of the Indian Seamen's Union Bombay, claimed to have interviewed twelve of the sixty Goan seafarers who had survived the *Egypt* disaster, all of whom had been employed in the 'saloon department'.[16] This occupational and ethnic selectivity reflected, on the one hand, the character of Bombay's early seamen's unions that restricted membership, before 1926, to Goan Christians only (presenting themselves thus as a mirror image of the 'white unionism' of British seafarers).[17] It was, on the other hand and more immediately, a response to the suspicion, formulated by Mazarello a few days earlier, that attempts to use the *Egypt* accident as a pretext for the exclusion of Indian seafarers from the British merchant fleet would focus most strongly on Goan stewards who were Portuguese, not British imperial subjects and, therefore, legally less protected.[18] Nor was this suspicion far-fetched:[19] two years earlier, a number of Goan seamen's clubs and unions had submitted a petition to the governor of Bombay seeking his 'gracious and exalted protection' against an agitation of British and other European seamen's unions 'to compel ship-owning companies to replace in an unfair proportion Goan and Indian saloon crew with European units'.[20] That the issue was still simmering was reflected in the piece the London *Times* had carried from their Calcutta correspondent only a week earlier, which has been quoted already: it had suggested that 'the trouble on board the Egypt after the collision was caused by a panic of Goanese stewards, not by lascars'.[21]

Baptista, in his account, seemed to follow the format of a legal inquiry, giving names of witnesses, numbers of lifeboats, and technical

---

16 '"Egypt" Disaster: The Lascars' Version'.

17 A. Colaco (ed.), *A History of the Seamen's Union Bombay*, Bombay: Pascoal Vaz, 1955, pp. 15f.

18 'The "Egypt" Disaster' (letter by A. Mazzarello), *Bombay Chronicle*, 6 June 1922.

19 British unions would seek exploit this differential status repeatedly for exclusionary purposes, e.g., when the Tramp Shipping Act of 1926 was framed. Cf. Gopalan Balachandran, 'Conflicts in the International Maritime Labour Market: British and Indian Seamen, Employers, and the State, 1890–1939', *Indian Economic and Social History Review* 39, no. 1 (2002), p. 132.

20 BL: OIOC/IOR/P/10793, A273f, Bombay Marine Proceedings ('Petition of the members of the Goa Portuguese Seamen's Club, the Portuguese Seafarer's Union and the Asiatic Seamen's (Saloon Crew) Union' to the Governor of Bombay, 23 July 1920).

21 'Lascars and Their Reputation', *The Times*, 29 May 1922.

details, attempting, moreover, to fix the precise spatial and temporal coordinates of the events unfolding in the twenty minutes between the collision and the foundering of the *Egypt*. The account invalidated the assumption that no coherent narrative could be constructed from the statements of the surviving Indian crew. Many of them were, as Baptista emphasized, seasoned seafarers – twenty of the seventy-nine Goan seafarers on board the *Egypt*, he claimed, 'had experienced similar disasters during the war when the "Arabia", "Medina" and "Malaya" were torpedoed'.[22] Baptista's report was corroborated by several of the statements made during the official inquiry in Britain in the following months.[23] The interviewed Goan stewards denied categorically any armed assault on passengers by Indian members of the crew and insisted that firearms had been used by one British passenger only – a claim that was later confirmed. The high loss of lives was due, in their opinion, to the belated realization on the part of the ship's officers of the gravity of the damages caused by the collision: Captain Collyer and his first officer, Cartwright, they claimed, had even countermanded the crew's efforts to lower the lifeboats in time, i.e., before the heavy list of the ship made this impossible for the boats on the starboard side.[24] Baptista's findings were published by the *Daily Herald* in Britain – that paper now distanced itself from 'those who circulated random accusations against the Lascars' and tacitly passed over its own failings on this count. It concluded: 'This is a direct negation of all the stories put about in the British press. It is a direct challenge to the P. and O. officials. It must be met.'[25] The latter, however, had little reason to do more than file the article as its claims failed to gain wider currency in British newspapers.[26]

The *Daily Herald* now also took up the plea that 'the Lascars must have fair representation [at the inquiry] through their chosen delegate or delegates'.[27] The demand for an 'open and impartial enquiry' through a committee including a representative of Indian seamen had been raised in a recent resolution of the Indian Seamen's Union in Calcutta.

22 '"Egypt" Disaster: The Lascars' Version'.

23 See the next chapter.

24 '"Egypt" Disaster: The Lascars' Version'.

25 'The Egypt', *Daily Herald*, 24 June 1922, p. 4. See also 'Who Blundered on the Egypt?', *Daily Herald*, p. 1.

26 NMM, Caird Library, P&O Collections, 65/1, f. 268.

27 'The Egypt', *The Daily Herald*, 24 June 1922, p. 4.

The resolution had been passed on the trade union's general meeting on 11 June. It was forwarded to the British Government's secretary of state for India by the union's general secretary, the lawyer and sometime politician Mohammed Daud, and was covered, through Associated Press, by newspapers in India and, more marginally, in Britain.[28] It insisted that the 'conflicting allegations against Indian seamen' required thorough investigation since the accused had 'discharged their functions during the great war with credit and bravery'.[29] The Bombay Seamen's Union, a separate body at the time, passed a similar resolution three days later at their annual general meeting, which was forwarded to the Government of India's Commerce Department. They demanded that 'a thorough investigation be made by an impartial and independent Commission appointed by Government and that on this Committee a representative of this Union recommended by the General Board be nominated'. Foregrounding the sectional interests of their ethnically circumscribed membership, the union repudiated 'the malicious and libellous allegations made against the Goan Seamen which are incredible, specially after their heroic conduct during the Great War when many Goan Seamen lost their lives'.[30] The demands of the seamen's unions were supported by the recently founded All-India Trade Union Congress (AITUC) and other trade union leaders such as K. C. Roy Chowdhury, who also served as the Labour member of

28 BL: OIOC, IOR/L/E/7/1123, F. 1989, Commerce & Revenue Department, Loss of the S.S. Egypt (letter by M. Daud to Secretary of State for India, 13 June 1922). For Daud see Frank Broeze, 'The Muscles of Empire: Indian Seamen and the Raj, 1919–1939', *Indian Economic and Social History Review* 18, no. 1 (1981), pp. 52–5; Kenneth McPherson, 'The Muslims of Calcutta, 1918 to 1935: A Study of the Society and Politics of an Urban Minority Group in India', doctoral dissertation, Australian National University, 1972, *passim*. 'Indian Seamen's Union', *Times of India*, 13 June 1922, p. 8; 'Abroad', *Manchester Guardian*, 4 July 1922, p. 16.

29 BL: OIOC, IOR/L/E/7/1123, F. 1989, Commerce & Revenue Department, Loss of the S.S. Egypt (letter by M. Daud to Secretary of State for India, 13 June 1922).

30 NAI: Commerce Department, Lascar Seamen, October 1922, F.Nos. 48–70 (resolution of Indian Seamen's Union, Bombay, 14 June 1922, forwarded by its president Joseph Baptista to the secretary to government of India, Commerce Department, 17 June 1922). The union appears to have considered to engage counsel to represent the 'saloon' crew at the inquiry, which commenced at short notice and earlier than anticipated, however, which left no time for implementing the measure. BL: OIOC, IOR/L/E/7/1123, F. 1989, Commerce & Revenue Department, Loss of the S.S. Egypt (telegrams between Government of India, Commerce Dept., and India Office, 1 and 3 August 1922).

the Bengal Legislature – a nominated and thus officially recognized labour representative.[31]

However, the call for participation of representatives of the Indian seafarers in an impartial inquiry into the *Egypt* disaster was raised not only by Indian trade unions. Purushottamdas Thakurdas, one of the heavyweights of Indian big business, sent a telegram to the Government of India on 16 June on behalf of the Indian Merchants' Chamber stating that it was 'imperative that the interests of lascars should be safeguarded by appointment of suitable Indians of recognized standing on Committee of Enquiry'.[32] Noticing that Indian public opinion was 'much disturbed over allegations against Lascars', the Government of India approached the India Office in London with the request of including 'at least one Indian of suitable standing to the Committee of Enquiry'.[33] The secretary of state for India forwarded the request to the future British prime minister Stanley Baldwin, then president of the Board of Trade. 'There are on my Council two Indian gentlemen of standing and ability, either of whom would I am sure prove useful members of the Committee', he wrote.[34] Baldwin responded that the inquiry was to be conducted not by a committee, but by a court with the wreck commissioner as the sole judge. The Board of Trade would make arrangements, however, 'that the lascar side of the question should receive the fullest fair play' and that there was 'nothing to prevent the India Office, if they so wish, being represented by Counsel at the Inquiry who would see that the interests of the lascars were properly safeguarded'.[35] Expecting that 'racial feeling would be roused' the India Office considered employing an Indian barrister as their legal counsel but contented themselves eventually by appointing a British lawyer.[36]

31 'All-India Trade Union Congress', *Bombay Chronicle*, 27 June 1922; '"Egypt" Disaster: Direct Lie to Allegations against Lascars', *Bombay Chronicle*, 26 June 1922.

32 NAI: Commerce Department, Lascar Seamen, October 1922, F.Nos. 48–70 (Purushottamdas Thakurdas, Indian Merchants' Chamber & Bureau, Bombay, to [Charles] Innes, Department of Commerce, Government of India, 19 June 1922).

33 BL: OIOC, IOR/L/E/7/1123, F. 1989, Commerce & Revenue Department, Loss of the S.S. Egypt (telegram from Government of India, Commerce Dept., to India Office, 17 June 1922).

34 Ibid. (Viscount Peel, Secry. of State for India, to Stanley Baldwin, Pres. Board of Trade, 28 June 1922).

35 Ibid. (Stanley Baldwin, Pres. of Board of Trade, to Viscount Peel, Secry. of State for India, 4 July 1922).

36 Ibid. (memorandum dated 6 September 1922).

The issue of 'representing the lascar' had thus been reformulated twice in the process: the initial demand for a representation of Indian seafarers through Indian trade unions was taken up by business interests and nationalists in India who turned it into a plea for the appointment of 'suitable Indians of recognized standing': the 'lascar' crew of the *Egypt* were to be represented as Indian nationals, not as workers. The India Office redefined the issue once more: if Indian seafarers could not be represented by their unions, they were to be represented by government as imperial subjects and not as citizens of an aspiring nation or, as they put it, on account of 'race'.

When the *Egypt* inquiry commenced on 24 July 1922, Indian nationalists continued to carp that 'any conclusions which the Committee might arrive at will not command as much weight as they would, if Indian seamen were represented on the body'.[37] Benjamin G. Horniman, the anti-imperialist English editor of the *Bombay Chronicle* whose forcible deportation from India had triggered Indian nationalist protests in 1919, attended several of the court hearings and decried the 'deplorable lack' of any 'organised representation of Indian interests in London'. This, he held, had resulted in the 'amazing and deplorable feature of the enquiry . . . that not a single question has been put to the witnesses . . . on behalf of the Indian sailors who have been made the butt and scapegoats of the occasion'. He complained that the legal counsel appointed by the India Office, the British barrister A. J. Bucknill, did 'nothing to counteract the mischievous activities of Mr. Cotter' – the representative of the Amalgamated Marine Workers Union at the inquiry – 'who behaves as though he had a brief for the prosecution of the Indian crew'. He criticized the Indian Seamen's Union for having 'taken no steps for the proper representation of the interests of the Indian sailors'. He went on to denounce the failure of the 'Workers' Welfare League of India' to fulfil its role at the inquiry as the official representative of the AITUC in Britain – a failure, he alleged, that was due to an attitude that sought 'to placate the prejudices of British Trade Unionists'. Horniman mentioned, however, that 'an Indian barrister appeared on behalf of the Islamic Society and protested against questions which had been put regarding the Lascars'. The barrister 'was told by the President to make a proper application on behalf of his Society to be made a party to the

37 'The "Egypt" Inquiry', *New India* (Madras), 25 July 1922.

proceedings'.[38] Yet no further trace of this intervention can be found in the court records.

Eventually, the issue of how the Indian crew of the *Egypt* was to be represented receded to the background: neither Indian trade unionists nor nationalists assigned much priority to pursuing the grievances and claims of the seafarers. And A. J. Bucknill, the legal representative of the India Office, seemed almost embarrassed when having recorded, towards the end of the inquiry, that the Government of India was informed about the commencement of the proceedings only three days in advance. This, he stated rather timidly, made it impossible to give the Indian crew 'any adequate opportunity of meeting the charges', as only six of them had been called before the court with most of their foremen excluded.[39] Effectively, the *Egypt*'s 208 South Asian deckhands, stokers, and stewards were assigned a passive, impersonal underpart in the judicial drama that was staged in the Court of Inquiry: the 'native' seafarer was presented and processed in a summary and generic way that helped to defend imperial interests and catered to the needs of shipping magnates as well as the concerns of the Government of India. On the one hand and in order to fend off attacks from the direction of rising Indian nationalism, he needed to be shown as being under the protection of imperial authorities against unfair victimization. On the other, and with an eye to counter the popular jingoistic particularism and racist exclusivism that British unions sought to harness, the 'native' seafarer had to be presented as a racially inferior, yet indispensable, perfectly functional, and fully controllable part of the imperial machine.

38 'London Letter' (dated 27 July 1922), *Bombay Chronicle*, 15 August 1922.

39 TNA, TS 34/10 'R.M.S. Egypt. Transcript of Court Proceedings', Eighth Day: 2 August 1922, pp. 126, 138.

5

Lines of Defence: 'Natives, Properly Led'

Even before the inquiry commenced in late July, an understanding had been reached on the *Egypt* issue between Britain's leading shipping concern and the government bureaucracies in India and, to some extent, at home. This imperial nexus concurred on the common goal of preventing an unmitigated condemnation of the Indian crew that might precipitate restrictions on 'lascar' employment. The major lines of defence had been spelled out in the public debate of the preceding weeks. Most obviously, the allegations originating from the French press and then circulated internationally of 'lascars' assaulting passengers with guns, knives, and clubs were discounted as 'sensationalism' and dismissed categorically in the course of the court proceedings.[1]

In an internal memorandum, the P&O's managing directors had stated confidently, already a few days after the accident, that 'the possession of a revolver by any lascar or member of the native crew is altogether improbable'.[2] When the issue was raised in the House of Commons, Alexander Shaw, Inchcape's son-in-law who managed the crisis at the P&O headquarters, added a postscript to a 'private letter' he sent on the matter to the president of the Board of Trade:[3] 'I need hardly say that the Indian crews are not permitted to possess firearms.'[4] K. C. Roy

1 See p. 34.

2 NMM, P&O/65/1, f. 210 ('Memorandum for Mr Shaw', 23 May 1922).

3 Hansard, vol. 154 (24 May 1922), col. 1200-1.

4 NMM, P&O/65/1, f. 339 ('Private letter by A. S. [Alexander Shaw] to [Stanley] Baldwin', 24 May 1922).

Chowdhury, who had earlier served as secretary of the philanthropic 'British Indian Seamen's Institute' in London, declared publicly that 'those who have any idea of the vigilance exercised in Tilbury and Victoria Docks and in British ports generally and the scrutinizing by customs officials of lascars' belongings in order to detect smuggling' could not credit theories suggesting a free availability of revolvers on board ship.[5]

Some contrary murmurs could be heard as well, for instance in the British daily *Pioneer* from Allahabad that had 'been assured on the authority of an officer of high standing, who happened to be on the Egypt on that voyage that he was informed that smuggling of firearms by Lascars was well-known to be taking place'.[6] And, indeed, the post-war decade saw some alarm in British security circles about an intensification of the illegal arms trade to India, often channelled through 'lascars', though mostly from German and other continental ports and much less so from Britain.[7] Yet not a single witness examined during the *Egypt* inquiry supported the allegation that Indian seafarers had used any kind of weapon to force themselves into a lifeboat. The affidavit by George Denne Franklin, a lieutenant-colonel of the Indian Medical Service and first-class passenger on the *Egypt*, typifies many of the testimonies submitted by white passengers and crew: 'I saw no firearms or knives in the possession of the native crew, they were not violent but terror stricken. This applies to all three departments, Deck, Engine, and Stewards. All the white crew behaved splendidly.'[8] Enid Corbould Southby, a first-class passenger, concurred, expressing her perceptions as follows:

---

5 '"Egypt" Disaster: Direct Lie to Allegations Against Lascars', *Bombay Chronicle*, 26 June 1922.

6 Quoted in 'Contemporary Opinion', *Times of India*, 20 June 1922.

7 For a detailed account, see Svenja von Jan's doctoral dissertation at the University of Göttingen: 'Exploring Migrant Lives: Non-elite South Asian Migration to Germany and Belgium from a Micro-Historical Perspective, c. 1920–1950'. See also Jonathan Hyslop, 'Guns, Drugs and Revolutionary Propaganda: Indian Sailors and Smuggling in the 1920s', *South African Historical Journal* 61, no. 4 (2011), pp. 838–46; Ali Raza and Benjamin Zachariah, 'To Take Arms across a Sea of Trouble: The "Lascar System," Politics, and Agency in the 1920s', *Itinerario* 36, no. 3 (2012), pp. 19–38.

8 TNA, TS 34/9 'R.M.S. Egypt. Exhibits' (affidavit by George Denne Franklin, 7 June 1922).

> I was jostled in the boat. I was not intentionally pushed by the natives in the boat and certainly not on deck. The natives were frightened – like beaten dogs – and intent on saving their own lives. They showed no personal animosity towards us. They were in fear of being drowned.[9]

Other 'white' passengers referred to some jostling for space in the lifeboats and to 'lascars' rowing boats away from the ship leaving passengers behind, and there was also the accusation that in one instance an Indian member of the crew had tried to grab a life jacket from a female passenger.[10] Yet even the latter kind of testimonies did not suggest any use of arms on the part of the Indian crew. If the statements of the 'white' witnesses displayed little congruence, those of the eight 'native' witnesses brought out a different perspective altogether as we shall see in the next chapter.[11] Yet the Indian testimonies were not given much weight by the court – the 'non-European witnesses' were clearly perceived as a nuisance one wished to 'get rid of' in as little time as possible, as the counsel for the Board of Trade, L. F. C. Darby, put it.[12]

Of the 'white' witnesses whose statements were taken more seriously, only a minority asserted that casualties could have been avoided with an all-'white' crew, though almost all emphasized the uniformly 'splendid' behaviour of 'white' passengers and seafarers.[13] Even among the British crew, few were as explicit as quartermaster Harry Scott, who claimed that 'as effective seamen in a crisis they [the 'lascars'] entirely failed', that 'their soft brains did not let them see that help was necessary' and that 'loss of life might have been avoided by having an European instead

---

9 TNA, TS 34/8 '"R.M.S. Egypt": Various Proofs and Documents' (depositions by passengers and crew: Enid Corbould Southby, p. 15).

10 TNA, BT 239/2 (deposition by Arthur Popple, joiner, 6 June 1922); TNA, TS 34/8 '"R.M.S. Egypt": Various Proofs and Documents' (depositions by passengers and crew: Roberto Florio Bevan, p. 4; Harold George Dalway Turnbull, p. 6); TNA, TS 34/9 'R.M.S. Egypt. Exhibits' (affidavit by Anthony Bado, 19 July 1922; deposition by Aima Stodart, second-class passenger).

11 See chapter 6.

12 TNA, TS 34/10 'R.M.S. Egypt. Transcript of Court Proceedings', Sixth Day: 31 July 1922, p. 2.

13 TNA, TS 34/9 'R.M.S. Egypt. Exhibits' (affidavits by William George, 19 July 1922; Anthony Bado, 19 July 1922; Betty Hansen, 19 July 1922). All three affidavits were taken in Gibraltar on the same day, and Betty Hansen declared that she was in communication with the other witnesses and aware of their testimonies.

of native crew'.[14] Three weeks earlier, Horniman had caustically anticipated in the *Bombay Chronicle* the stanzas that were to be recited in court:

> There were individual acts of heroism no doubt. There always are and always will be as long as British ships go to sea and British survivors are left to tell the tale, and the British press is there to report them, of British heroism and cowardice and incompetence on the part of the foreigners.[15]

The shipmaster, Captain Collyer, however, defended himself by stating that the 'abnormal list' of the foundering ship had caused a general panic, a '*sauve qui peut*' situation: it had 'terrified evidently the crew, not only the natives but a great many of the Europeans'. 'Even if we had had a white crew . . .', he insisted, 'they could not have done any more than the Lascars did, because the whole secret of the accident was that everybody seemed to me to be crouched with terror.' 'The loss of life,' Collyer held, 'was due to the passengers and crew flinging themselves overboard before the ship actually turned turtle on them.'[16]

The inquiry brought out that only one pistol had featured during the *Egypt* accident – the one owned and fired by one Captain Douglas G. Carr of the 120th Prince of Wales's Rajputana Infantry. This Indian Army officer had taken refuge in lifeboat no. 17, one of the six lifeboats the crew succeeded in lowering from the heavily listing steamer.[17] Carr fired at least a couple of rounds 'over the heads' of the 'natives' in order, as he and other European passengers claimed later, to make space for further 'Europeans' and prevent the 'natives' from rowing the boat away from the ship. To his deposition, Carr himself added the telling admission 'that he did not see an actual physical interference' of 'natives' 'with any European. *The fact that they were there did in itself prevent*

14 TNA, TS 34/8 '"R.M.S. Egypt": Various Proofs and Documents' (depositions by passengers and crew: quartermaster Harry Scott, p. 43f). See also ibid., Arthur Popple, joiner, p. 61; Herbert Cyril Cullingford, First Saloon Deck Steward, p. 70.

15 'The Egypt Disaster and the Lascars', *Bombay Chronicle*, 4 July 1922.

16 TNA, TS 34/10 'R.M.S. Egypt. Transcript of Court Proceedings', Second Day: 25 July 1922, pp. 15f, 33–36.

17 BL: OIOC, IOR/L/E/7/1123, F. 1989, Commerce & Revenue Department, Loss of the S.S. Egypt (Report of Court on the loss of the S.S. Egypt, 4 September 1922, with Annex), pp. 4, 9. See also chapter 11.

Europeans getting near.'[18] The implied subtext of this statement was clearly that 'natives' were less entitled to make use of the lifeboats than 'Europeans'. Lucy Delap's perceptive analysis of shipwreck narratives in the nineteenth and twentieth centuries may explain why Carr saw no reason to explicate this subtext to the court: 'class and racial dimensions of precedence', Delap concludes, 'were better established than the supposedly universal norms of chivalry'.[19]

Be that as it may, this British officer of the Indian Army merely admitted to having unintentionally injured two Indian seafarers. When the P&O's solicitor, Bateson, pointed out that, in fact, four Indian seafarers including at least one member of the lifeboat's designated rowing crew had received gunshot wounds, Captain Carr simply responded that this 'was unfortunate, but it had an effect on the others'.[20] Captain Collyer, the shipmaster, was eventually pulled into the boat, took possession of the weapon, and ended the shooting. Some of the European witnesses celebrated Carr as the courageous and determined saviour of British women – a version that was readily taken up by sections of the British press.[21] Indian testimonies suggest, however, that he merely compounded the fear of being drowned with that of being shot.[22] The Punjabi fireman Baram Mustafa remembered having crouched down in the lifeboat to avoid further bullets after having being shot in his shoulder, and Carr himself boasted that 'it had the desired effect as the natives immediately dropped into the bottom of the boat and

---

18 TNA, TS 34/8 '"R.M.S. Egypt": Various Proofs and Documents' (depositions by passengers and crew: Captain Douglas Gerald Carr, p. 26). Emphasis added.

19 Lucy Delap, '"Thus Does Man Prove His Fitness to Be the Master of Things": Shipwrecks, Chivalry and Masculinities in Nineteenth- and Twentieth-Century Britain', *Cultural and Social History* 3, no. 1 (2006), p. 53.

20 TNA, TS 34/10 'R.M.S. Egypt. Transcript of Court Proceedings', Eighth Day: 2 August 1922, p. 28 (examination of Captain Douglas Gerald Carr). For accounts of the shooting from Indian crew members, one of whom confirmed that four men had been injured, see TNA, BT 239/2 '"Egypt" in Collision with "Seine"' (deposition by: Moossa Fackeer, 2 June 1922; Abdool Rassol, n.d.; Mahomed Adam, 2 June 1922; Barrum Mustapha, 2 June 1922); NMM, Caird Library, P&O Collections, 65/3, ff. 280, 308 ('draft statements' of Moosa Fackeer, Barrum Mustapha).

21 TNA, TS 34/8 '"R.M.S. Egypt": various proofs and documents' (depositions by passengers and crew: Alison Joyce Moore, p. 12; quartermaster Harry Scott, pp. 43f); *Manchester Guardian*, 26 May 1922, p. 9.

22 TNA, BT 239/2 '"Egypt" in Collision with "Seine"' (depositions by Barrum Mustapha and Moossa Fackeer, 2 June 1922).

remained quiet'.[23] A petrified crew was not the best precondition, however, for surviving a situation requiring swift action. Captain Collyer accordingly reported that he had great difficulty in getting out the oars in time to escape from the suction of the sinking ship, and lifeboat no. 17 appears to have been saved eventually only by the happenstance of a wave that pushed it away from the capsizing steel hull of the *Egypt*.[24] Yet the court showed little interest in either examining the shooting incident or in challenging the comforting publicized view that 'all the British [men, apparently] were splendid' while 'the women behaved very bravely'.[25] Establishing the fact that no weapons had been used *by Indian seafarers* on board a British ship seemed to serve the purpose.

There was clearly an 'imperial angle' to the official approach to the *Egypt* inquiry, which sought to avoid an outcome that would provide further ammunition to campaigners for the exclusion of Indian seafarers from employment on British merchant ships. This 'imperial angle' shaped, as we will see subsequently, both strategic choices and the lines of argument. Alexander Shaw, Inchcape's son-in-law and future successor as P&O supremo, had pointed out some of the issues in his 'private letter' to the president of the Board of Trade:

> There is considerable agitation going on in India that ships in the Indian trade should be manned and officered by Indians alone. Indian Chambers of Commerce are passing Resolutions and the subject has already been touched on in the Legislative Assembly. Any agitation here for the exclusion of our Indian fellow subjects from the ships trading with India would have a very bad effect on Indian opinion which is very touchy on these matters at present. It would be considered (and I think rightly) as a great and undeserved slur to exclude from our ships a class of men of a sea-faring race who have proved their worth and have a splendid record over a very long term of years; and retaliation would very likely be demanded. If we were ever to set

---

23 Ibid. (deposition by: Barrum Mustapha, 2 June 1922); TNA, TS 34/8 '"R.M.S. Egypt": Various Proofs and Documents' (depositions by passengers and crew: Captain Douglas Gerald Carr, p. 24).

24 TNA, TS 34/10 'R.M.S. Egypt. Transcript of Court Proceedings', Second Day: 25 July 1922, pp. 9f.

25 '"Egypt" Survivors', *Times of India*, 27 May 1922 (quoting first-class passenger Mrs Turnbull).

> the example of exclusion and antagonism on racial lines, our position in India will be seriously undermined.[26]

There were other connected issues, which Shaw chose not to foreground in his letter to Baldwin: The BISN, under the same management as the P&O since 1914 and largely in control of Indian Ocean coastal steam shipping, was involved at that time in a fierce rate war to prevent the market entry of a new competitor: the Scindia Steam Navigation Company. This enterprise had been founded in 1919 and was owned exclusively by Indian shareholders who secured the public support of Indian nationalists in their – ultimately successful – struggle against this goliath of imperial shipping.[27] The imperial shipping nexus was thus not only openly critiqued but directly challenged. B. G. Horniman brought out with characteristic clarity some of the business worries that likely bothered the P&O directors in the wake of the *Egypt* disaster:

> As for the monstrous suggestion that Indian seamen are not entitled to serve in British ships depending on the Indian trade and receiving a subsidy from the Government of India for carrying the Indian mail, one can only be amazed by its audacity. If Indian sailors are to be excluded from vessels flying the British flag for the benefit of British sailors, it had better be understood that it is within the power of the Indian people to see that their Government places its mail contracts elsewhere and closes its ports to ships that refuse to employ Indian seamen.[28]

The P&O management was quite aware of these implications: if jingoists back home in Britain were allowed to undermine the logic of empire by denying colonial subjects their carefully calibrated inferior rights,

26 NMM, P&O/65/1, ff. 338f ('Private letter by A. S. [Alexander Shaw] to [Stanley] Baldwin', 24 May 1922).

27 Cf. Frank Broeze, 'Underdevelopment and Dependency: Maritime India during the Raj', *Modern Asian Studies* 18, no. 3 (1984), pp. 448–51; N. G. Jog, *Saga of Scindia: Struggle for the Revival of Indian Shipping and Shibuilding*, Bombay: Scindia Steam Navigation Company, 1969, pp. 28–31 and *passim*; M. A. Master, 'The Story of Indian Shipping', in K. V. Hariharan (ed.), *So I Rest on My Oars: Collection of Writings and Speeches, 1947–1970*, vol. 2, pp. 1–10.

28 'The Egypt Disaster and the Lascars', *Bombay Chronicle*, 4 July 1922.

British imperial business monopolies would be much harder to defend against resurgent and increasingly nationalist competitors from the colonies. Walchand Hirachand, one of the founders of the Scindia Company, later recalled how outrageous this challenge to imperial legitimacy had seemed to his main adversary, Lord Inchcape, who, on one occasion, had burst out in anger: 'Motherland! Whose motherland? We are all children of the British Empire!'[29] Hence, a week after the commencement of the *Egypt* inquiry, a concerned P&O management sent a letter, probably dictated by Inchcape himself, to the company's solicitors suggesting that at some stage of the court proceedings

> it might be very useful to call someone from the India Office who would give general evidence with regard to native crews, showing that although there may be isolated cases in which they have not behaved so well as European crews, yet generally speaking they are most splendid sailors, and that it is most essential from an Empire point of view that their employment should be continued.[30]

The author of these lines seemed confident that the India Office could be fully relied on in the matter and 'would give general evidence' along entirely predictable lines. Shaw, in his earlier letter to Baldwin, had skilfully included two key phrases that neatly circumscribed this predictable 'Empire point of view' on the employment of Indian seafarers on British ships: 'our Indian fellow subjects' and 'a seafaring race who have proved their worth'.[31] We will explore the implications of these phrases in the remainder of this chapter.

Ten days after the accident, the *Egypt* shipwreck was raised as an issue in the House of Commons for the second time. Questions were forwarded by the Labour MP William Thorne and his liberal colleague James Gilbert to the president of the Board of Trade as to the

29 *Opening Ceremony of Scindia House*, Bombay, 1938, p. 38 (This rare publication may be preserved in the Erulkar Collection held at the University of Perth, where, however, it cannot be traced at present. It is here quoted from Broeze, 'Underdevelopment and Dependency', p. 445, fn 35). See also Jog, *Saga of Scindia*, p. 32.

30 NMM, P&O/65/2, ff. 84f (unsigned letter to ? Taylor of Freshfields Leese and Munns solicitors, 2 August 1922).

31 NMM, P&O/65/1, ff. 338f ('Private letter by A. S. [Alexander Shaw] to [Stanley] Baldwin', 24 May 1922).

'advisability of carrying no more lascars' and whether mail steamers were 'allowed to carry lascar or other foreign crews.' Baldwin responded:

> I am informed that in all contracts entered into by the Post Office with steamship companies for the carriage of mails a Clause is inserted to the effect that the master and officers and at least three fourths of the crew of every mail ship shall be British subjects. The majority of the seamen described as 'lascars' are British subjects.[32]

Baldwin thus not only tried to cut short further discussion by pointing out that the question was conclusively dealt with in legally binding mail contracts, but also clarified that the larger part of the 'lascars' could not be treated as 'foreigners' or 'aliens': they had to be recognized as imperial subjects and could not be barred, for this reason, from employment on British merchant vessels, including mail steamers like the S.S. *Egypt*.

The 'Empire point of view' was brought home to the British public not solely or mainly through legal reasoning, however. It was more often justified in terms of a moral obligation Britain had incurred as Indian seafarers had 'proved their worth' and their loyalty not only to British employers, but also to the empire, particularly during the Great War. The 'war services of "the modest, efficient and quietly courageous Lascars"' had entered discourses of imperial self-celebration even as the global slaughter was still under way.[33] When the *Egypt* foundered, a 'Lascar War Memorial' was under construction on the Calcutta *maidan*: it was to honour the 896 Indian seafarers recruited from that port who were reported to 'have made the supreme sacrifice in the service of the Empire'; the monument was eventually inaugurated by the Earl of Lytton, governor of Bengal, early in 1924.[34] While legal entitlements of Indian seafarers to compensation in the event of accident had been (and would continue to be) largely unenforceable, meagre compensation

---

32 Hansard, vol. 154 (29 May 1922), col. 1655-8.

33 See, e.g., 'Lascars' War Services', *Times of India*, 15 April 1918.

34 'Indian Sailors Hold Fine War Record', *Christian Science Monitor*, 1 April 1924; see also 'Lascars in the War: Bengal's Enviable Record', *Times of India*, 8 February 1924; *Bombay Chronicle*, 9 February 1924, p. 13 and the webpage of the memorial, which was renovated, after a long period of neglect, in the 1990s: lascarwarmemorial.com. The number quoted is that given on the inauguration plaque of the memorial.

payments were doled out, for the first time, towards the end of the war to families of 'lascars' who had been maimed or killed in the course of naval warfare.[35] No petition or memorandum submitted by Indian seafarers and their none too radical trade unions during these years left out the opportunity to appeal to imperial common sense: loyal 'war services' had gained them entitlements, they believed, and legitimized their demands.[36] We have seen already, that both the Calcutta and the Bombay seamen's unions framed their protests in this loyalist vein against the international vilification of Indian seafarers after the *Egypt* disaster.[37] So did most of the newspaper articles, parliamentary interventions, and employer statements that opposed employment restrictions for 'lascars' on British ships.[38] And in the course of the *Egypt* inquiry, when cross-examined by Joseph Cotter, Sir Frank Bartlett Stewart Notley, the P&O's marine superintendent, responded in much the same way:

35 Indian seafarers employed by shipping companies registered in Britain had been entitled to compensation according to the British Workmen's Compensation Act (1906), but these claims could rarely be recovered. Even though an Indian Workmen's Compensation Act was passed in 1923, this situation did not change for the majority of Indian seafarers. Cf. L/E/7/1163, File 2886 (1923–31); Dinkar D. Desai, *Maritime Labour in India*, Bombay: Servants of India Society, 1940, pp. 177–8; Gopalan Balachandran, *Globalizing Labour? Indian Seafaring and World Shipping, c. 1870–1945*, New Delhi: Oxford University Press, 2012, pp. 109f. During the World War, however, a 'War Risks Compensation Scheme' for Indian seafarers was found necessary in the face of a maritime labour shortage. OIOC, Bombay Marine Proceedings (hereafter: BoMP) P/10546, B15 (December 1919).

36 For a particularly elaborate specimen see BL: OIOC/IOR/P/10793, A273f, Bombay Marine Proceedings ('Petition of the members of the Goa Portuguese Seamen's Club, the Portuguese Seafarer's Union and the Asiatic Seamen's (Saloon Crew) Union' to the Governor of Bombay, 23 July 1920).

37 See pp. 66–7.

38 'Notes of the Day', *Bombay Chronicle*, 16 June 1922; 'The Lascars', *Bombay Chronicle*, 20 June 1922; 'Lascars and their Reputation', *The Times*, 29 May 1922; 'The Loss of the Egypt', *Times of India*, 25 May 1922, p. 6; 'Panic on "Egypt"', *Times of India*, p. 7; 'Current Topics', *Times of India*, 5 June 1922, p. 8. See, e. g., Major Glyn's reference in the House of Commons to the 'coastal seafaring people of India' and their 'gallant service to the country in the late War and in times of peace': Hansard, vol. 157 (31 July 1922), col. 1025. See, e. g., the speech of Glasgow shipowner W. S. Workman on occasion of the launch of the *City of Nagpur*, which quoted various incidents of 'lascars' acting 'most bravely' under war conditions: 'New City Liner: Tribute to Lascars', *Times of India*, 23 June 1922.

Q Do you contend in your experience that the Lascar and Goanese in case of emergency are equal to the British seaman?
A I contend that on many occasions, and I have been in many tight corners myself in the past, I should never wish for better men than the Lascar seamen.
Q And the Goanese?
A And the Goanese, Yes; I will bring them in equally with the Lascar. I do not know so much of them, but I should never submit to the Lascar being put down as a sailorman. We had them all through the war in the Western Ocean, and they have done magnificently.[39]

A few weeks earlier, when the formal investigation of the *Egypt* disaster was ordered by the Board of Trade, a detailed brief for the board's legal counsel had specified the questions to be looked into with particular care. Even without further investigation, the authors of the brief were already convinced that the 'natives or foreigners or some of them, appear to have completely lost their heads and given way to abject panic and their behaviour no doubt hampered the Officers and seamen in their work of getting out and lowering the boats'. The panic, they believed, 'may have been due solely to the natural temperament of the race to which they belong' though more specific reasons needed to be looked into as well since 'most, if not all, of these men had served in their various capacities in other ships before and had had the benefit of having seen what discipline meant to a European crew'. Having left no doubt about the inborn 'temperamental' feebleness of the 'darker races', much space was given to elaborate that different 'classes' of Indian seafarers needed to be distinguished carefully in the course of the investigation:

> The lascars have been accused of rushing the boats and keeping out the passengers and women, and Questions have been asked in the House of Commons with regard to 'the alleged misconduct of the lascars of the "Egypt"', and 'to lascars and Goanese sailors rushing the boats'.

39 TNA, TS 34/10 'R.M.S. Egypt. Transcript of Court Proceedings', First Day: 24 July 1922, p. 55.

> There were no Goanese sailors on board the Egypt and the term 'lascar' is often loosely used to include all sorts and conditions of dark men serving on board ship in any capacity.
>
> The real lascars call themselves 'khalashis' (i.e., free or freed men). They are true British-Indian seamen – sailors by profession from youth upwards and for the most parts descendants of the men who manned the old India navies. They form part of the Deck crew and have their own Sarangs and Tindals or native Quartermasters over them and lascars have quite a fair reputation for discipline.
>
> A different class of coloured person to the Deck lascar is employed below Deck in various capacities – firemen, trimmers, greasers in the Engine-room department, cooks, bathroom attendants, Steward servants and other ratings in the Purser's department etc. These men include natives of India of a lower class than the lascar, also Portuguese and often many other nationalities. They practically know nothing of the sea and sea life beyond a continuous existence below Decks in the engine-room, stoke-hold etc., but being units of the native part of the crew they are all sometimes confused with and referred to as 'lascars'.
>
> In this case it would seem only fair to differentiate and determine, if possible whether in fact the true lascar or native deck-hands of the Egypt formed any part of the panic-stricken crowd who rushed the boats and against whom the accusations of lack of discipline are made.[40]

Even if panic was not to be ascribed to identifiable individuals but to an ethnically defined 'crowd', the brief insisted that not all 'dark men' were the same: the 'panic' on the *Egypt* was likely to have been caused not by all 'coloured persons' jointly but by *sub-collectivities* distinguished by markedly diverging behavioural patterns and defined by their 'lower class' status or by lack of maritime ancestry. The solicitor general, in his opening statement during the inquiry, made clear that he intended to follow this line of investigation: 'The question of the behaviour of

---

40 TNA, TS 34/8 '"R.M.S. Egypt": Various Proofs and Documents' ('The British Steamship "Egypt" of Greenock, Official No. 105581. Formal Investigation ordered by the Board of Trade . . .', n. d.), detailed brief for the legal counsel of the Board of Trade, pp. 43–5.

various members of the crew who were not white men, is one that calls for careful consideration and possibly for differentiation between the different classes of natives, the Goanese stewards, for instance.'[41] In the Board of Trade's brief, the criterion of categorization shifted uneasily between notions of ethnicity, class, and hereditary occupational status. The lack of coherence and the confused artificiality of this practice of categorization become fully apparent, however, only if one takes account of the messy range of contradictory voices that tried to define the criteria.

Already a week after the *Egypt* disaster, the Calcutta correspondent of the London *Times* had written, as has been mentioned before, that 'Calcutta opinion insists that there should be no general condemnation of lascars until the inquiry shall disclose from what class the accused Indian were recruited'. He distinguished the 'Chittagong lascars' who were 'descended from pirates and retain the best traditions of seamanship' from the 'Pathans' (Pashtuns) who were often enlisted in Bombay as firemen since the advent of steam and from the 'Goanese stewards' who, he alleged, had caused a panic on the *Egypt*.[42] In the Indian press, colonial luminaries quarrelled over whether the 'Bombay lascar' could measure up to the 'Bengal lascar' in terms of 'courage, discipline and devotion to duty' – that seafarers recruited from the colonial port cities of Calcutta and Bombay could be reduced to the singulars of an essentializing anthropology seemed uncontroversial, however: if you knew one such labourer, you knew, apparently, the moral mettle and market value of all.[43] The *Times of India*, published from Bombay, had their own regional version to tell when they informed their readers that it was 'necessary to make a distinction between the different classes of seamen' who had been called 'lascars' indiscriminately in English newspaper reports on the *Egypt* disaster:

> There are men among them who are properly termed 'lascars' or sailors, who are picked up from the Indian coast. These are born seamen and have made their mark for bravery and fearlessness in

41 TNA, TS 34/10 'R.M.S. Egypt. Transcript of Court Proceedings', First Day: 24 July 1922, p. 23.

42 'Lascars and their Reputation', *The Times*, 29 May 1922.

43 'Current Topics', *Times of India*, 5 June 1922.

> emergencies. Then there are the Goanese people who serve mostly as cabin boys, stewards, cooks and waiters. These men are also known to be good seamen and susceptible to discipline. There is a third class of people who hail from northern India and away from the sea coast. This class of people is almost entirely employed as firemen and stokers. They are by nature fierce and not amenable to discipline even in normal times and they have no great reputation as seamen.[44]

In the House of Commons, Major Glyn asked for a clearer definition of the term 'lascar', which was to be confined, in his opinion, to 'the coastal seafaring people of India', which included, in his view too, the Goans recruited for the 'saloon department'.[45] Glyn was not the first to raise this issue in Parliament: J. D. Rees, formerly a colonial bureaucrat in South India and then 'one of the most indefatigable members [of Parliament] who make it their special business to watch over the interests of Britons in India', had referred to the 'safety of passengers on British ships' ten years earlier when he asked 'whether there is any guarantee that lascars engaged on British ships really belong to *Asiatic maritime seafaring races, castes, and tribes*, and do not include coolies, ex-sepoys, and others unaccustomed to the sea'. He had also inquired whether the recruitment of 'lascars' was under the supervision of the Government of India.[46]

Rees, by referring to 'races, castes, and tribes', the key categories of a thriving colonial anthropology, explicitly linked up the 'lascar' question to colonial practices of knowledge production and statecraft: a chaotic mass of 'native' humanity was to be filtered through a taxonomic grid and then allocated to their appropriate positions of utilization, both processes supervised by a scientific-administrative bureaucracy bred in British public schools. Colonial anthropology was clearly omnipresent in the cultural and intellectual history of British imperialism – a dimension much explored in recent critical scholarship.[47] What has been

44 '"Egypt's" Crew. Arrival in Bombay', *Times of India*, 17 June 1922.

45 Hansard, vol. 157 (31 July 1922), col. 1025.

46 'Current Topics', *Times of India*, 5 June 1922; Hansard, vol. 38 (9 May 1912), col. 575. Emphasis added.

47 For an overview see Peter Pels and Oscar Salemink (eds), *Colonial Subjects: Essays on the Practical History of Anthropology*, Ann Arbor: University of Michigan Press, 1999.

examined less is that colonial anthropology also provided a managerial theory for 'making the Empire work': a method of gauging the 'human resources' of the empire, of arranging them according to a racial taxonomy, and of mobilizing them for the purposes of imperial expansion, civilizational progress, and associated profits. Just as taxonomies of cotton fibres and other primary products enabled the allocation of raw materials to the far-flung industries of a capitalist world economy, racial taxonomies of labour 'resources' were to facilitate the incorporation of disparate populations into the empire's increasingly transcontinental, hierarchically segmented, and non-equalizing labour markets.[48] The anti-egalitarian backlash of the age of modern imperialism thus permitted the interweaving of ideologies of class and race not merely in existential meditations like those of Joseph Conrad but also in enunciations of 'scientific' managerial knowledge. This form of knowledge interwove structures of class with those of race; it inserted racist typologies into the parameters of measuring labour power; it merged myth with management: the calculating logic of commodification, when applied to labour, was expressed in the irrational idioms of ethnicity – of 'race', 'tribe', or 'caste'. Racialized managerialism expressed, in other words, a core paradox of the age of imperialism that would reach a genocidal climax in the 1940s: it fulfilled the criteria of a Weberian 'formal rationality' in its attempt to optimize the allocation of labour 'resources' by means of calculation and accountancy, while the content of its reasoning was derived, to a large extent, from deeply irrational racist premises.[49]

As for their more direct impact on the world of labour, theories of 'racial management' can perhaps be described as a kind of sociological alchemy in search of the formula of the perfect composition and organization of workforces – a composition and organization that aimed at balancing productivity with subordination: the employer strove, in other words, to accomplish the most effective combination of skills and

48 I owe this thought to Frank Perlin's innovative analysis of and theoretical reflections on preindustrial commodity culture, though the link to the racial taxonomies of the late nineteenth century is not discussed in his book (and is also clearly beyond its scope). Frank Perlin, *City Intelligible: A Philosophical and Historical Anthropology of Global Commoditisation before Industrialisation*, Leiden: Brill, 2020.

49 Cf. Max Weber, *Wirtschaft und Gesellschaft. Grundriss der verstehenden Soziologie* (5th revised ed. by Johannes Winckelmann), Tübingen: J. C. B. Mohr, 1972, pp. 44f.

capabilities while seeking to prevent, at the same time, any unmediated, autonomous combination on the part of the workers.[50] Explicit theories of 'racial management' had been in the making since the nineteenth century. Elizabeth Esch and David Roediger have shown in a brilliant essay how such theories linked the US history of slavery with that of wage labour, and how these theories were inducted into Taylorist 'scientific management' rather than being replaced by it in the early decades of the twentieth century. Theories of 'racial management' governed, despite their glaring inconsistency, 'human resource' management in American steelworks and were even turned into an export item when US mining engineers advertised themselves as the leading experts of labour deployment across the globe – men who 'claimed an ability to know and to boss "native" and racially divided labor worldwide'.[51] Yet 'racial management' was not as original a contribution of US post-slavery society to capitalist civilization as Esch and Roediger's analysis may suggest.

In the British Empire, the military, that great innovator of social forms, provided a blueprint for 'racial management' techniques: the theory of so-called 'martial races' had legitimized and regulated since the 1880s a selective recruitment policy of the colonial armed forces in India. It ascribed military abilities, unperturbed by pervasive historical evidence to the contrary, to certain regions and social groups only. The practical application of this theory resulted in the creation of highly segmented military labour markets. Taxonomic approaches to 'races, castes, and tribes' were thus well established and had acquired, through cranial measurements and other academic rituals, the status of a scientific theory. The theory had entered the syllabus preparing British officers for deployment in India and led a respectable and long-lasting shelf life in the form of official handbooks and gazetteers.[52] When the

---

50 Cf. Elizabeth Esch and David R. Roediger, '"One Symptom of Originality": Race and Management of Labor in US History', in D. R. Roediger, *Class, Race and Marxism*, London: Verso, 2017, p. 122. In this argument, the authors rely on Michael Lebowitz's analysis in 'The Politics of Assumption, the Assumption of Politics', *Historical Materialism* 14, no. 2 (2006), pp. 29–47. See also Michael Lebowitz, *Beyond Capital: Marx's Political Economy of the Working Class* (2nd ed.), Basingstoke: Palgrave Macmillan, 2003, pp. 84–7 and *passim*.

51 Ibid., p. 138 and *passim*.

52 The classical colonial handbook is: George MacMunn, *The Martial Races of India*, London: Sampson Low, Marston & Co., 1933. For an overview see Heather

labour requirements of the imperial state diversified during the First World War to include, apart from unprecedented numbers of soldiers, an enormous non-combatant workforce of 'labour corps' and maritime workers, racial taxonomies were further expanded and linked, as Radhika Singha shows, to projects of enhancing 'efficiency':

> One of the key tenets of war propaganda was the assertion that the ruling race had the ability to make use of different races and castes, at different levels of civilisation, with different skills and dispositions, and then to send them back as assets to the society from which they had been drawn.[53]

This managerial ability to allocate, combine, and mould the empire's racially categorized labour resources in the most 'efficient' way was also claimed for non-military segments of India's colonial world of labour, which included the plantation economy as much as the shipping industry.[54] Whenever the debate over the exclusion of colonial workers from the British maritime labour market escalated, as was the case in the weeks of the *Egypt* inquiry, this theory of 'racial management' proved its political utility: it was employed by the spokesmen of shipping circles and imperial government to beat back an economically harmful and politically dangerous alliance that British trade unionists tried to forge with the most jingoist milieus of British society – a cross-class alliance based on a binary racism that juxtaposed gallant and seaworthy 'whites' with savage and incompetent 'natives'. The imperial shipping nexus countered this blunt dichotomy with a presumably more rational, scientific, and nuanced racial taxonomy – a genteel racism that behoved the better-bred guardians of the British Empire.

While this taxonomic approach did by no means question assumptions of a racial inferiority of 'coloured' seafarers, it posited them as a

Streets, *Martial Races: The Military, Race and Masculinity in British Imperial Culture, 1857–1914*, Manchester: Manchester University Press, 2017.

53 Radhika Singha, *The Coolie's Great War: Indian Labour in a Global Conflict, 1914–1921*, London: Hurst, 2020, p. 311.

54 Cf. Kaushik Ghosh, 'A Market for Aboriginality: Primitivism and Race Qualification in the Indentured Labour Market of Colonial India', in G. Bhadra, G. Prakash, and S. Tharu (eds), *Subaltern Studies X: Writings on South Asian History and Society*, New Delhi: Oxford University Press, 1999, pp. 8–48.

managerial challenge and not as a justification for absolute exclusion: handling and combining the presumably inbred differential capabilities of a racially heterogeneous workforce was presented as a key imperial skill, which officers of the British merchant marine were expected to excel in no less than colonial officials. As in the US case of 'managerial folklore' studied by Esch and Roediger, such imaginative conjurations of differential capabilities included racially defined levels of physical strength and technical prowess; a differential temperamental proneness to docility or recalcitrance, timidity or courage; and inborn resilience towards oppressive heat or biting cold.[55] In a popular account written by an influential writer on maritime matters and published in 1900, we thus read that the trimmer and stoker's

> work in tropical seas is so utterly unfit for white men to do that, in spite of the hardship attendant upon loss of employment at first, it would be a good thing if stokeholds were entirely manned by negroes, who, from their constitutional experience of heat, must be far better fitted to endure the conditions of the stokehold.[56]

During the *Egypt* inquiry, Captain Collyer stated similarly, just as numerous British shipping spokesmen had done for many years, that 'lascars' were better suited than white crews to the hot climatic conditions of the London–Bombay route in particular and that Indian seafarers were 'no trouble at all' '*if officers lead them well*'.[57] He insisted that even in emergencies there was 'not much to choose . . . between a Lascar crew, *if you lead them all right*, and a white crew'.[58] At the end of the inquiry, as we shall see, the judgment accepted that 'non-European' crews and especially 'lascars', '*if properly led*, discharge their duties with efficiency and a ready obedience to orders'. This assumption was turned

55 Cf. Esch and Roediger, '"One Symptom of Originality"', pp. 135–51.

56 Frank T. Bullen, *The Men of the Merchant Service Being the Polity of the Mercantile Marine for 'Longshore Readers*, London: Smith, Elder & Co., 1900, p. 327. Three years later, Bullen was called before the Mercantile Marine Committee and interviewed extensively as an expert: *MMC*, vol. 2, Evidence, pp. 617–23, 635–44.

57 Cf. *MMC*, vol. 2, Evidence, pp. 9, 21, 28, 61, 67, 73, 98, 129, 283, 310, 531, 586.

58 TNA, TS 34/10 'R.M.S. Egypt. Transcript of Court Proceedings', Second Day: 25 July 1922, pp. 15f. The emphases are added in these quotations as well as in the following one.

against Collyer and his first officer, Cartwright, however: the wreck commissioner ruled that one of the reasons for the high casualties had been precisely that the 'native' crew of the foundering *Egypt* was 'not properly led'.[59]

59 BL: OIOC, IOR/L/E/7/1123, F. 1989, Commerce & Revenue Department, Loss of the S.S. Egypt (Report of Court on the loss of the S.S. Egypt, 4 September 1922, with Appendix), pp. 5, 9.

6

Discomforting Testimonies: Eight 'Native Seamen' in Court

The political controversy, which the *Egypt* disaster had raised both in Britain and India, meant that eight members of the Indian crew had to be heard in court, too, even though none of the British gentlemen assembled to assume the roles of judge, assessor, prosecutor, and legal counsel seemed particularly keen to do so. Initially, the *Egypt*'s chief officer had picked out only two witnesses from among the 159 Indian crew who had been rescued and detained in a storehouse in Brest. The company headquarters then sent instructions, however, that all 'three native departments' had to be represented.[1] The eight Indian witnesses chosen eventually included two men (an experienced sailor and a fireman) who had received bullet wounds when Captain Carr fired his 'warning shots'. As for the others, we can only guess which selection criteria were applied by the *Egypt*'s chief officer and the P&O's representative in France. Certain imbalances stand out: preference had been given to 'lascars' from the deck department (four out of eight witnesses) and to long-term employees of the P&O (six witnesses had a service record with that company of nine to twenty-one years). There was also a bias towards crew that had joined the *Egypt* already in Bombay for its previous 'home journey' to London in April, while the sizeable section of the Indian crew that had been transferred to the *Egypt* from the

1 NMM, Caird Library, P&O Collections, 65/1 (letter to P&O directors from James Beveridge, Brest, 25 May 1922).

Palermo shortly before its departure from London (87 men out of 208) was only represented by the two firemen. Most conspicuously, the three *serangs*, the powerful foremen in charge of the Indian deck crew, the firemen, and the trimmers respectively, all of whom had been transferred from the *Palermo* to the *Egypt* a few days earlier, were left out even though all had survived.[2] This omission was all the more striking as these foremen were supposed to act as the main intermediaries between the Indian crew and the British officers on the bridge and in the engine room. We shall return to this issue when deepening the analysis.

Two of the witnesses, Antonio de Silva and Phillip Azevedo, originated from Goa and had been employed as stewards on board the *Egypt*.[3] Forty and thirty-seven years old, both had worked at sea for about two decades and been in the P&O's service most of that time.[4] In the course of the inquiry, they appear to have made their depositions in English and were cross-examined in the same language, which curtailed their ability to express themselves. Their typed depositions were thus extremely short, confined to rough and simplified narratives, and diverged markedly from the eloquent statements Goan stewards made on their return to India according to Baptista's letter to the *Bombay Chronicle*, which has been discussed already.[5] De Silva's English language skills were rather limited apparently – he was examined in court as the first Goan survivor and Cotter felt justified, after just two offhand questions, to generalize in exasperation: 'I do not know what we are going to do with these Goanese witnesses.' The wreck commissioner agreed ('I do not think you will get very far with this one') without

---

2 NMM, Caird Library, P&O Collections, 65/3, ff. 256-316 ('draft statements' of Mohammed Adam, Phillip Azevedo, Moossa Fackeer, Moossa Ismail, Abdool Rasched [Rasool], Sabdeen Fazuldeen, Barrum Mustaffa, Antonio Phillip de Silva, n. d.); TNA, TS 34/9 'R.M.S. Egypt. Exhibits' ('List of Native Crew of P. & O. S. S. "Egypt"', 20 May 1922).

3 Spellings of names often vary in the sources indicating a somewhat muted need for precise identification. Hence 'de Silva' is used interchangeably with 'da Silva,' for instance. For the politics of naming see chapter 12.

4 NMM, Caird Library, P&O Collections, 65/3, ff. 256-316 ('draft statements' of Phillip Azevedo and Antonio Phillip de Silva, n. d.).

5 TNA, BT 239/2 '"Egypt" in Collision with "Seine"' (depositions by Antonio Philip de Silva and Phillip Azevedo, 2 June 1922); '"Egypt" Disaster: The Lascars' Version' (letter by Joseph Baptista), *Bombay Chronicle*, 19 June 1922.

considering the option of engaging an interpreter.[6] Azevedo stood his ground better during the cross-examination, but either chose or was equally compelled to confine himself to brief and bare factual responses. A glint of resistance was briefly perceivable only when he responded, on being probed by Cotter whether he knew anything about boat drills, that he had been on board the P&O liner *Arabia* when it was sunk by German torpedoes in 1917 and when most passengers were saved.[7]

The remaining six Indian witnesses, two firemen representing the engine-room crew and four khalasis from the deck department, were all Muslims. Most were between twenty-five and thirty-five years old and, like their Goan shipmates, experienced seafarers. Two of the deck hands, Musa Faqir and Musa Ismail, hailed from Daman, a coastal enclave under Portuguese control about 170 kilometres north of Bombay. Both introduced themselves as '*panjari wallahs*', as 'top men' on full pay (the counterparts of European 'ABs', i.e., 'able-bodied seamen'). They looked back on work experience – beginning in their late childhoods – of two decades or more and long years of service on P&O steamers. Mohammed Adam, stating Bombay as his birthplace and his age as twenty-five, had been employed by the P&O for fourteen years and had served on the *Egypt* as a 'lascar tindal', as a sub-foreman in the deck department. Abdul Rasul was a young adult from Calcutta who had been hired in Bombay as a 'bhandary's mate', i.e., as a helper for the cook of the *Egypt*'s Indian deck crew – he was returning to India from his first sea voyage when the ship foundered. The two '*ag wallahs*' or firemen had been recruited from the landlocked northern province of Punjab: Sabdin Fazuldin hailed from the district of Campbellpur (today's Attock in Pakistan), had been a ship worker for fifteen years, mostly in the employ of the P&O, and had signed on as a 'fireman tindal' – a foreman in the stokehold. Baram Mustafa originated from Mirpur, then in the princely state of Kashmir, one of the main recruitment areas for Bombay stokehold crews. He was a fireman of the 'first class according to pay' and had been with the P&O nine out of his ten years at sea.[8]

---

6 TNA, TS 34/10 'R.M.S. Egypt. Transcript of Court Proceedings', Sixth Day: 31 July 1922, pp. 2–5 (examination and cross-examination of Antonio de Silva).

7 TNA, TS 34/10 'R.M.S. Egypt. Transcript of Court Proceedings', Sixth Day: 31 July 1922, p. 10 (examination and cross-examination of Phillip Azevedo).

8 TNA, BT 239/2 '"Egypt" in Collision with "Seine"' (depositions by Moossa Fackeer, Abdool Rasched [Rasool], Moossa Ismail, Mahomed Adam, Sabdeen Fazuldeen

For these six witnesses, an unusually competent and conscientious linguist was employed who translated their depositions and interpreted their oral statements in court. Abraham Challis had been working as a 'lay missionary' for the London City Mission among Indian seafarers in the docklands for more than two decades, had campaigned for improving their conditions on board British ships, and stood out from among his fellow missionaries in that he had shown an unusual propensity to perceive 'lascars' not merely as dull-witted objects of proselytism, but as individuals with critical minds of their own.[9] 'The typical lascar', he had once written, 'is far shrewder a person than many people give him credit for.'[10] This may explain the careful renditions and Challis's repeated interjections in the cross-examinations, whenever he felt that unclear questions, terminological difficulties, or the inadequacy of his own translation rather than the witnesses' responses themselves had led to misunderstandings and ambiguity.[11] Challis's efforts allow us to catch some glimpses at least of what Indian seafarers wished to express about the *Egypt* disaster and how they inserted these statements into the rigid frame of the testimonies they were allowed to give.

A tenacious self-will is perceivable, for instance, in the refusal of Indian deckhands to refer to themselves as 'lascars' – a term carrying connotations of military service and of legally sanctioned racial discrimination. They showed a clear preference for the term 'khalasi', common among Indian Ocean seafarers for centuries, that implied the

---

and Barrum Mustapha, 2 June 1922); NMM, Caird Library, P&O Collections, 65/3, ff. 256-265, 274-310 ('draft statements' of Mohammed Adam, Moossa Fackeer, Moossa Ismail, Abdool Rasched [Rasool], Sabdeen Fazuldeen, Barrum Mustaffa, n. d.); TNA, TS 34/10 'R.M.S. Egypt: Transcript of Court Proceedings', Fifth Day: 28 July 1922, pp. 70–104 (examinations and cross-examinations of Sabdeen Fazuldeen, Barrum Mustapha, Musa Fakir, Abdul Rasoul, Mohammed Adam, Moosa Ismail).

9 Lahiri, 'Patterns of Resistance', pp. 171, 178 (fn. 89); Lahiri quotes an article by Challis on his missionary experiences with 'lascars' that was published in 1900. Between 1911 and 1913, Challis wrote a number of letters to the Board of Trade, which denounced the maltreatment of Indian seafarers on board British ships and particularly the exaction of bribes by British engineers. The letters were based on the complaints of Indian seafarers and are remarkably precise and detailed. See BL, OIOC, IOR, Bombay Marine Proceedings P/9083, A468-470, A473-476; BL, OIOC, IOR, Bombay Marine Proceedings P/9342, A215f.

10 Quoted in Lahiri, 'Patterns of Resistance', p. 168.

11 TNA, TS 34/10 'R.M.S. Egypt: Transcript of Court Proceedings', Fifth Day: 28 July 1922, pp. 71f, 97, 102.

maritime worker's claim to independence and freedom – a claim that conferred a respectability that was, however, largely unenforceable.[12] A seemingly inconspicuous sequence of the prosecutor general's abrupt interrogation of Abdul Rasul, the youngest of the witnesses, brings this out rather strikingly:

> [Abdul R.]: I should suppose there were 100 men perhaps there trying to lower the boats, but they failed in lowering them.
> [Prosecutor]: Were there any Lascars there?
> [Abdul R.]: Yes, there were khalasis there; there were Europeans there.
> [Prosecutor]: Were there lascars at your boat?
> [Abdul R.]: We tried to lower that boat to which I went and we could not lower it, and I went over to the other side.
> . . .
> [Prosecutor]: Will you answer my question? Were there any Lascars at the boat you tried to lower?
> [Abdul R.]: Yes, there were khalasis there.
> [Prosecutor]: Were there Lascars at the boat in front of the one that you tried to lower?
> [Abdul R.]: Yes there were khalasis there. They were with the crowd.[13]

Each time the prosecutor asked for 'lascars' he was implicitly corrected by a twenty-year-old kitchen helper who insisted on using the designation 'khalasi'. Abdul could not have been unfamiliar with the term 'lascar': it had been used commonly in maritime India since the age of sail and he himself had been hired on 'lascar articles', the contracts that prescribed the reduced rights and entitlements of South Asian

12 For a brief discussion of the etymology of the term 'lascar' see Amitav Ghosh, 'Of Fanás and Forecastles: The Indian Ocean and Some Lost Languages of the Age of Sail', *Economic and Political Weekly*, 21 June 2008, pp. 56f and 62 (fn 2). Ghosh's characterization of 'lascar' as a generic colonial term for Indian Ocean and East Asian sailors is valid for the eighteenth and much of the nineteenth century. By the end of the nineteenth century, as the designation became a term of British mercantile marine law, its meaning was narrowed down regionally to South Asia and sometimes occupationally to deckhands. For connotations of the term 'khalasi' and the legal implications of the term 'lascar' in the early twentieth century see also chapter 3, footnote 10, p. 44.

13 TNA, TS 34/10 'R.M.S. Egypt: Transcript of Court Proceedings', Fifth Day: 28 July 1922, p. 94.

seafarers.[14] Nevertheless, and perhaps even for this very reason, he had obstinately shunned what had become a discriminatory term in the nomenclature of colonial maritime law.

If Challis's conscientious translations are a stroke of luck already for our investigation, we are even more fortunate to have three documents for each Indian witness that were produced by different authorities during the various stages of the inquiry: First came the depositions that were taken from them by a government official, the deputy receiver of wreck, in the Mercantile Marine Office in the London docklands on 2 June 1922, shortly after their arrival from Brest, with Abraham Challis acting as interpreter.[15] Subsequently, when the solicitors of Freshfields, Leese and Munns were engaged as legal counsel by the P&O, their preparations for the inquiry included a detailed 'mock interrogation' of the Indian witnesses that resulted in the second, extremely rich series of testimonies the clearly competent translator of which is not mentioned.[16] Third and last there are the minutes of their oral examination and cross-examination in court on 28 July 1922, which identify Challis again as the sworn interpreter.[17]

The two earlier questionings of the Indian witnesses, the depositions and the 'mock interrogation', focused, to a considerable extent, on the question whether 'natives' had physically manhandled or even used weapons to attack 'Europeans' in their attempt to escape from the foundering ship. If white passengers, crew, and officers concurred that

---

14 Cf. Ravi Ahuja, 'Networks of Subordination – Networks of the Subordinated: The Case of South Asian Maritime Labour under British Imperialism (c. 1890–1947)', in Harald Fischer-Tiné and Ashwini Tambe (eds), *Spaces of Disorder: The Limits of British Colonial Control in South Asia and the Indian Ocean*, London: Routledge, 2008, pp. 14–16.

15 TNA, BT 239/2 '"Egypt" in Collision with "Seine"' (depositions by Moossa Fackeer, Abdool Rasched [Rasool], Moossa Ismail, Mahomed Adam, Sabdeen Fazuldeen, Barrum Mustapha, Antonio Phillip de Silva and Phillip Azevedo, 2 June 1922).

16 NMM, Caird Library, P&O Collections, 65/3, ff. 256-316 ('draft statements' of Mohammed Adam, Phillip Azevedo, Moossa Fackeer, Moossa Ismail, Abdool Rasched [Rasool], Sabdeen Fazuldeen, Barrum Mustaffa, Antonio Phillip de Silva, n. d.).

17 TNA, TS 34/10 'R.M.S. Egypt: Transcript of Court Proceedings', Fifth Day: 28 July 1922, pp. 70–104 (examinations and cross-examinations of Sabdeen Fazuldeen, Barrum Mustapha, Musa Fakir, Abdul Rasoul, Mohammed Adam, Moosa Ismail); ibid., Sixth Day: 31 July 1922, pp. 2–12 (examinations and cross-examinations of Antonio de Silva and Phillip Azevedo).

no pistols had been fired nor knives wielded by 'natives' and most of their testimonies agreed that no aggression could be observed, all Indian witnesses were questioned, too, and uniformly confirmed that finding.[18] Nobody had seen a gun in the hand of an Indian and yes, khalasis needed pocket-knives for their work, but none had been drawn on the sinking ship.[19] To the court, the submitted testimonies seemed to appear sufficiently conclusive to make a further interrogation of the Indian witnesses on the matter largely unnecessary. Even so, the Indian witnesses offered several uncomfortable observations on the possibility and reality of violence on board the *Egypt* – observations that neither court nor press chose to take up subsequently.

Hence, several of the witnesses hinted at the unlikeliness of the notion that Indian seafarers were carrying arms and some barely concealed their irritation with this proposition. Mohammed Adam explained that the possession of weapons was an unlikely risk: 'I know that if I had a pistol in my possession and it was found on me, I should be arrested and taken to prison. Everybody knows that.' He added: 'I saw nobody with a pistol, neither white nor black man.'[20] Apparently, he felt that the issue could not be settled in general terms: since the possession of arms was linked to racial status, he chose to make explicit that his statement applied to both sides of a harsh black-and-white racial divide. Musa Ismail, in his draft statement, explained his reasons for staying away from firearms: 'I am under the Portuguese law and both in Bombay and my own country, Daman, the only men that are allowed to carry revolvers are the police. I have never had a revolver in my possession.'[21] His impatience with the question was palpable in his deposition that ended with the following terse sentences: 'I did not have a pistol. Where should I get one? I did not see any pistol. I did not have a knife.'[22] Sabdin Fazuldin merely pointed out that the consequences awaiting colonial subjects who violated the law were known in full detail: 'If I or any other

18 See the preceding chapter.

19 See footnotes 15–17 of this chapter, above.

20 NMM, Caird Library, P&O Collections, 65/3 ('draft statement' of Mohammed Adam, n. d., f. 265).

21 NMM, Caird Library, P&O Collections, 65/3 ('draft statement' of Moossa Ismail, n. d., f. 291).

22 TNA, BT 239/2 '"Egypt" in Collision with "Seine"' (deposition by Moossa Ismail, 2 June 1922).

native had a pistol we should be liable to six months imprisonment.'[23] Musa Faqir gave the same response to the P&O's legal counsel during the 'mock interrogation':

> Q[uestion:] Have you ever had a pistol in your possession?
> A[nswer:] I have never had a pistol in my hand.
> Q[uestion:] Have you any reason?
> A[nswer:] I never wanted or would like to have one because if it was discovered that I had one I would get six months gaol.[24]

Musa Faqir had been selected as a witness, together with Baram Mustafa, most probably because these two seafarers had been hit by bullets in their neck and shoulder respectively, when Captain Carr 'fired two shots over their heads' – adding thereby another instance to the long list of colonial 'shooting accidents', one of the standard justifications of British gentlemen in India to avoid legal prosecution for acts of personal violence against 'natives'.[25] 'The only pistol I saw', declared Musa Faqir, 'was the one fired at me and I have never known one of the natives have a pistol[.] How can they?'[26] He had joined the *Egypt* in Bombay and this experienced khalasi had been assigned to the accident crew in charge of handling and rowing lifeboat no. 17. He gave the following account of how he received his bullet wound: After lowering the boat into the water together with two European quartermasters, Musa Faqir followed them going down a lifeline to take his place at the oars. As he reached the boat, he heard a shot, saw a passenger with a revolver in his hand, and felt blood running down his neck. He quickly scrambled up the rope again to the now heavily listing ship, which was about to turn turtle. When he saw Captain Collyer taking Carr's revolver, he felt it was

23 TNA, BT 239/2 '"Egypt" in Collision with "Seine"' (deposition by Sabdeen Fazuldeen, 2 June 1922, p. 2). See also NMM, Caird Library, P&O Collections, 65/3, f. 303 ('draft statement' of Sabdeen Fazuldeen, p. 6).

24 NMM, Caird Library, P&O Collections, 65/3 ('draft statement' of Moossa Fackeer, n. d., f. 284).

25 TNA, TS 34/8 '"R.M.S. Egypt": Various Proofs and Documents' (depositions by passengers and crew: Captain Douglas Gerald Carr, p. 24). See also Elizabeth Kolsky, *Colonial Justice in British India: White Violence and the Rule of Law*, Cambridge: Cambridge University Press, 2010, pp. 186–96 and *passim*.

26 TNA, BT 239/2 '"Egypt" in Collision with "Seine"' (deposition by Moossa Fackeer, 2 June 1922, p. 2).

sufficiently safe to jump into the water next to the lifeboat and was pulled in by some of his Indian shipmates.[27] If Rajputana rifleman Carr had admitted that he felt justified to use his gun because of the sheer *presence* of 'natives' in the lifeboat and not by what they *did*, Musa Faqir offered the following remarkably restrained comment in his deposition:[28] 'I do not know why Captain Carr fired but I suppose he thought there were enough people in the boat. I thought I was doing right as it is a part of my work to help lower and get the boat away.'[29]

Baram Mustafa, a fireman who had sought refuge in the same boat, had received a more serious bullet wound and expressed his sense of grievance more aggressively than Musa Faqir. 'I had not a pistol', he stated in his deposition and asked: 'How can a black man get a pistol? The only one I saw was the one I was shot with by the passenger.'[30] Racial discrimination, the condition of being a *kala admi*, a black man, and not a *gora*, a white man, was pointed at directly. Examined in court, Baram Mustafa was bold enough to respond to the Board of Trade counsel's question whether he had been armed on board ship with a counter-question: 'Is it likely if a man stands a chance of getting six months in gaol that he is going to have a pistol with him?'[31] During the 'mock interrogation' by the P&O's solicitors he had expressed his irritation even more openly and gave an account of the shooting incident that was neither confirmed by other testimonies nor repeated by him when examined in court:

> [Baram M.]: When I came down this passenger had a pistol in his hand and ordered us to get out of her saying the boat was only for passengers.

---

27 This narrative is reconstructed from Musa Faqir's three statements: TNA, BT 239/2 '"Egypt" in Collision with "Seine"' (deposition by Moossa Fackeer, 2 June 1922); NMM, Caird Library, P&O Collections, 65/3 ('draft statement' of Moossa Fackeer, n. d., ff. 274-285); TNA, TS 34/10 'R.M.S. Egypt: Transcript of Court Proceedings', Fifth Day: 28 July 1922, pp. 88–93 (examination and cross-examination of Musa Fakir).

28 Cf. pp. 74–5.

29 TNA, BT 239/2 '"Egypt" in Collision with "Seine"' (deposition by Moossa Fackeer, 2 June 1922, p. 2).

30 TNA, BT 239/2 '"Egypt" in Collision with "Seine"' (deposition by Barrum Mustapha, 2 June 1922).

31 TNA, TS 34/10 'R.M.S. Egypt: Transcript of Court Proceedings', Fifth Day: 28 July 1922, p. 87.

Q[uestion]: Did you get out?
[Baram M.]: The ship was sinking and there was nowhere for us to go[,] so I stayed in the boat. The passenger shot me in the shoulder, another man in the neck, and another man in the head. He also shot another man who was standing at the side of the boat, and he fell overboard and I did not see him again. He shot four altogether.
Q[uestion]: The man who fell overboard – as the boat was so crowded and he was standing, couldn't he have fallen over by accident?
[Baram M.]: The passenger fired at and shot him and he fell overboard.
Q[uestion]: Who was the man who went overboard?
[Baram M.]: He was one of the Palermo men who had been with me. I do not know his full name. He was known to us as Kara.[32]

Five of the twenty-two firemen transferred from the S.S. *Palermo* to the *Egypt* days before her last journey went missing and all we know about them are the names under which they were registered when they signed on: 'Mohamed Ahmed', 'Khairdeen Imamdeen', 'Amadkhan Khamaskhan', 'Haja Mustaken', and 'Moonakmud Gool Akmud'.[33] One of them may have been called by the nickname 'Kara'. One of them may not have survived because he sustained an 'accidental' bullet wound. We cannot know whether Baram Mustafa inflated the incident in a moment of fury or whether the solicitors convinced him to drop an accusation that could not be proved and was unlikely to be investigated by a British court but might have stirred up political trouble back in India. 'Kara's' body went missing when the *Egypt* sank to the bottom of the sea, and so did his name after making a single appearance in the extensive *Egypt* files.

The P&O company's solicitor accepted Baram Mustafa's version that four Indian seafarers had received gunshot wounds and cross-examined Captain Carr accordingly.[34] But when all was said and recorded, the Indian crew's depositions regarding the unfolding of events during the twenty minutes after the collision of the two steamers were tacitly yet

32 NMM, Caird Library, P&O Collections, 65/3 ('draft statement' of Barrum Mustapha, n. d., f. 308).

33 TNA, TS 34/9 'R.M.S. Egypt: Exhibits' ('List of Native Crew of P. & O. S. S. "Egypt"', 20 May 1922).

34 TNA, TS 34/10 'R.M.S. Egypt: Transcript of Court Proceedings', Eighth Day: 2 August 1922, p. 28 (examination of Captain Douglas Gerald Carr).

almost entirely disregarded by the wreck commissioner and the court's assessors. The synoptic narratives of the rescue operations, which the court had compiled in preparation of their judgment for each of the lifeboats were, for instance, based exclusively on the testimonies of British officers and crew. Unsurprisingly, under the circumstances, these testimonies were contradictory in many ways, but tended to highlight the 'failings' of the 'natives' and remained largely silent about the contributions of the latter to the rescue operations, which were emphasized more in the testimonies of Indian crew.[35] 'Horniman's law', his prediction about the public representation of the *Egypt* disaster, could be applied to the court proceedings also: as long as British courts showed partiality for the testimonies of British witnesses, the judicial certification of British heroism and of the 'cowardice and incompetence on the part of the foreigners' was a foregone conclusion.[36] Yet Indian seafarers made the point that the *sauve qui peut* situation on board the sinking ship had resulted in assertions of racial superiority and privilege to the detriment of the Indian crew. 'I saw some white people pulling natives out of the boats', reported Abdul Rasul, the young kitchen helper, while stoker Baram Mustafa recalled that 'this passenger had a pistol in his hand and ordered us to get out of her saying the boat was only for passengers' – accounts that could not be excised entirely from the records even though they were passed over silently in the court's final report.[37] However, the Indian seafarers' statements regarding the safety provisions and procedures on the *Egypt* since her departure from the Tilbury docks were, as we shall see presently, more difficult to ignore and had a greater impact on the judgment.

In the course of the inquiry, the conclusion became unavoidable that basic safety procedures, which were commonly followed at the time on British ocean liners including those of the P&O, had been neglected on board the S.S. *Egypt*.[38] This neglect was particularly grave in all

35 TNA, TS 34/9 'R.M.S. Egypt: Exhibits' (schematic narratives for lifeboats). This will be analysed more thoroughly in chapter 11, below.

36 See p. 74, above.

37 NMM, Caird Library, P&O Collections, 65/3 ('draft statements' of Abdool Rasched [Rasool], n. d., f. 294 and Barrum Mustapha, n.d., f. 308).

38 BL: OIOC, IOR/L/E/7/1123, F. 1989, Commerce & Revenue Department, Loss of the S.S. Egypt (Report of Court on the loss of the S.S. Egypt, 4 September 1922, with Annex), pp. 1f, 5.

matters concerning the Indian crew. Crucially, deck and engine room crew had not been provided with lifebelts ever since the ship had left Bombay in April. The seafarers were aware of this default, since lifebelts were usually stored in lockers in their living quarters as well as in boxes on the decks of the P&O ships on which they had served previously. On earlier voyages, they had also been regularly instructed on where to find their lifebelts. On the *Egypt*, however, food stores had been kept in the lockers, by the serang as some witnesses alleged, and no other place had been pointed out to them where they could find their lifebelts.[39] Few appear to have ventured to address the issue before the accident, but many assembled on the bridge immediately after the collision to ask Captain Collyer and Chief Officer Cartwright for lifebelts. According to their testimony, they were told there were none and then left to their own devices.[40] Chief Officer Cartwright denied this outright: 'After the collision occurred none of the native crew asked me for a life jacket neither did I hear them ask the Captain.'[41] However, the testimonies of the Indian witnesses were particularly clear and consistent on this issue – even the more cautious and timid ones were unambiguous in this regard. In the brief prepared for the Board of Trade's legal counsel in preparation of the inquiry, it was observed already that 'some of the officers appear to have been very

39 NMM, Caird Library, P&O Collections, 65/3 ('draft statements' of Mohammed Adam, ff. 258f; Moossa Fackeer, f. 276; Moossa Ismail, f. 288; Abdool Rasched [Rasool], f. 293; Sabdeen Fazuldeen, ff. 299f; Barrum Mustapha, f. 306); TNA, BT 239/2 '"Egypt" in Collision with "Seine"' (deposition by Abdool Rasool, 2 June 1922); TNA, TS 34/10 'R.M.S. Egypt: Transcript of Court Proceedings', Fifth Day: 28 July 1922 (examinations and cross-examinations of Sabdeen Fazuldeen, p. 73; Barrum Mustapha, pp. 85f; Moossa Fackeer, p. 89; Mohammed Adam, p. 100; Moosa Ismail, p. 104). See also TNA, TS 34/8 '"R.M.S. Egypt": Various Proofs and Documents' ('The British Steamship "Egypt" of Greenock, Official No. 105581. Formal Investigation ordered by the Board of Trade . . .', n. d.), detailed brief for the legal counsel of the Board of Trade, pp. 25–8; BL: OIOC, IOR/L/E/7/1123, F. 1989, Commerce & Revenue Department, Loss of the S.S. Egypt (Report of Court on the loss of the S.S. Egypt, 4 September 1922, with Annex), pp. 1f, 5.

40 TNA, BT 239/2 '"Egypt" in Collision with "Seine"' (depositions dated 2 June 1922 by: Abdool Rasool, Mahomed Adam, Sabdeen Fazuldeen, Barrum Mustapha); TNA, TS 34/10 'R.M.S. Egypt: Transcript of Court Proceedings', Fifth Day: 28 July 1922 (examinations and cross-examinations of Barrum Mustapha, p. 86; Moossa Fackeer, p. 90; Mohammed Adam, p. 100).

41 TNA, TS 34/8 'R.M.S. Egypt' (deposition of Chief Officer Charles Walter Cartwright, p. 7).

hazy as to the whereabouts of the life-jackets, except those for the European crew and the passengers'.[42] The court refrained nevertheless from any insistent examination of Collyer and Cartwright on the issue, but had to take note of the issue in their report: 'Certain Indian members of the crew (other than the Goanese stewards) stated that they were not told where their life-jackets were stored and had none allotted to them. The Court thinks this is true.'[43]

This was not all. The lack of lifebelts had not been the only reason why many khalasis and firemen assembled on the bridge deck after they became aware of the collision: they were also asking for orders.[44] According to the P&O's own safety rules and to general practice, each member of the crew on joining a ship was to be 'told off', i.e., assigned, to a certain lifeboat where they were to assemble in the event of an emergency. In some ships brass tallies with the number of the lifeboat were distributed among the crew – not so on the *Egypt*, even though Captain Collyer incorrectly claimed that this had been the case in his original statement, which he was forced to revoke.[45] Weekly boat drills were prescribed, when the boat crews were to be mustered at the falls in order to swing out and lower their respective boats.[46] Boat drills of

42 TNA, TS 34/8 '"R.M.S. Egypt": Various Proofs and Documents' ('The British Steamship "Egypt" of Greenock, Official No. 105581. Formal Investigation ordered by the Board of Trade . . .', n. d.), detailed brief for the legal counsel of the Board of Trade, p. 42.

43 BL: OIOC, IOR/L/E/7/1123, F. 1989, Commerce & Revenue Department, Loss of the S.S. Egypt (Report of Court on the loss of the S.S. Egypt, 4 September 1922, with Annex), p. 5.

44 TNA, BT 239/2 '"Egypt" in Collision with "Seine"' (deposition by Moossa Fackeer, 2 June 1922); NMM, Caird Library, P&O Collections, 65/3, f. 278 (draft statement of Moossa Fackeer); TNA, TS 34/10 'R.M.S. Egypt: Transcript of Court Proceedings', Fifth Day: 28 July 1922 (examinations and cross-examinations of Barrum Mustapha, p. 86; Moossa Fackeer, p. 90).

45 TNA, BT 239/2 '"Egypt" in Collision with "Seine"' (deposition by Mahomed Adam, 2 June 1922); TNA, TS 34/8 '"R.M.S. Egypt": Various Proofs and Documents', deposition by Captain Andrew Collyer, p. 2, and additional deposition by Charles Cartwright, Chief Officer, on brass tallies; TNA, TS 34/10 'R.M.S. Egypt: Transcript of Court Proceedings', Second Day: 25 July 1922 (examination and cross-examination of Captain Andrew Collyer), p. 5.

46 TNA, TS 34/8 '"R.M.S. Egypt": Various Proofs and Documents' ('The British Steamship "Egypt" of Greenock, Official No. 105581. Formal Investigation ordered by the Board of Trade . . .', n. d.), detailed brief for the legal counsel of the Board of Trade, pp. 13–16.

some description had, in fact, been held during the *Egypt*'s voyage from Bombay to London and again on 18 May, two days before the ship sailed from Tilbury, even though the trouble of actually lowering the boats was largely avoided.[47]

On reaching the latter port more than half of the deck and the engine room crews were exchanged, moreover: twenty-five of the forty-six khalasis who served in the deck department at the time of the collision had been transferred to the *Egypt* in London from another vessel, the S.S. *Palermo*, and so were fifty-three of the eighty-three Indian engine room crew.[48] These new crew members, including all three senior foremen or serangs, had not been informed about their respective 'boat stations', and the mandatory boat stations drill before the departure from London had been performed in an even more perfunctory way: instead of being assembled at their boats, the crew were simply asked to stand in lines according to their department, and while some boats were swung out, none were lowered into the water.[49] Sabdin Fazuldin claimed that he 'received no instructions about the boat I was to go to'. He recalled having 'asked the Engineer "What about the boat stations" and having received as an answer to "never mind about boat stations[,] stand on one side."'[50] Baram Mustafa declared similarly to have asked the engine room serang for the number of his lifeboat, who presumably responded that he had not been informed either.[51] The fact that none of the serangs was selected

47 BL: OIOC, IOR/L/E/7/1123, F. 1989, Commerce & Revenue Department, Loss of the S.S. Egypt (Report of Court on the loss of the S.S. Egypt, 4 September 1922, with Appendix, pp. 1f); TNA, BT 239/2 '"Egypt" in Collision with "Seine"' (deposition by Moossa Fackeer, 2 June 1922); NMM, Caird Library, P&O Collections, 65/3, ff. 274–6 (draft statement of Moossa Fackeer).

48 TNA, TS 34/9 'R.M.S. Egypt: Exhibits' ('List of Native Crew of P. & O. S. S. "Egypt"', 20 May 1922).

49 TNA, TS 34/8 '"R.M.S. Egypt": Various Proofs and Documents' ('The British Steamship "Egypt" of Greenock, Official No. 105581. Formal Investigation ordered by the Board of Trade . . .', n. d.), detailed brief for the legal counsel of the Board of Trade, pp. 25–8, 42.

50 TNA, BT 239/2 '"Egypt" in Collision with "Seine"' (deposition by Sabdeen Fazuldeen, 2 June 1922, p. 1); NMM, Caird Library, P&O Collections, 65/3 ('draft statement' of Sabdeen Fazuldeen, ff. 298f).

51 TNA, BT 239/2 '"Egypt" in Collision with "Seine"' (deposition by Barrum Mustapha, 2 June 1922, p. 1); NMM, Caird Library, P&O Collections, 65/3 ('draft statement' of Barrum Mustapha, ff. 305f).

as a witness suggests that the P&O officials soon understood that the officers' negligence would be a sore point during the impending inquiry.

The effects of these violations of safety procedure were compounded by further omissions. Many of the passengers were equally unaware of which lifeboat they had been assigned to and crucial time was lost after the collision when large parts of the *Egypt*'s human load wandered about desperate and aimless, crowding the boats on the fore of the ship, while those swung out aft got away almost empty.[52] Further, when the fatal fog came up in the channel, Captain Collyer refrained from the precautionary measure of swinging out more of the lifeboats.[53] For this reason, even those European as well as Indian seafarers who knew their boat stations often discovered that their assigned boats were jammed and could not be hoisted.[54] This takes us to the next, perhaps most complex issue: the collapse of hierarchical communication or of the ship's structure of command during the twenty minutes between the collision and the sinking of the ship.

52 TNA, TS 34/9 'R.M.S. Egypt: Exhibits' (depositions by Aima Stodart, second-class passenger, p. 1; Colonel George Denne Franklin, first-class passenger, p. 2; Roberto Florio Bevan, passenger, p. 2; Francis Henry Chancellor, first-class passenger, p. 1; William George, passenger, p. 1); TS 34/8 '"R.M.S. Egypt": Various Proofs and Documents' (depositions by Walter Frederick Randall, second-class passenger, p. 18; Mildred Alice Steward, second-class passenger, p. 2; Captain Douglas Gerald Carr, passenger, p. 26).

53 TNA, TS 34/9 'R.M.S. Egypt: Exhibits' (plan and schematic narrative of lowering of lifeboats); BL: OIOC, IOR/L/E/7/1123, F. 1989, Commerce & Revenue Department, Loss of the S.S. Egypt (Report of Court on the loss of the S.S. Egypt, 4 September 1922, with Annex), pp. 3f. For a more detailed discussion of these issues see chapter 11 below.

54 Ibid.; TNA, TS 34/9 'R.M.S. Egypt: Exhibits' (plan and schematic narrative of lowering of lifeboats).

7

Communication Collapse: The Steamship and 'Naval Hindustani'

The signal for 'boat stations' was five short blasts from the ship's fog whistle, which was operated with steam from the engine room. Indian seafarers were familiar with this signal and expected to hear it after a collision.[1] It never came on the S.S. *Egypt*, however, and could no longer be given within minutes as seawater flooded the stokehold and extinguished the boilers.[2] Chief Officer Cartwright, according to his statement, 'sang out' the order 'clear away boats' but 'did not sound the signal on the steamer's whistle as [he] did not think it was necessary as everybody seemed to be on deck'.[3] Testimonies by British members of the deck crew confirmed Cartwright's version by stating that he had ordered them orally to 'boat stations' within minutes of the collision.[4] Indian witnesses did not confirm this assertion, however, and some of them, including experienced deck crew, even insisted that no orders had been given whatsoever.[5] How do we explain these starkly irreconcilable

1 TNA, BT 239/2 '"Egypt" in Collision with "Seine"' (depositions by Mahomed Adam and Moossa Fackeer, 2 June 1922).

2 TNA, TS 34/8 'R.M.S. Egypt' (depositions by Sidney Herbert French, Supernumerary Second Mate, p. 18; Gordon Dixon Brown, Third Officer, p. 81).

3 Ibid. (deposition by Chief Officer Charles Walter Cartwright, p. 8).

4 Ibid. (depositions by Donald Lennox Gates, boatswain, p. 39; Edward W. Ruskin, quartermaster, pp. 47, 49; Cecil Charles Nelson, quartermaster, p. 55).

5 TNA, BT 239/2 '"Egypt" in Collision with "Seine"' (deposition by Moossa Fackeer, 2 June 1922); NMM, Caird Library, P&O Collections, 65/3, f. 261 (draft statements of

accounts? Was this a matter of miscommunication at a basic linguistic level? Were the Indian seafarers simply unable to understand the chief officer's command? This explanation was explicitly ruled out in court. When cross-examining fireman Sabdin Fazuldin, the P&O's legal counsel asked: 'Is "Boat stations" the same in your language as in English?' The reply had been a terse 'Everybody says "boat stations".' When this translation was challenged, interpreter Challis repeated: 'I was asked if there was a difference in the language, and he said everyone understood boat stations as it was spoken in English.' The matter was settled by the judge himself who remarked that the witness's statement 'was intelligible to me'.[6]

Another explanation for the discrepancy of the testimonies might have been that the Indian crew had not paid attention to the officers' commands in their state of panic – an explanation suggested by more than one British witness.[7] Yet the fact, confirmed in both Indian and British testimonies, that large sections of the Indian crew initially proceeded to the bridge deck casts doubt on this version of the story. Indian witnesses stated explicitly that they had turned to the bridge not only for life jackets but also with the purpose of asking the captain and the chief officer for orders. However, no order had been given, they insisted, leaving them to fend for themselves.[8] A clamour for commands would not have been an unusual reaction in a situation of crisis. The memoirs of the communist stoker Amir Haider Khan show that even the most rebellious seafarers accepted the obligation to fulfil their 'sea duty' out of an 'instinctive sense of discipline'. They acquiesced in principle to a

---

Mohamed Adam, f. 261; Moossa Fackeer, f. 278); TNA, TS 34/10 'R.M.S. Egypt: Transcript of Court Proceedings', Fifth Day: 28 July 1922 (examinations and cross-examinations of Barrum Mustapha, p. 86.

6 TNA, TS 34/10 'R.M.S. Egypt: Transcript of Court Proceedings', Fifth Day: 28 July 1922, pp. 79f.

7 TNA, TS 34/8 'R.M.S. Egypt' (depositions by Roberto Florio Bevan, passenger, p. 4; Alexander Nicol Cameron, 2nd Officer, p. 12; Sidney Herbert French, Supernumerary 2nd Mate, p. 16; Harry Scott, quartermaster, p. 43; Thomas Harvey, quartermaster, p. 51; Arthur Popple, joiner, p. 60; William John Hamilton, 3rd Engineer, pp. 84, 86).

8 TNA, BT 239/2 '"Egypt" in Collision with "Seine"' (deposition by Moossa Fackeer, 2 June 1922); NMM, Caird Library, P&O Collections, 65/3, f. 278 (draft statement of Moossa Fackeer); TNA, TS 34/8 'R.M.S. Egypt' (depositions by Moossa Fackeer, p. 85, and Mohammed Adam, p. 90; TNA, TS 34/10 'R.M.S. Egypt: Transcript of Court Proceedings', Fifth Day: 28 July 1922 (examinations and cross-examinations of Barrum Mustapha, p. 86; Moossa Fackeer, p. 90; Mohammed Adam, p. 100).

hierarchical structure of command on board ship since dangers were a permanent presence at sea and emergencies required swift and closely coordinated action.[9] The Indian crew of the *Egypt* was no exception apparently.

The suspicion that the *Egypt*'s officers had failed to put their commands through to the Indian crew, that language barriers had impeded effective rescue operations, had lingered on ever since the *Egypt* disaster made headlines: newspapers had referred to this issue severally.[10] In the course of the inquiry, the solicitor general received an anonymous letter suggesting that the proficiency of the ship's officers in Indian languages and, more particularly, their ability to convey orders to the crew ought to be examined in court:

> Dear S-G,
>
> You are probably aware of the cause of the trouble – perhaps you are not.
>
> LANGUAGE.
>
> Lascars. Native Indian Language – Gujerathi and other Indian languages.
>
> Lascars also speak a few words of 'Hindustani' (a lingua franca).
>
> P.[&]O. Officers speak a few words 'Hindustani' and no other Indian language.
>
> They are not required by Company to pass any language test. They could not write or read names of Crew in any Indian language.
>
> Now you have had some P.[&]O. Officers in the box who swore they spoke the native language.

9 Amir Haider Khan, 'I Break with the Old World' (Part I: Nasik manuscript 1939–1942, typed copy with editorial markings by Hasan Gardezi, Pakistan Study Centre, University of Karachi), p. 252. For a brief discussion see Ravi Ahuja, 'A Freedom Still Enmeshed in Servitude: The Unruly "Lascars" of the S.S. City of Manila or, a Micro-History of the "Free Labour" Problem', in Ravi Ahuja (ed.), *Working Lives and Worker Militancy: The Politics of Labour in Colonial India*, Delhi: Tulika, 2013, pp. 111f. A moderately edited version of this important autobiographical text has been published in Hasan N. Gardezi (ed.), *Chains to Lose: Life and Struggles of a Revolutionary. Memoirs of Dada Amir Haider Khan*, Karachi: Pakistan Study Centre, 2007. In this book, I refer to the unedited manuscript version for reasons explained in chapter 12.

10 'Discipline of Egypt's Crew', *Manchester Guardian*, 2 August 1922, p. 3; 'Ships' Officers and Hindustani', *Dundee Advertiser*, 7 August 1922 (see below for details).

> Recall all of them and ask if they will act as interpreters when you examine the lascar witnesses, ask them to write a native mans [*sic*!] name. Ask them to say to the lascars:
>
> 'There is no need for alarm. Keep calm. Do exactly as you are told and every one will be saved. If you disobey I will shoot you.'
>
> The fact is there is only one medium of communication between officers and lascars[,] the translator – the 'sorrang'. There is only one of him.
>
> The lascars did nothing: they were waiting for orders – but the sorrang could not be everywhere.[11]

The last sentence with its claim that the 'lascars' 'were waiting for orders' corroborates the Indian witnesses' version and suggests that the author may have been an eyewitness him- or herself and, with some probability, a British member of the *Egypt*'s deck crew. The phrases proposed for the 'language test' betray assumptions on how 'coolie sailors' were to be dealt with properly on board a British ship: they do not contain any specific orders or technical terms connected to the lowering of boats or other rescue operations, but merely an unspecific assertion of absolute authority backed up with the threat of armed violence. The letter was duly filed, but the prosecutor general chose not to look too deeply into the matters it raised when he examined the *Egypt*'s officers.

Despite its coarseness, the letter was well-informed and concerned a politically contentious issue: British trade unionists, supported by sections of the British public, had used for long – and would continue to use for many years – the argument of linguistic barriers to substantiate their claim that the employment of 'lascars' and other 'alien' seafarers involved high risks, especially in emergency situations, and should be restricted for this reason.[12] The tactical use of this argument for

11 TNA, TS 34/8 'R.M.S. Egypt' (anonymous letter to the Solicitor General).

12 The topic cropped up time and again as early as in the inquiries of the Manning Committee of 1896 but resulted in a restriction on the employment of 'alien' seafarers only ten years later. A coalition of shipping and imperial interests made sure, however, that 'lascars' were excluded from these restrictions on the grounds that they were 'imperial subjects' and thus technically not 'aliens'. For a concise overview see Marika Sherwood, 'Race, Nationality and Employment among Lascar Seamen, 1660 to 1945', *Journal of Ethnic and Migration Studies* 17, no. 2 (1991), pp. 233–41.

exclusionary purposes does not disprove by itself the validity of the claim that restricted communication channels among the crew created additional safety risks in times of emergency. The claim needs to be examined on its own merits and cannot be disregarded merely on account of the self-interested reasons for its employment.

Turning to the testimonies of the Indian witnesses we find, however, that they did not refer to any incident of linguistic miscommunication on board the *Egypt* but rather to a communication *refusal* on the part of the officers, whether caused by inability or by unwillingness. Moreover, they even recounted orders that were comprehensible in terms of language but did not seem to make sense otherwise. Several khalasis and stokers reported that the captain and other officers had ordered them out of the lifeboats, insisting that the ship was not foundering and that there was no need for rescue operations.[13] These testimonies are corroborated by the statements of surviving Goan stewards that were recorded by Joseph Baptista in even greater detail immediately after their return to Bombay, i.e., independently from the depositions that were taken in far-away London almost simultaneously from the eight selected witnesses – a congruence that is even more striking if we consider that most of the latter belonged to different linguistic segments of the crew.[14]

Yet, if the captain had intended to reassure the crew, he failed: a number of the Indian seafarers had previously served, as has been mentioned already, on ships torpedoed by German submarines and knew a foundering steamer when they went down with one.[15] 'The ship is finished', Baram Mustafa remembered telling the second engineer when seawater flooded the stokeholds, even before he scrambled up the engine room ladder to find a life jacket, a boat, or any other means of

13 TNA, BT 239/2 '"Egypt" in Collision with "Seine"' (deposition by Barrum Mustapha, 2 June 1922); NMM, Caird Library, P&O Collections, 65/3, f. 278 (draft statement of Moossa Fackeer); TNA, TS 34/10 'R.M.S. Egypt: Transcript of Court Proceedings', Fifth Day: 28 July 1922 (examinations and cross-examinations of Barrum Mustapha, p. 86; Moossa Fackeer, p. 90).

14 '"Egypt" Disaster: The Lascars' Version' (letter by Joseph Baptista), *Bombay Chronicle*, 19 June 1922.

15 Ibid.; TNA, TS 34/10 'R.M.S. Egypt: Transcript of Court Proceedings', Sixth Day: 31 July 1922, p. 10 (examination and cross-examination of Phillip Azevedo); TNA, TS 34/8 'R.M.S. Egypt' (deposition by William John Hamilton, 3rd Engineer), p. 34.

saving his life.[16] Then orders were either not forthcoming from the officers or merely seemed to serve the goal of getting the 'natives' out of the way rather than involving them in rescue operations either actively or passively. Consequently, many of the crew hurled themselves into the sea just as numerous passengers did, with or without wooden gratings or boxes to cling to.[17] Others crowded the lifeboats – even those that were hopelessly jammed in their davits.[18] When hierarchical communication collapsed and the ensuing chaos fuelled desperation, it was *sauve qui peut* indeed.

No mention is made of this clamour for commands or of the failure to give them in the testimonies of Captain Collyer and his chief officer, Cartwright, nor did the prosecutor general or even the India Office's legal counsel choose to press them for an explicit response to this allegation by several Indian witnesses. 'Horniman's law' applied again. When the court had the two officers recount their actions in the decisive twenty minutes after the collision, Collyer reported to have mainly tried to assess the damage and then instruct the wireless operator to call for help. Cartwright claimed to have seen only a single 'lascar' when supervising the rescue operations and attending to the lowering of some lifeboats.[19] The second officer, Alexander Cameron, did mention, in distinction to Cartwright and only when asked directly, that 'lascars' helped to lower the boats.[20] Yet, even in their own testimonies, there is little evidence for an attempt on the part of the deck officers to coordinate rescue operations – of distributing crew and

16 TNA, BT 239/2 '"Egypt" in Collision with "Seine"' (deposition by Barrum Mustapha, 2 June 1922); TNA, TS 34/10 'R.M.S. Egypt: Transcript of Court Proceedings', Fifth Day: 28 July 1922 (examination of Barrum Mustapha), p. 83.

17 See, e.g., NMM, Caird Library, P&O Collections, 65/3, f. 264 (draft statement of Mohamed Adam); ibid., f. 270 (draft statement of Phillip Azevedo).

18 TNA, TS 34/10 'R.M.S. Egypt: Transcript of Court Proceedings', Second Day: 25 July 1922 (examination of Captain Collyer), p. 8; TNA, BT 239/2 '"Egypt" in Collision with "Seine"' (deposition by Thomas Whyte, 30 May 1922); TNA, TS 34/8 'R.M.S. Egypt' (deposition by Gordon Dixon Brown, 3rd Officer), pp. 21f.

19 TNA, TS 34/8 'R.M.S. Egypt' (depositions by Andrew Collyer, Master, and Charles Walter Cartwright, Chief Officer), pp. 1–6; TNA, TS 34/10 'R.M.S. Egypt: Transcript of Court Proceedings', First Day: 24 July 1922 (examination of Captain Collyer), pp. 87–90; ibid., Second Day: 25 July 1922 (examination of Captain Collyer), pp. 7f; ibid. (examination of Charles W. Cartwright), pp. 62–4, 67.

20 TNA, TS 34/10 'R.M.S. Egypt: Transcript of Court Proceedings', Second Day: 25 July 1922, pp. 108f (examination of Alexander Cameron, Second Officer).

passengers more evenly between the swung-out lifeboats or of establishing command over the Indian crew through the usual conduit of the serangs. Among the *Egypt*'s officers, only the second engineer, Thomas Whyte, recounted a successful effort to mobilise Indian crew for the lowering of boats.[21] The suspicion, raised by Joseph Baptista in Bombay after the *Egypt* disaster, that the commanding officers had at first underestimated the gravity of the damage and thus lost crucial minutes for the initiation of rescue operations may not have been entirely off the mark.[22]

If the testimonies of the Indian witnesses provide direct evidence for the collapse of hierarchical communication, this finding is confirmed indirectly not only by the gaps in Collyer's and Cartwright's testimonies, but also by the decision to exclude from the Indian witnesses the serangs – an absence that was hardly lost on the court but explicitly raised as an issue only at the very end of the proceedings by the India Office's legal counsel.[23] As a result, the crucial link in the chain of command between the British officers and the Indian crew was removed from the examination. This decision was taken, whether or not in communication with the P&O headquarters, in Brest and with the consent of the company's representative in France by the first officer, Cartwright, who had been in charge of the rescue operations.[24] The latter was thus given the opportunity to pre-empt uncomfortable questions concerning his own performance as a commanding officer. The court could, however, reconstruct that the khalasi serang, i.e., the senior foreman of the 'lascars' in the deck department, had been sent away in the first lifeboat that left the sinking *Egypt* – a decision 'greatly to be regretted' in the court's opinion.[25] The assumption underlying this statement was

21 TNA, BT 239/2 '"Egypt" in Collision with "Seine"' (deposition by Thomas Whyte, 30 May 1922).

22 '"Egypt" Disaster: The Lascars' Version'; '"Egypt" Disaster' (letter to the editor by Joseph Baptista), *Bombay Chronicle*, 21 June 1922. See also 'The Egypt', *Daily Herald*, 24 June 1922.

23 TNA, TS 34/10 'R.M.S. Egypt: Transcript of Court Proceedings', Eighth Day: 2 August 1922, p. 126.

24 NMM, Caird Library, P&O Collections, 65/1 (letter to P&O directors from James Beveridge, Brest, 25 May 1922).

25 BL: OIOC, IOR/L/E/7/1123, F. 1989, Commerce & Revenue Department, Loss of the S.S. Egypt (Report of Court on the loss of the S.S. Egypt, 4 September 1922, with Annex), p. 3.

never spelled out explicitly but is easy enough to grasp: when the khalasi serang went, the linguistic tie between the chief officer and the 'lascar' crew snapped, the chain of command broke, and the khalasis were either ignored or dismissed. Neither had they been provided with life jackets, nor were they given meaningful orders, which may well have created the impression among the Indian crew that the task of securing their survival was rather low on the list of priorities of the *gora malum*, the 'white' officers. Our evidence suggests that the collapse of communication may have raised to an existential level the suspicion of racial subordination – a suspicion that was nurtured by the structure of 'racial management' Indian seafarers were subjected to whenever they signed up on a British steamer.

Of course, there is no possibility of an ex post examination of Captain Collyer's and Chief Engineer Cartwright's linguistic abilities or willingness to communicate with the Indian crew. Our 'cold case' will remain cold in this regard. We can merely reconstruct the expectations which British shipping concerns employing large numbers of Indian crew had in regard to the language skills of their officers. If the British India Steam Navigation Company had asked their officers in the early years of the century to acquire a knowledge of 'Hindustani' – a language that could be mastered, their spokesman asserted, in about three months – the P&O Company would continue to formulate similar demands in later years.[26] The officers' actual knowledge of a very basic maritime Hindustani, the so-called 'lascari bat' ('lascar' talk, 'lascar' argot), remained unexamined, however, and chains of communication could be fragile as a consequence. In 1912, when examining the loss of the P&O Liner *Oceana*, the Board of Trade's Court of Inquiry was, on the one hand,

> satisfied that the officers of the ship had observed the company's rule to make themselves conversant with Lascari. On the other hand the quartermasters had to admit that their directions to a lascar boat's crew would have to be given largely by signs, and this cannot be considered satisfactory in an emergency.

26 *MMC*, vol. 2, Evidence, p. 586 (examination of Captain Walter Ernest Hutchinson, Marine Superintendent to the British India Steam Navigation Company).

They suggested that the acquisition of language skills should be 'stimulated by the prospect of some small extra reward', which would encourage the attainment of a 'working knowledge of the simple tongue used by the native seamen'.[27] No formalization of obligations was considered at the time. Ten years later, in the case of the *Egypt*, Captain Collyer asserted before another Court of Inquiry that he was to report regularly to the company on the knowledge of 'Hindustani' of all senior officers in the deck and the engine-room departments and that a lack of that knowledge could be an impediment to promotion.[28] The court, however, appeared to be unimpressed with the level of implementation of this company policy:

> The ship's Officers all stated that they could speak Hindustani, by this they meant Lascari Bat as spoken on board ship. The P. and O. Company encourage their officers to learn the language, but do not make it essential. The Court thinks it of high importance that the Company should insist upon a knowledge of the language.[29]

The matter, on which they commented, had regained public attention already in the weeks after the *Egypt* disaster. The P&O's management took notice, for instance, of a letter to the *Dundee Advertiser* written apparently by an 'old India hand' who declared that in twenty voyages between Britain and India 'in not a single instance have I run [into] ships' officers who had anything but the very merest acquaintance with colloquial Hindustani'. The letter writer referred to the practice of some of the major railway companies in India who demanded that officers were to 'pass the colloquial test within eighteen months of his appointment' and recommended a similar regulation for the merchant marine.[30] A Royal Navy officer, Lieutenant Commander Frederick Southwell

27 TNA: MT 23/264 'Behaviour of Lascars at Loss of "Oceana"', 1912 (excerpts from *Lloyds List*, 26 June 1912).

28 TNA, TS 34/10 'R.M.S. Egypt: Transcript of Court Proceedings', Second Day: 25 July 1922 (examination of Captain Collyer), pp. 13f.

29 BL: OIOC, IOR/L/E/7/1123, F. 1989, Commerce & Revenue Department, Loss of the S.S. Egypt (Report of Court on the loss of the S.S. Egypt, 4 September 1922, with Annex), p. 5.

30 'Ships' Officers and Hindustani', *Dundee Advertiser*, 7 August 1922 (the press cutting is preserved in NMM, Caird Library, P&O Collections, 65/2).

Piper, wrote to the P&O's chairman with the proposal for the establishment by the company of a 'School of instruction in Lascari Bat' in London, recommending himself as a qualified teacher and offering, 'as the prospects of promotion are poor', to resign from 'His Majesty's service' if he was given the job.[31] The managing directors did not waste time on considering the offer; they declined with polite promptness.[32]

Primers and dictionaries of 'lascari bat' had been published in Britain for more than a century, the first being Thomas Roebuck's 'English and Hindoostanee Naval Dictionary' of 1811. Apart from a short grammar of 'Hindustani', this volume contained a list of technical vocabulary and of 'sea phrases' – the key commands required to navigate a sailing vessel. This dictionary had been compiled with the help of a British shipmaster with decades of experience in the Indian Ocean 'country trade' and, crucially, of four equally seasoned Indian serangs, all of them bearing Muslim names but originating from various shores of the subcontinent, mainly from the West Coast (Kutch in the Northwest, Gogha in Gujarat, Kolaba on the Konkani coast South of Bombay) but one also from Chittagong in East Bengal.[33] The dictionary reflected, in its own specific form, the communication patterns, problems, and needs of an age of sail when the proverbial 'motley crew', consisting, in the Indian Ocean, of sailors who originated from anywhere between Sumatra and East Africa, was still the rule.[34] This was a time when sailors needed to 'know the ropes' of a sailing ship: this complex, multipartite, and manually regulated early modern machine was mirrored in an equally intricate vocabulary, the knowledge of which was part of the seafarer's skill.[35]

31 NMM, Caird Library, P&O Collections, 65/2 (letter by Lieutenant Commander F. Southwell Piper, 9 September 1922).

32 NMM, Caird Library, P&O Collections, 65/2 (letter by Managing Directors to Lieutenant Commander F. Southwell Piper, 12 September 1922).

33 Thomas Roebuck, *An English and Hindoostanee Naval Dictionary of Technical Terms and Sea Phrases* . . . , London: Black, Parry & Co., 1813 (London reprint of the original Calcutta edition), pp. ii–iii, vi–vii.

34 For a brief account of a 'motley' 'lascar' crew of a British sailing ship in 1858 that combined seafarers from all coasts of the Indian Ocean between Sumatra and East Africa see Amitav Ghosh, 'Of Fanás and Forecastles: The Indian Ocean and Some Lost Languages of the Age of Sail', *Economic and Political Weekly*, 21 June 2008, p. 56. See also Aaron Jaffer, *Lascars and Indian Ocean Seafaring, 1780–1860: Shipboard Life, Unrest and Mutiny*, Woodbridge: Boydell, 2015, pp. 10–16.

35 On the technological status of sailing vessels as a manually regulated but complex machine see Heide Gerstenberger and Ulrich Welke, *Vom Wind zum Dampf.*

This vocabulary had roots in various Indian languages as well as in naval English but contained also numerous words of Portuguese origin – Iberian maritime technology had been appropriated by Indian Ocean shipbuilders for centuries and its terminology had entered a lingua franca understood by sailors across this extended maritime landscape.[36]

Yet Roebuck's dictionary, as Amitav Ghosh rightly pointed out, hardly provided a key to that link language: rather it combined a vocabulary of multiple linguistic roots with the grammar of North Indian 'Hindustani' (or, Urdu) to create a *language of command*, a means of unidirectional communication that British officers could acquire quickly and that allowed them to manage their Indian Ocean crews effectively.[37] Hence according to its extended title, the book was 'calculated to enable the Officers of the Hon. East India Company's and Country Service, to give their orders to the Lascars with that Exactness and Promptitude, which, upon many Occasion, must prove of the greatest Importance'.[38] In the short grammar introducing the dictionary, the section on verbs began, quite consistently, with the following sentence: 'The imperative, in the second person singular, is the root of every verb in the Hindoostanee Language; and it is this portion of the verb which is most required by the Officers and others, in giving their commands to the Lascars.'[39] Roebuck's dictionary thus combined a glossary of maritime hardware, mainly nouns denominating the parts of a sailing vessel and its rigging, with verbs in their imperative form.

'Lascari bat', then, was a specialized and simplified language of command, akin to the latinized 'military Hindustani' that was studied and used by the British officers of the 'British Indian Army' during that period.[40] Patterns of lived communication went beyond this narrowly

---

Sozialgeschichte der deutschen Handelsschiffahrt im Zeitalter der Industrialisierung, Münster: Westfälisches Dampfboot, 1996, p. 184 and *passim*. On the linguistic aspects see Ghosh, 'Of Fanás and Forecastles', p. 58.

36 Cf: Ghosh, 'Of Fanás and Forecastles', p. 59; Kirti Narayan Chaudhuri, *Trade and Civilisation in the Indian Ocean: An Economic History from the Rise of Islam to 1750*, Cambridge: Cambridge University Press, 1985, p. 151 and *passim*.

37 Ghosh, 'Of Fanás and Forecastles', p. 60.

38 Roebuck, *An English and Hindoostanee Naval Dictionary*, title page.

39 Ibid., p. xxxix.

40 For a systematic examination of 'Anglo-Hindustani' including its military variety see Alison Safadi, 'The Colonial Construction of Hindustani 1800–1947', doctoral dissertation, Goldsmiths' College, University of London, 2012. See also Nile

restricted language of command, however, and we can also assume that multilingualism was not uncommon among skilled Indian sailors who spent their working lives among 'motley crews' with long waiting periods in foreign ports. Herman Melville recalled, for instance, from his seafaring days in the 1830s, that he had encountered in Liverpool 'several men' who spoke 'very good English' among the 'lascar' crew of an India-built British sailing vessel, the 'country boat' *Irrawaddy*. He particularly remembered in graphic detail a long conversation on matters of shipbuilding with one of the Indian sailors.[41]

Roebuck's dictionary was revised, enlarged, and republished numerous times, the most extensive edition being that of 1882 by George Small, a missionary associated with the 'Asiatic Strangers' Home' in Limehouse, London. By then, the sailing vessel was increasingly being replaced by the steamship. This process went along with a complex process of partial 'deskilling' and 'reskilling' that affected large sections of the crew, while only a minority acquired higher formal and certified levels of technical skill for the operation and maintenance of the new machineries of propulsion, loading, and hauling. Quite strikingly, the technical vocabulary of Small's dictionary of 'lascari bat' remained unaffected by these momentous technological changes: it continued to provide translations for every sail, spar, and rope, but maintained a curious silence on the gratings, rakes, and flame tubes of the fireroom.[42]

A. I. Valentini, an employee of the P&O Company, compiled a new phrasebook and dictionary of 'lascari bat' towards the end of the century, which aimed at the 'young officers' serving his employer and other shipping companies, but remained, to a large extent, in the framework provided by Roebuck almost a century earlier.[43] 'Lascari bat' was still

Green, *Islam and the Army in Colonial India: Sepoy Religion in the Service of Empire*, Cambridge: Cambridge University Press, 2009, p. 143.

41 Herman Melville, *Redburn: His First Voyage*, New York: Harper & Brothers, 1855, pp. 216–20.

42 George Small, *A Laskari Dictionary or Anglo-Indian Vocabulary of Nautical Terms and Phrases in English and Hindustani* . . . , London: W. H. Allen & Co., 1882.

43 A. I. Valentini, *Lascari-Bât: A Collection of Sentences Used in the Daily Routine of Modern Passenger Steamers, Where Lascars Are Carried as the Deck Crew; Also a Copious English-Lascari Vocabulary*, London: Miller & Sons, 1896 (2nd ed.). I have only been able to trace the second and third editions of 1896 and 1901 respectively, but we can assume that the second edition was published shortly after the first as its preface refers to the 'rapid sale of the first edition'. Ibid., p. 5.

conceived as a language of command based on a deliberately simplified 'Hindustani' and the terminology of the sailing ship was meticulously itemized even now. Yet the transformed structure of the work that seamen were now expected to execute on the decks of a steamer was to some extent taken into account. The phrasebook thus included new chapters with detailed and precise commands concerning the unending paint work required to protect steel-built ships from corrosion, the more complex cargo work on much larger vessels, but also the handling of lifeboats and other safety issues that assumed a greater urgency when mail steamers carried unprecedented passenger loads.

Some of these commands appear, in the light of the *Egypt* disaster, acutely pertinent even as they suggest standards that were not always met: 'For each man on board there is a lifebelt' (15), 'When the fire bell rings, then must go quickly each to their station' [*sic*] (37), 'They must be daily drilled, in order to get the boat away quick when wanted' (43). However, the boiler and engine rooms at the bottom of the steamer's hull did not seem to exist even in Valentini's thoroughly revised version of *Lascari-Bât*. While the *ag-vala* (literally 'fireman') was mentioned at least in the vocabulary, even the extended subtitle that Valentini chose left no doubt that 'lascari bat' was meant to be the language of command on the decks and not below: 'A collection of sentences used in the daily routine of modern passenger steamers, where lascars are carried as the deck crew . . .'[44]

When Norwood Harrison's *Manual of Lascari Hindustani* appeared in its fifth edition in 1928, the age of sail was positively over: now, oil-fuelled and diesel-motorized ships were progressively replacing the once-revolutionary coal-burning steamer. Another revolution of shipping technology had thus occurred since the publication of Valentini's *Lascari-Bât* three decades earlier, but the transformation of ship-work was reflected even less in Harrison's *Manual* than in the older book: the ship's changed hierarchy of command was accounted for – '*bura mistery sahib*' (roughly, the 'great master mechanic') being the title invented for the chief engineer – but the technical vocabulary remained solidly that of the age of sail.[45] Even though Harrison claimed that the book was

44 Ibid., p. 136; inside title page.

45 Norwood Harrison, *A Manual of Lascari-Hindustani with Technical Terms and Phrases* (5th extended ed.), London: Imray, Laurie, Norie & Wilson, 1928, p. 3. The first edition of this book was published in 1905.

'written more especially for the use of Officers and Engineers of steamers carrying lascar crews', its reduced engagement with the technical terminology of contemporary shipping allowed Harrison to extend its readership to 'those who have the management of lascars and of other uneducated natives of British India' and include decidedly non-maritime yet apparently useful 'Hindustani' translations of sentences like: 'I want a solar hat', 'Coachman, go back to the hotel' or 'Shikari [hunter], is there any game near here?'[46]

A late addition to this corpus of naval dictionaries was Shedden Chalmers Parry's *Lascar Hindustani for Ship-Surgeons*, published in London in 1930. This thin booklet of forty-eight pages confirms the paradox pattern that the need for translating the terminology of maritime technology between European and South Asian languages appears to have declined just at a time when the employment of Indian seafarers on British merchant vessels reached its historical climax. Parry's flimsy brochure barely contained specific references to maritime work: even the particularly relevant section entitled 'Accidents' merely mentioned falls down the hatch or overboard, but not, for instance, the heat cramps or the burns that clenched and branded the bodies of firemen. The booklet was also more careless in matters of transliteration (and thus less concerned with ensuring the comprehensibility of commands) than earlier dictionaries: if the first seven entries in the 'Regimen' section were all concerned with sending 'lascar' patients back to their duties, the order 'You must go to work immediately' was translated, for instance, as '*Ubhi toom karm kurner hoenga, jow*.'[47] Alison Safadi's observation that the quality of the language training British officers received in 'military Hindustani' declined steeply in the early decades of the twentieth century can be extended to 'lascari Hindustani' also.[48]

It was not as if the technology of a steamer was less complex than that of a sailing vessel or required a less differentiated vocabulary. A brief glance at the parallel history of maritime dictionaries mediating between European languages makes this clear. Such works had been published since the early 1700s, assembling terminologies of navigation and of the

46 Ibid., pp. iii, 118–20.

47 Shedden Chalmers Parry, *Lascar Hindustani for Ship-Surgeons*, London: W. J. Clark, 1930.

48 Cf. Safadi, *The Colonial Construction of Hindustani*, pp. 76–9.

sailing ship's 'machine parts' just like Roebuck's 'English and Hindoostanee' dictionary about a century later. Yet the historical trajectory of European language dictionaries diverged as they came to be adapted to the changes in shipping technology almost immediately. Karel Pieter ter Reehorst's multilingual *The Mariner's Friend or Polyglot Indispensable*, published simultaneously in the Netherlands, Britain, and Germany in 1849 and clearly designed for the practical use of navigators, already included twenty-two entries that were compounds of the word 'steam'.[49] Across the Atlantic, 'an Illustrated Nautical Polyglot Containing Drawings and Descriptions in English, German, French, Spanish, Italian and Scandinavian [*sic*]' was published in New York in 1883 – a large-sized if slim volume that referred even in its title not only to sailing vessels but also to 'steamers, engines and boilers'.[50]

Two years later, Heinrich Paasch, surveyor to *Lloyd's Register* in Antwerp and a leading maritime expert of the time, published a substantial and hands-on trilingual 'marine dictionary' in English, French, and German that, too, covered sailing technology as much as that of steam. Paasch dedicated a full quarter of its 203 amply illustrated pages to the vocabulary of the stokehold and the engine room – almost exactly as many as he reserved for the conventional terminology of masts and spars, sails and rigging.[51] This work would set the standard for maritime dictionaries and 10,000 copies of its various editions were reportedly sold during the author's lifetime.[52] When its fourth edition was posthumously published in 1908, Spanish and Italian translations were provided as well. The dictionary now comprised more than 800 pages

49 Karel Pieter ter Reehorst, *The Mariner's Friend or Polyglot Indispensable, and Technical Dictionary, of . . . Nautical-, Steam- and Shipbuilding-terms, Commercial and Scientific Expressions . . . in Ten Different Languages: English, Dutch, German, Danish, Swedish, French, Italian, Spanish, Portuguese and Russian . . .*, Amsterdam: 1849.

50 J. C. Coxe, *An Illustrated Nautical Polyglot: Containing Drawings and Descriptions in English, German, French, Spanish, Italian and, Scandinavian, of the different classes of sailing vessels, also of steamers, engines and boilers, to which is added a complete list of ship chandlery, stores, engineers' supplies, tools, &c., also rendered into the above six languages*, New York: n.a., 1883.

51 Heinrich Paasch, *From Keel to Truck: A Marine Dictionary in English, French and German*, Antwerp: Ratinckx Frères, 1885.

52 Christiane Villain-Gandossi, 'De Robert Estienne a Heinrich Paasch: La place du vocabulaire maritime dans les dictionnaires plurilingues', in D. L. Newman and M. v. Campenhoudt (eds), *Maritime Terminology: Issues in Communication and Translation*, Brussels: Hazard, 1999, pp. 22–46.

to which an extensive appendix of plates and indices in all five languages had been added. The author had felt obligated, in his preface to the third edition, to justify the continued attention to the terminology of the sailing vessel, even though the relevant sections were now dwarfed by those dealing with the machinery of the steam ship.[53]

Yet the new technical vocabulary of steam propulsion was used and mastered only by the ship's engineers and a small number of qualified engine-room mechanics, while the greater part of a steamer crew, even those employed in the stokehold, did not require this terminology to fulfil the role they were assigned to in the labour process. If dictionaries of 'lascari bat' lost much of their maritime specificity, and most glaringly in regard to the ship's propulsion, this may well have mirrored the transformed, more segmented, and on the whole reduced communication requirements on board a late nineteenth-century steamship. Ship engineers had risen, in the course of the latter half of the nineteenth century, from humble artisan origins to become a highly qualified, specialized, and powerful section of the maritime workforce.[54]

At the same time, everyday work processes had become less uniform, less complex, and perhaps less communication-intensive for the large majority of the sizeable crews of coal-burning steamers: while the sailor of old days had to know the numerous parts of the ship's rigging by name to follow the mate's orders, the range of tasks of a steamer's deck crew had been narrowed down considerably, which made it less problematic to channel much of the communication required on a day-to-day basis through middlemen-translators – the much-quoted serangs and tindals.[55] Down below the waterline, in the steamer's coal bunkers and stokehold, large numbers of trimmers and firemen moved coal, fed the most advanced steam engines in a surprisingly low-tech way, and were prevented by rigid shipboard hierarchies from enhancing and diversifying their skills.

53 The full preface of the third edition was reproduced in the German version of the fourth edition: *From Keel to Truck: Marine-Wörterbuch englisch-französisch-deutsch-spanisch-italienisch*, Hamburg: Eckardt und Messtorff, 1908. This edition was simultaneously published in Britain as Heinrich Paasch, *From Keel to Truck: Dictionary of Naval Terms, English-French-German-Spanish-Italian*, 4th ed., revised and enlarged, London: David Nutt, 1908.

54 Conrad Dixon, 'The Rise of the Engineer in the Nineteenth Century', in G. Jackson and D. M. Williams (eds), *Shipping, Technology and Imperialism*, Aldershot: Scolar Press, 1996, pp. 231–41.

55 See p. 169.

The dramatic collapse of communication during the last twenty minutes on the S.S. *Egypt* that is revealed so clearly in the minutes of the Board of Trade inquiry, I conclude, may well have had deeper causes that followed from the modalities of labour management on board coal-burning British steamers at that time. The following three chapters, therefore, turn specifically to the hierarchically organized labour processes in coal bunkers and firerooms of large steam vessels. For these were the daily work-routines the Punjabi coal trimmers and firemen of the S.S. *Egypt* found themselves subjected to – the very men singled out as the main perpetrators of panic in many of the European narratives on the ship's foundering.

8

Fireroom Hierarchy: Stoking, Skill, and Status

For two generations, comprising the latter half of the nineteenth and the pre-war years of the twentieth century, the steamship epitomized the cutting edge of industrial technology: ever more giant steel hulls propelled by enormous batteries of coal-devouring boilers and increasingly powerful steam engines.[1] Almost half a century before the British-German competition for the largest, fastest, and most luxurious transatlantic liner dominated newspaper headlines,[2] Karl Marx had argued that the technological requirements of the propulsion machinery of steamships (as much as of railways) had revolutionized industrial production itself: the machinery as well as the enormous steel hulls of steamers could no longer be built by skilled artisans using preindustrial technologies. Instead, their production required 'cyclopean machines'. As a result, machinery ceased to merely imitate the artisan's work process and large-scale industry began to stand 'on its own feet' technologically. Being both a launch pad and a product of this revolutionary 'machine system', steamships could apparently be scaled up to ever more monstrous proportions.[3]

1 Daniel R. Headrick, *The Tentacles of Progress: Technology Transfer in the Age of Imperialism*, 1850–1940, Oxford: Oxford University Press, 1988, pp. 27–30.

2 Douglas R. Burgess Jr., *Engines of Empire: Steamships and the Victorian Imagination*, Stanford, CA: Stanford University Press, 2016, pp. 249–69; Stephen Fox, *The Ocean Railway: Isambard Kingdom Brunel, Samuel Cunard and the Revolutionary World of the Great Atlantic Steamships*, London: HarperCollins, 2003, ch. 15.

3 Karl Marx, *Capital: A Critique of Political Economy*, vol. 1, transl. Ben Fowkes, Harmondsworth: Penguin, 1976, p. 506.

Marx ascribed a greater 'objectivity' to a production process depending on these 'cyclopean machines' and, conversely, a decline of the individual labourer's subjective ability to shape the organization of work.[4] More than a century later, Raphael Samuel found, however, that this transformation had been limited and patchy, in fact, even in highly advanced industries like shipbuilding.[5] When the steel-hulled steamers were launched from the shipyards this unevenness became even more pronounced. The analysis of work processes within the stokeholds and engine rooms shows that the prevalent division of labour here was by no means a direct outgrowth of technology: even though the scope for appropriating (or 'subjectifying') technology may have been narrowed down for the *individual* worker if compared to earlier ship-work, labour processes were nevertheless mediated by social relations of property and power or, in other words, *collectively subjectified*. This has been demonstrated clearly in Heide Gerstenberger and Ulrich Welke's brilliant but barely recognized study. They show, in considerable detail, that excessively steep hierarchies between engineers and firemen were no quasi-natural consequence of technological compulsions but resulted, to a large extent, from efforts on the part of shipowners – in the British merchant marine as much as its German counterpart – to assert an effective 'remote control' over the fault-prone engine rooms of their increasingly capital-intensive as well as spatially dispersed fleets. These hierarchies, they argue, emerged only over the nineteenth century and turned the initially artisanal 'mechanic' into a certified 'engineer'.[6]

By the 1920s, the British shipping industry looked for new recruits who had undergone a five-year apprenticeship 'preferably in a marine engineering establishment', gained some work experience, and had then been trained 'in a good technical college' either as a full-time student or, more likely, in evening classes.[7] Engineers competed with the deck officers – rather successfully in regard to pay though less so in terms of

---

4 Ibid., p. 508.

5 Raphael Samuel, 'Workshop of the World: Steam Power and Hand Technology in Mid-Victorian Britain', *History Workshop* 3 (1977), pp. 6–72.

6 Heide Gerstenberger and Ulrich Welke, Vom Wind zum Dampf. *Sozialgeschichte der deutschen Handelsschiffahrt im Zeitalter der Industrialisierung*, Münster: Westfälisches Dampfboot, 1996, pp. 183–87.

7 John G. Liversidge, *Engine-Room Practice: A Handbook for the Royal Navy and Mercantile Marine*, London: Charles Griffin & Co., 1923 (11th ed.), p. 23.

shipboard status.[8] The rise of the engineer went along, at the same time, with the cultivation of a status difference between engineers and the bulk of the engine- and boiler-room crew.[9] Detailed instructions of the P&O Company to their chief engineers thus directed them to 'keep proper subordination by not mixing too freely or familiarly' with 'those employed in your department', to 'always have a watchful eye' over their subordinates, to 'never pass unnoticed an act of wilful misconduct', to report on any 'refusal to work', and to give 'on a man's Discharge' only such character assessments 'which he really deserves, and no other'.

The chief engineer was also held fully responsible for the preservation 'of the machinery under his care in the highest possible state of efficiency' and for 'carry[ing] out the strictest economy'.[10] Crew other than engineers were to be excluded from the performance of certain 'skilled' work tasks in order to centralize accountability for potentially sensitive technical operations and cut back costly repairs.[11] As work tasks were separated and circumscribed more narrowly, the stokers' ability was curtailed – though, as well shall see, never fully suppressed – to adapt the work process to their needs. 'De-skilling' or, more precisely, a hierarchical segmentation of skills was thus an intended and regulated process, even though the appointment of 'head firemen' or other intermediate overseers (or, in the case of South Asian seafarers, of serangs and tindals) and the establishment of highly specialized non-officer ranks (like that of the boiler maker or refrigeration mechanic) suggests that the strict separation of 'skilled' from 'unskilled' work required some mitigation and reached hard, practical limits when it militated against requirements of cooperation inherent in the labour process itself.[12]

---

8 Conrad Dixon, 'The Rise of the Engineer in the Nineteenth Century', in G. Jackson and D. M. Williams (eds), *Shipping, Technology and Imperialism*, Aldershot: Scolar Press, 1996, pp. 231–41. See also Tony Lane, 'Neither Officers nor Gentlemen', *History Workshop Journal* 19, no. 1 (1985), pp. 128–43.

9 Gerstenberger and Welke, *Vom Wind zum Dampf*, pp. 183–7.

10 NMML, P&O/9/2/1, 'Peninsular & Steam Navigation Company: Instructions for Chief Engineers', London: 1873, pp. 9–10.

11 Ibid., pp. 22f.

12 Ibid., p. 25. See also Alston Kennerley, 'Stoking the Boilers: Firemen and Trimmers in British Merchant Ships, 1850–1950', *International Journal of Maritime History* 20, no. 1 (2008), p. 199; Alston Kennerley, 'The Seamen's Union, the National Maritime Board and Firemen: Labour Management in the British Mercantile Marine', *Northern Mariner* 7, no. 4 (October 1997), p. 16; Gerstenberger and Welke, *Vom Wind zum Dampf*, p. 242.

This intentional, owner-managed division of the workforce along lines of status and skill was not necessarily marked out racially but *could* be articulated in the language of racial difference. This possibility turned into a reality when South Asian, African, Yemeni, and Chinese ship-workers were recruited in large numbers to toil as trimmers and stokers in coal bunkers and boiler rooms even beyond the Indo-Pacific rim from the latter half of the nineteenth century onwards.[13] More qualified engine-room jobs and particularly the ship engineer's profession remained largely a 'white' preserve. Even 'the winchmen employed on the auxiliary machinery', insisted a British engine-room manual as late as 1923, 'are always European'.[14] The sharpness of racial exclusion was slightly dulled only in shipping operations confined to the East of Suez: a limited number of Indians, mainly Parsis, served as engineers on smaller coastal steamers in India or on vessels of the Royal Indian Marine, though always in subaltern capacities.[15] The consequent ethnicization of boiler- and engine-room hierarchy, then, goes a long way in explaining the glaring terminological 'gaps' in Anglo-Hindustani maritime dictionaries.

If the division between the 'skilled' engineers and 'unskilled' coal trimmers and firemen resulted thus, to a large extent, from efforts of establishing managerial control over the labour process through centralized, 'remote-controllable' structures of accountability, we are still left with the question whether coal-bunker and stokehold work afforded, in fact, merely large quantities of 'raw' muscle power bare of any specific quality (or 'skill') acquired either through experience or training. Historians and social scientists have been content too often with accepting the epithet 'unskilled' without any serious examination of actual labour processes in the stokehold,[16] though some insightful analyses

13 Cf. Janet Ewald, 'Crossers of the Sea: Slaves, Freedmen, and Other Migrants in the Northwestern Indian Ocean, c. 1750–1914', *American Historical Review* 105, no. 1 (2000), pp. 84–9.

14 Liversidge, *Engine-Room Practice*, p. 32.

15 This issue was considered at length in the deliberations of the Indian Mercantile Marine Committee. See *Report of the Indian Mercantile Marine Committee (1923–24)*, Delhi: Government Central Press, 1924, pp. 16f and *passim*. See also *Minutes of the Evidence Recorded by the Indian Mercantile Marine Committee*, n.l., n.d., p. 309 and *passim*.

16 See for instance Jonathan Hyslop, '"Ghostlike" Seafarers and Sailing Ship Nostalgia: The Figure of the Steamship Lascar in the British Imagination, c. 1880–1960',

exist that have made use, among other material, detailed accounts of boiler-room work in autobiographical writings.[17] Of particular interest are the seafaring memoirs of Karl Helbig, who had worked as a fireman on German steamers time and again over a period of more than thirty years. Having signed on first in 1923, he kept rejoining the 'black gang' in order to self-fund his research as an anthropologist. The trained eye of the ethnographer served him well when he sat down eventually to write about his own work experiences 'at the fires'.[18] At the most basic quotidian level, these experiences were shaped by handling rakes, pokers, prickers, brushes, shovels, and tongs – the instruments that firemen continued to use the world over until the end of the age of the steamer in the mid-twentieth century. Helbig understood the significance of sketching these simple tools, when engineering manuals saw no reason to waste pages on them while carrying intricate technical drawings of boilers, triple expansion engines, turbine plants, and winches.[19]

De Kerbrech notes that the 'rake' (or 'slice bar') used for removing hot coals and clinker from the grates of the furnace was 'similar in appearance and construction to a garden hoe'.[20] Yet this very simplicity is significant in more than one way for our appreciation of the work processes in the stokehold. To begin with, it underlines the importance allotted to the extraction of sheer physical energy from human bodies in the organization of the labour process or, in other words, the low priority of inventing or implementing labour-saving devices. A trimmer was expected to move between 2.4 and 4 tons of coal each four-hour watch, running along planks with a shaky wheelbarrow, frequently scorching

Journal for Maritime Research 16, no. 2 (2014), p. 214. For a cliometric account built on similarly shallow conceptions of 'skill' see Aimee Chin, Chinhui Juhn, and Peter Thompson, 'Technical Change and the Demand for Skills during the Second Industrial Revolution: Evidence from the Merchant Marine, 1891–1912', *Review of Economics and Statistics* 88, no. 3 (2006), pp. 572–8.

17 Gerstenberger and Welke, *Vom Wind zum Dampf*; Kennerley, 'Stoking the Boilers'; Richard P. de Kerbrech, *Down amongst the Black Gang: The World and Workplace of RMS Titanic's Stokers*, Stroud: History Press, 2014; Eric W. Sager, *Ships and Memories: Merchant Seafarers in Canada's Age of Steam*, Vancouver: University of British Columbia Press, 1993, pp. 44–53.

18 Karl Helbig, *Seefahrt vor den Feuern. Erinnerungen eines Schiffsheizers*, Hamburg: Hans Georg Prager Verlag, 1987.

19 See, e.g., Liversidge, *Engine-Room Practice*.

20 de Kerbrech, *Down amongst the Black Gang*, p. 65.

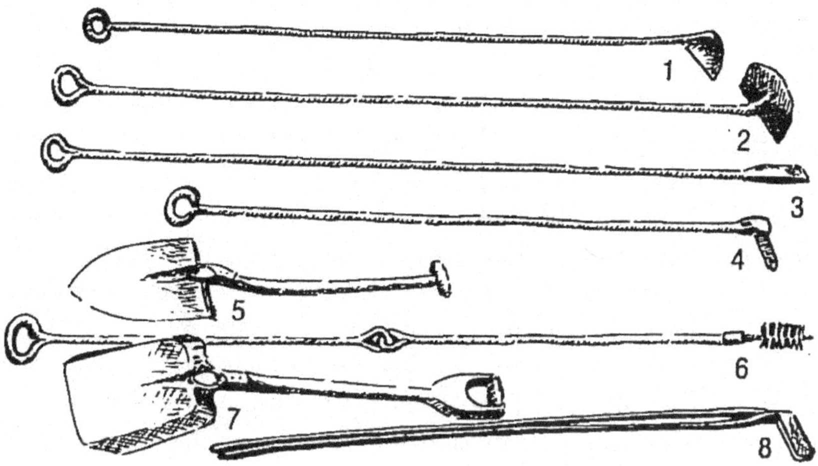

Figure 8.1. Tools of a fireman. Source: Karl Helbig, *Seefahrt vor den Feuern. Erinnerungen eines Schiffsheizers*, Hamburg: Hans Georg Prager Verlag, 1987, p. 62.

his shoulders as he squeezed past the searing hot boilers.[21] He also needed to break up oversized lumps of coal, while the distances he had to cover grew as the voyage progressed and coal had to be carried from more remote depths of the bunkers.

As for firemen, estimates vary greatly, but, according to the 1923 edition of Liversidge's engine-room manual, one ship worker could shovel up to 5.6 tons per day in two four-hour watches.[22] In the mid-1890s, several engineers stated similarly that a fireman could handle up to 5 tons of coal per day, though the Manning Committee recommended that the minimum requirement of boiler room crew (including trimmers and firemen only) should be fixed in proportion to the respective vessel's daily consumption of coal at the rate of one man for 3 tons of coal, allowing for a reduction of half a ton in hot climates.[23] In the 1950s,

21 Liversidge, *Engine-Room Practice*, pp. 25–7.

22 Hope claims that a fireman would 'shovel two tons of coal into a furnace in every four-hour watch', while Gerstenberger and Welke arrive at the double amount in their calculations as a standard for the entire period of steam shipping: Ronald Hope, *A New History of British Shipping*, London: John Murray, 1990, p. 342; Gerstenberger and Welke, *Vom Wind zum Dampf*, pp. 188 and 300n3. Liversidge, *Engine-Room Practice*, pp. 25–7.

23 *Manning Committee*, vol. 1, Report, pp. 28f, 34, 249, 467.

towards the end of the maritime steam age, another technical manual observed likewise that even a sturdy, experienced stoker could manage no more than 3.2 tons of coal in two four-hour watches if he took proper care of the attendant cleaning tasks also.[24] For, apart from stacking coal onto the fire bars, he also needed to tear apart large and heavy clinkers, rake them out from the furnaces along with the smouldering ashes, remove scale from within the boilers and soot from the flues, as well as pump out and scrape the bilges. Less frequently but inescapably, burnt-through bars and grates needed to be replaced with the help of unwieldy, long-armed tongs.[25] The latter was one of the 'most arduous tasks of the fireman's work', wrote Helbig: 'We fear it more than a heavy gale.'[26] Most of these tasks had to be handled in the blazing heat since the boiler pressure, on which the propulsion and the safety of the ship depended, had to be kept up at all times.

In addition, the removal of ashes was a never-ending chore 'like a curse from hell', as former engineer and novelist William McFee put it.[27] Depending on fuel quality, the weight of the ashes could amount to as much as one-fifth of that of the burnt coal.[28] For discharge into the sea, the ashes were hoisted to the deck – often in buckets, not always with a hand-winch, and seldom with an ash ejector.[29] Accordingly, this was a laborious duty in itself: each bucket weighed about six kilograms to be heaved up steep iron ladders, sometimes slipping from an exhausted

24 Wilhelm Leder, *Schiffsmaschinenkunde. Band I: Schiffsdampfkessel*, Leipzig: Fachbuchverlag Leipzig, 1956 (2nd ed.), p. 66 (the calculation assumed 400 kg per hour as a realistic workload).

25 For a detailed analytic account of the work process and regular repair tasks in the stokehold see Gerstenberger and Welke, *Vom Wind zum Dampf*, pp. 187–92, 204–10. Several graphic descriptions of such work can be found in *Manning Committee*, vol. 2, Minutes of Evidence, see esp. the interrogation of fireman Thomas McCarthy, p. 394. See also Kennerley, 'Stoking the Boilers', pp. 208–12; de Kerbrech, *Down amongst the Black Gang*, pp. 65–84; John Guthrie, *A History of Marine Engineering*, London: Hutchinson, 1971, p. 193; Helbig, *Seefahrt vor den Feuern*, pp. 121–4.

26 Ibid., p. 124 [my translation, RA].

27 William McFee, 'Oil, and the Hairy Ape', *Fortnightly Review*, May 1932, p. 567.

28 de Kerbrech, *Down amongst the Black Gang*, p. 35. The *Titanic* reportedly consumed 850 tons of coal per day, which produced about 100 tons of ashes. Ibid., p. 78.

29 Kennerley, 'Stoking the Boilers', p. 198f. See also Frank T. Bullen, *The Men of the Merchant Service Being the Polity of the Mercantile Marine for 'Longshore Readers*, London: Smith, Elder & Co., 1900, pp. 326f.

hand and causing severe injuries.[30] The boiler-room crew often found themselves unable to cope with the ashes during their regular working hours and had to let them pile up beside the boilers. In smaller ships, deck crew frequently helped out and at times even engineers removed their shirts to shovel ashes. More commonly, however, the discharge of ashes and other ancillary tasks compelled the 'black gang' to do overtime either before or after their watch, often elongating their two regular four-hour watches by a further two hours. However, working days of up to fifteen hours were reported in cases of severe undermanning that were increasingly common towards the end of the nineteenth century.[31]

Ship workers, both on deck and in the stokehold, were furthermore regularly required to perform work in addition to their regular tasks and sometimes even outside their respective departments: engine-rooms, stokeholds, but also freight holds were, for instance, regularly cleaned during so-called 'field days' at sea to reduce lay days in port.[32] The physical strain of overlong working hours was compounded by inadequate lighting occasioning work accidents and by ubiquitous coal dust injuring eyesight and the respiratory system.[33] In hot climates, and particularly in the Red Sea, temperatures rose above 50 degrees Celsius in ill-ventilated stokeholds and were reported to have exceeded, in extreme cases, even 60 degrees Celsius.[34] Excessive sweating caused painful and debilitating heat cramps – a condition affecting solely the 'black gang'

30 *Report of the Manning Committee*, vol. 2, Minutes of Evidence, and Appendices, London: Eyre and Spottiswood, 1896, pp. 91, 214.

31 This issue was brought out clearly in the testimonies of several firemen called before the Board of Trade's Manning Committee in 1896. See *Manning Committee*, vol. 2, Minutes of Evidence . . . , pp. 39, 41, 47, 52f, 57f, 62, 76, 407. Working days in the stokehold of fourteen or fifteen hours are reported, ibid., pp. 69, 400, 443. See also Gerstenberger and Welke, *Vom Wind zum Dampf*, p. 197; Gavin Douglas, *Seamanship for Passengers*, London: John Lehmann, 1949, pp. 17f.

32 *Manning Committee*, vol. 1, Report, p. 21; *Manning Committee*, vol. 2, Minutes of Evidence . . . , pp. 88, 101f, 106, 108, 269, 535. See also Conrad H. Dixon, 'Seamen and the Law: An Examination of the Impact of Legislation on the British Merchant Seaman's Lot, 1588–1918', doctoral thesis, University College London, 1981, p. 203; Valerie Burton, 'The Work and Home Life of Seafarers with Special Reference to the Port of Southampton 1871–1921', doctoral dissertation, London School of Economics, 1988, p. 117.

33 *Manning Committee*, vol. 2, Minutes of Evidence . . . , pp. 58, 73, 76.

34 Two firemen reported, independently from each other, to the Manning Committee to have been exposed to a scorching 145 degrees Fahrenheit, i.e., more than 60 degrees Celsius. Ibid., pp. 63, 396.

on board ship.[35] A 'Special Sanitary Commission' set up by the medical journal *Lancet* to inquire into 'sanitation at sea' concluded in 1890 that 'six or seven years' constant work as a firemen [*sic*!] on board a steamer seems sufficient to ruin the health of a strong man'. Undermanning and overwork were perceived, by that commission, as the main causes of ill-health: stokehold labour was clearly considered, as Michael Quinlan puts it, an 'expendable resource'.[36] Conditions appear to have been particularly harsh on 'tramp' cargo steamers owned by smaller limited liability shipping companies: a retired shipmaster alleged, in 1894, that they 'treat[ed] their people as if they were pegs in a machine, and if one peg breaks off they put in another peg'.[37]

While stylized drawings of 'firemen at work' or posed photographs of ship workers before artificially illuminated Scotch boilers generally fail to give a sense of the pulse and ferocity of this labour process, the Swedish artist and seasoned stoker Torsten Billman succeeded in conveying some of the scorching heat, the oppressive gloom, and the draining exertion defining this work environment in his 1936/37 woodcut *Across the Red Sea: Change of Watch in the Boiler Room* (Figure 8.2).[38]

In the foreground, the tools of the 'relieved' watch lean against the ladder; the men approach it, drained of all energy. One of them has climbed a few rungs already, heaving up a bucket of ashes; another gathers his remaining strength to follow him with the next bucket; more cinder has piled up before the furnace during their watch. The woodcut appears to give visual expression to the statement of Thomas Cummings, a forty-five-year-old fireman, who reported, more than four decades earlier, on the strain of a six-hour watch in the Red

35 Ibid., pp. 69, 72, 243f, 735. See also 'White Men and Work in the Tropics', *Lancet*, 5 January 1924, p. 51; 'Heat Cramp on Shipboard', *Lancet*, 3 November 1928, p. 935.

36 'The Lancet Special Sanitary Commission: Report on Sanitation at Sea', *Lancet*, 20 September 1890, pp. 635f. Michael Quinlan, 'Precarious and Hazardous Work: The Health and Safety of Merchant Seamen 1815–1935, *Social History* 38, no. 3 (2013), pp. 281–307 (305 and *passim*).

37 *Manning Committee*, vol. 2, Minutes of Evidence . . . , p. 134.

38 See, e.g., W. W. Lloyd's coloured drawings of the stokehold as 'Tartarus' and of 'Seedie boys' in the boiler room, published in 1891, or Reinhold Thiele's often reproduced photograph of 'lascar' stokers in the hold of a P&O steamer in 1900: W. W. Lloyd, *P&O Pencillings*, London: P&O, 1891; Getty Images, Robert Fox, *Liners: The Golden Age*, Potsdam: H. F. Ullmann, 2011, p. 28.

Figure 8.2. Torsten Billman, *Across the Red Sea: Change of Watch in the Boiler Room* (woodcut, 1936/37, reproduced under its original Swedish title, *Genom Röda havet – Vaktombyte I eldrummet,* in Dan Lennervald [ed.], *Torsten Billman Bildmakaren*, Kungsbacka: ABF Norra Halland, 2010, p. 117).

Sea: 'Gentlemen, if you believe me, I have seen the time when I have hardly been able to get up the ladder . . .'[39] Their 'relief', close to the furnace and in a whirl of heat, is exposed at once to the unrelenting compulsion of keeping up the pressure in the boilers. This requirement to feed the furnaces continuously meant that informal breaks were barely possible. Resonances are perceivable, once again, with Cummings's testimony:

> You are continually going round her; as soon as you fire her you have to get your pricker and slicer, and you are always working, continually working, your four hours; you cannot get five minutes to spare out of the four hours. You are working and working very hard all the time.[40]

The two watches, on Billman's woodcut, connect fleetingly by way of a glance over the shoulder, not through words. One of the most common nonverbal signals that replaced oral communication to a large extent was the sound of the fireman's shovel when it was banged against the iron ladder. The trimmer then knew he was to hurry up with getting more coal to the furnace, and that he would end up clearing away the ashes well after his four-hour shift had ended.[41] By then, trimmers and firemen often reached a state of physical exhaustion that left them slumped on the deck and panting for air.[42]

Even so, in some large vessels, Tayloristic devices such as 'Kilroy's Stoking Indicator', which sounded a gong in regular intervals, were installed to further intensify the labour process.[43] The exploitation of the stokers' vital force was pushed to such extremes that physical fatigue could turn into mental crisis: the superintendent of Liverpool's Mercantile Marine Office speculated on 'a kind of heat insanity' when questioned, in 1902, about the causes for frequent suicides

39 *Manning Committee*, vol. 2, Minutes of Evidence . . . , p. 408.

40 Ibid., p. 407.

41 Kennerley, 'Stoking the Boilers', p. 211. See also Douglas, *Seamanship for Passengers*, pp. 17f; McFee, 'Oil, and the Hairy Ape', p. 576.

42 See again, for instance, Cummings's statement: *Manning Committee*, vol. 2, Minutes of Evidence . . . , p. 408, 426. See also de Kerbrech, *Down amongst the Black Gang*, pp. 82, 84; Kennerley, 'Stoking the Boilers', p. 213.

43 de Kerbrech, *Down amongst the Black Gang*, pp. 67–8.

among stokehold crew.[44] For trimmers and firemen, reportedly, were on average about four times more likely to take their own lives – and 'native' stokers even more so – while serving on a steamer than other crew, often by jumping overboard into the open sea. Suicide rates were sufficiently high to raise mild concern in British government circles around the turn of the century and induce them to at least keep track statistically of the phenomenon.[45] The rate of 'suicides at work and disappearances at sea' appears to have tailed off only from the 1930s, however, when oil-fuelled ships had become more common.[46]

Less conspicuous effects of overexploitation were, of course, unlikely to leave any paper trail. However, Amir Haider Khan, in his autobiography, remembered an episode of protracted physical exhaustion and mental depression, which he experienced as a sixteen-year-old coal trimmer for several months in the wake of a strenuous voyage on a British merchant vessel: 'I was so young and inexperienced . . . that I did not know what was wrong with me. All I knew was that I was indifferent to everything . . .'[47] Life-draining exploitation in the boiler room was not only experienced by stokers, however, but an open secret even in literary circles. 'Always in those days it was "blood for steam"', remembered William McFee, and explained:

> The extraordinary feature of the situation, as engines became more efficient, as steam pressures became higher and higher, and as the size, splendour, and speed of ships increased, was that no change seemed possible in the fire-room . . . the intolerable clumsiness and

---

44 *MMC*, vol. 2, Evidence, p. 28. Gerstenberger and Welke, drawing upon enquiries of German 'Seeämter' (Maritime Boards), likewise state that, in many cases, 'extreme physical and psychological strain' was a regular component of the work regime. Gerstenberger and Welke, *Vom Wind zum Dampf*, p. 202.

45 *MMC*, vol. 2, Evidence, p. 4; Kennerley, 'Stoking the Boilers', pp. 217–19. See also Jonathan Hyslop, 'British Steamship Workers, c. 1875–1945: Precarious before Precarity', *Labour History* 116 (May 2019), p. 25.

46 Stephen E. Roberts et al., 'Suicides among Seafarers in UK Merchant Shipping, 1919–2005', *Occupational Medicine* 60 (2010), p. 58.

47 Amir Haider Khan, 'I Break with the Old World' (Part I: Nasik manuscript 1939–1942, typed copy with editorial markings by Hasan Gardezi, Pakistan Study Centre, University of Karachi), p. 262.

waste of human effort in the business of stoking seemed to remain for ever.[48]

Even though automatic stokers – a technical adaptation of the conveyor belt to the steamship – had been invented around the turn of the century, they were never developed to a stage when they were considered sufficiently reliable or cost-saving. Ash ejectors were recommended in engineering manuals but failed likewise to establish themselves as a technical standard in merchant shipping and, too, appear to have remained rather fault prone.[49]

If Karl Marx had argued – somewhat too sanguinely as we know today – that the *production* of steel-hulled steam ships had enabled large-scale industry to stand 'on its own feet' technologically by generating machines premised on machines, the *propulsion* of these ships never ceased to require the harnessing of colossal amounts of muscle energy to shovel and rake, to hand barrow and bucket.[50] This combination of cutting-edge technology with a cannibalistic overexploitation of labour power, this pairing of capital-intensive machinery with labour-intensive drudgery may have been visible in the most compressed form in the narrow space of the steamship's boiler room, but it was not specific to this work environment. Rather it was the hallmark, as Raphael Samuel documented meticulously, of Britain as the nineteenth century's 'workshop of the world'.[51] McFee's observation, for the steamship, that even the most advanced machinery did not by necessity imply the pervasive mechanization of labour processes had been recognized by Karl Marx already in the 1860s as a more widespread phenomenon: only a few pages after highlighting the far-reaching social impact of the novel 'machine' system, he propounded in exasperation that 'we nowhere find a more shameless squandering of human labour-power for despicable purposes than in England, the land of machinery'.[52] This was, then, a labour regime that seemed almost entirely indifferent to the social costs

48 McFee, 'Oil, and the Hairy Ape', pp. 566, 568–9.

49 Liversidge, *Engine-Room Practice*, pp. 27, 87; Kennerley, 'Stoking the Boilers', pp. 198f; Gerstenberger and Welke, *Vom Wind zum Dampf*, pp. 220f.

50 Marx, *Capital*, vol. 1, p. 506. But see also Samuel, 'Workshop of the World', pp. 41f.

51 Ibid., pp. 6–72.

52 Marx, *Capital*, vol. 1, p. 517.

of sustaining and reproducing the labour force – though only *almost*, as we shall see.

Even so, the excessive reliance on muscle power, and the technological simplicity of the tools necessary for this work, should not be confused with an absolute redundancy of skill among the workers who used these tools. Frederick Winslow Taylor's famous formulation that, at least in regard to simple manual work, it was 'possible to train an intelligent gorilla so as to become . . . more efficient' than any human worker expressed, not more and not less, management *objectives* that were pursued in practical terms but could never be implemented comprehensively in actual labour processes.[53] Even Taylor's own phrase '*intelligent* gorilla' contained the admission, as Antonio Gramsci pointed out, that 'in any physical work, even the most degraded and mechanical, there exists a minimum of technical qualification, that is, a minimum of creative intellectual activity'.[54] If this was true even for Taylor's condescendingly typified Mr Schmidt ('he shall be so stupid and so phlegmatic that he more nearly resembles in his mental make-up the ox than any other type') who was made to haul forty-seven tons of pig iron in a working day, the fact that stokers were expected to move 'only' about a tenth of that weight in two watches suggests that there was much more to their job than 'shovelling and raking coal' and skills that 'could be picked up quite quickly'.[55]

Gerstenberger and Welke emphasize that 'there is no algorithm for the upkeep of optimal fires'.[56] Or, in the less academic but equally perceptive language of a former stoker: 'That's one of the hardest things to teach a guy, how to burn coal. You know in burning coal you have to say to a guy "I'll show you how the job is done, but it's entirely up to your mind how it works and how that fire's going to burn."'[57] The scarcity in maritime engineering manuals of precise descriptions of stoking procedures together with the limited success of Tayloristic

53 Frederick Winslow Taylor, *The Principles of Scientific Management*, London: Harper & Brothers, 1915 (1st ed. 1911), p. 40.

54 Antonio Gramsci, *Selections from Prison Notebooks*, ed. Q. Hoare and G. Nowell Smith, London: Lawrence & Wishart, 1991 (1st ed. 1971), p. 8.

55 Taylor, *The Principles*, p. 59. The other quotes are from Hyslop, '"Ghostlike" Seafarers', p. 214.

56 Gerstenberger and Welke, *Vom Wind zum Dampf*, p. 196; see also pp. 188f.

57 Len (Smiler) Underhill, former seaman interviewed in the Canadian Seamen's Union History Project and quoted in Sager, *Ships and Memories*, p. 47.

management practices in the stokehold indicate an organizational 'zone of uncertainty':[58] attempts to separate decision-making processes from manual labour, as reflected in the above-mentioned rise of the engineer, were largely confined to the technically most elaborate and sensitive parts of the machinery and focused more on the engine room than on the stokehold.[59] Before the furnace, the widely varying combustion qualities of different types of coal as well as the particularities and high susceptibility to failure of the machinery were among the multiple variables requiring a deep experiential, even sensory knowledge that defied verbalization and was, therefore, not recognized as a formally teachable and certifiable 'skill'. Yet such mastery of the intricacies of the work process was crucial to avoid pressure drops, wastage of fuel, damage to the boilers, and, since they were the most dangerous component of the machinery, risks for the security of the ship. All this required *knowledge* or, as the old fireman had put it, it was a matter of the *mind*.

Stokers had to be able to *interpret*, for instance, the texture of the coal and the colour of the flames as much as the sounds and vibrations of the machinery.[60] Moreover, 'considerable dexterity is often displayed by the stoker when feeling the moving parts, such as crossheads, crankheads, etc.', observed Liversidge, advising young engineers that they 'should also acquire this dexterity'. He was quick to add a cautionary note that 'considerable care is required in the operation, and many personal injuries have resulted from careless procedure'.[61] Even the cleaning of fires, one manual exhorted, required 'judgment and experience'.[62] Such skills, required to keep the ship under steam and the

58 For a rare attempt indicating the complexity of the matter see William F. Durand, *Practical Marine Engineering for Marine Engineers and Students*, New York: Marine Engineering Inc., 1901, pp. 277–87. Gerstenberger and Welke, *Vom Wind zum Dampf*, pp. 195–9. For the notion of organizational 'zones of uncertainty', Gerstenberger and Welke refer to the work of Michel Crozier and Erhard Friedberg; see especially their *Actors and Systems: The Politics of Collective Action*, Chicago: Chicago University Press, 1980, pp. 37, 44, and 53.

59 See p. 120.

60 Gerstenberger and Welke, *Vom Wind zum Dampf*, pp. 195–7. See also Kennerley, 'Stoking the Boilers', pp. 197–8; Sager, *Ships and Memories*, pp. 47–53. For attempts at Taylorization see, however, Guthrie, *A History of Marine Engineering*, p. 193, and de Kerbrech, *Down amongst the Black Gang*, pp. 67–70.

61 Liversidge, *Engine-Room Practice*, p. 47.

62 Durand, *Practical Marine Engineering*, p. 283.

machinery in repair while avoiding wastage of fuel, serious injury, or physical breakdown, were learned on the job and not from manuals or in evening classes: stokehold crew, often in their late teens or early twenties when hired for the first time, toiled as trimmers for some time before they were put in charge of boiler furnaces as firemen.[63] Hence the prevalent labelling of stokehold labour as 'unskilled' – or the deprecatory reference to skill as mere 'dexterity' – does not reflect an actual absence of mental work, of specialized occupational knowledge, and of ability. Rather, it indicates absent or weak standards of certification and, more than anything else, the low social status assigned to this work.

The division of labour on board ship was also much deeper now and skill profiles less homogeneous: from the point of view of work organization, regulated communication and close coordination between the deck and the engine-room departments were clearly of crucial importance, but mostly restricted to the officers. The 'donkey man' who was in charge of the smaller steam engine used for hauling purposes (and hence called 'donkey') was a rare intermediary figure: a workman connecting the 'black gang' with the deck crew.[64] Even so, the cleavage within the ship's communication patterns was sufficiently deep to imply the emergence of two at times competing centres of authority on board ship that were focused on the shipmaster and the chief engineer respectively.[65] Shipping companies could use this departmental divide to curb the autonomy of the shipmaster at sea and reenforce 'remote control' over their fleets.[66] Moreover, the division between the deck and

63 Kennerley thus suggests for British stokehold crews between 1850 and 1950 that trimmers were on average five years younger than firemen, and that there was a preference for new recruits in their twenties. See Kennerley, 'Stoking the Boilers', p. 202. Among Indian crews, the recruitment of trimmers in their late teens, at times even at the age of ten or twelve, appears to have been more common than in the British case. See, e.g., *Minutes of the Evidence Recorded by the Indian Mercantile Marine Committee*, n.l., n.d., p. 643.

64 Kennerley, 'Stoking the Boilers', p. 199; Kennerley, 'The Seamen's Union', p. 16; see also Helbig, *Seefahrt vor den Feuern*, pp. 22f.

65 Gerstenberger and Welke, *Vom Wind zum Dampf*, pp. 229–31; Valerie Burton, 'The Making of a Nineteenth-Century Profession: Shipmasters and the British Shipping Industry', *Journal of the Canadian Historical Association* 1, no. 1 (1990), pp. 108–10; Ewald, 'Crossers of the Sea', p. 85.

66 For a denouncement of the 'departmental system' as one undermining shipboard discipline in general and the power of deck officers and shipmasters in particular

engine-room crews encumbered fraternization between departments and status groups, and facilitated, conversely, the imposition of managerial authority and labour discipline. The labour process of a steamer thus allowed, much more than that of a sailing vessel, for the division of the workplace into segments and the erection of what might be called a structure of social bulkheads.

Such socially engineered divisions went along with (sometimes fictitious but by no means ineffective) expectations regarding the social profile of the various status groups: if a 'middle-class' background was valorized for deck officers, 'respectable' artisanal or working-class origins were considered desirable for engineers and deck crew, while 'unskilled' employment in the stokehold denoted the lowest rung on the occupational ladder and casual employment patterns, and suggested the likelihood of pauperism and social defectiveness.[67] In Liverpool, a major recruitment area for stokers in Britain, 'black gangs', as compared to deck crew, were recruited from poorer urban districts, and included fewer workers with an artisan background and a considerably larger proportion of men categorized as illiterate.[68]

The work of trimmers and firemen, as we shall see in the next chapter, was *stigmatized labour*, branded both with a lack of social respectability and a propensity for unruliness. Stokehold work carried a racial stigma already when Irish Catholic immigrants were hired for such jobs in the port of Liverpool, as was often the case in the late nineteenth century. When shipowners subsequently recruited Asian and African trimmers and firemen in growing proportions,

while being promoted by all major liner companies, see 'Departments. Ashore and Afloat' (by 'Observer'), *The Nautical Magazine: A Technical and Critical Journal for the Officers of the Merchant Marine* LXXXI (1909), January to June, pp. 422–9.

67 For an astute account of the contradictions of this hierarchical culture in mid-twentieth century Britain that combines memory with historical research see Tony Lane, 'Neither Officers nor Gentlemen', *History Workshop Journal* 19, no. 1 (1985), pp. 128–43. For an analytical account see Burton, 'The Making of a Nineteenth-Century Profession'. These social profiles were powerful as ideology, but at least partly fictitious in terms of actual social composition. Burton thus alerts us to a tendency of deck crew migrating to the engine room around the turn of the century on account of higher wages. Valerie Burton, 'Counting Seafarers: The Published Records of the Registry of Merchant Seamen', *Mariner's Mirror* 71, no. 3 (1985), p. 316.

68 Kennerley, 'Stoking the Boilers', pp. 213–14. See also de Kerbrech, *Down amongst the Black Gang*, p. 110.

heavy manual toil in coal bunkers and engine rooms came to be associated with racial inferiority even more strongly.[69] This stigma was not only a pervasive feature of shipboard order, it also became an issue of wider public reflection extending even to literary circles.

69 For the view that the Irish were acceptable as sailors 'if well led', but 'awful' as firemen see, e.g., W. H. Hood, *The Blight of Insubordination: The Lascar Question and Rights and Wrongs of the British Shipmaster*, London: Spottiswoode & Co., 1903, p. 20.

9

Stoker's Stigma: The Two Lives of the 'Hairy Ape'

In 1922, the year when the S.S. *Egypt* went down, Eugene O'Neill's play *The Hairy Ape* was premiered in New York City. O'Neill had been attracted to seafaring life and had briefly, in 1911, worked as a deckhand. He succeeded, at that time, in gaining the certificate of 'able-bodied seaman' but chose the stokehold of a steamer as the central locus of this play.[1] It is here that the tragedy begins to unfold when Mildred, the philanthropically inclined daughter of a steel baron, 'goes slumming' by climbing down from the upper deck to the fireroom to explore the infernal heat, noise, and gloom of that workplace. She finds herself stunned and unprepared for the kind of human existence that confronts her in this maritime underworld. 'The filthy beast!' she exclaims as she encounters the menacing physicality and sexualized abusiveness of Yank, the stokers' muscular and sooty boss man. However, as Mildred's philanthropic posture falls apart, Yank's swagger and self-assurance dissipate also: O'Neill represents relations of class as an irresolvable dilemma since even their exposure spells disaster. For it is only through the encounter with Mildred that Yank realizes that he 'does not belong', that he cannot find a dignified place for himself within humanity. On shore, bourgeois society denies or, more likely, altogether ignores his humanity, as he now realizes more clearly when roaming the streets of

1 Robert M. Dowling, *Eugene O'Neill: A Life in Four Acts*, New Haven, CT: Yale University Press, 2014, pp. 68–70.

New York City after being paid off. Even the militant syndicalists of the Industrial Workers of the World (IWW) whom he seeks out in his quest for revenge appear to engage in disgraceful mendicancy only as they can neither offer direct retribution for his humiliation nor an immediate escape from alienation. Yank, finally and in despair, seeks to shed his humanity altogether by attempting to join the animal kingdom where he hopes to find a dignified place for himself in a more inclusive community of the physically strong. His wanderings end, therefore, at the zoo, where he releases a gorilla from the cage. But, when the anguished animal crushes Yank's ribs in a deadly embrace, it stands confirmed that, while alive, he cannot 'belong'.[2]

Numerous interpretations of O'Neill's play have been offered. Some have read it as a challenge to contemporary notions of racism: when class relations were thrown into sharp relief, labels of 'racial degeneration' that were most commonly applied to African Americans moved effortlessly to 'white' workers.[3] As Yank's 'whiteness' and claim to full humanity was undermined, it is argued, ethnic essence revealed itself as socially manufactured or, in Roediger's words, as a product of the 'white look'.[4] Another attempt to explore O'Neill's stance towards the working class has done so mainly from the top-down perspective of the 'slumming' Mildred foregrounding an assumed impossibility of transcending class identity as the central motif of the play.[5]

Yet, for our purposes, it seems more significant that O'Neill chooses the stokehold as the allegorical locus of an irreversible *and twofold* loss of 'belongingness': trimmers and firemen were, for one, alienated by economic relations of class that turned them into maimed and deformed appendices of the ship's machinery. Secondly, as Mildred's entry revealed, they were also alienated through a political culture of class that made them unrecognizable as members of 'civilized' humanity. They appeared not only as the degraded offspring of progressive industrial deskilling but as branded by their work with a dehumanizing stigma. Borrowing

2 Eugene O'Neill, *Early Plays*, New York: Penguin, 2001, pp. 355–95.

3 John Nickel, 'Racial Degeneration and "The Hairy Ape"', *Eugene O'Neill Review* 22, nos 1/2 (1998), pp. 33–40.

4 David R. Roediger, 'White Looks: Hairy Apes, True Stories and Limbaugh's Laughs', *Minnesota Review* 47 (1996), pp. 37–47, especially pp. 40f.

5 Patrick J. Chura, '"Vital Contact": Eugene O'Neill and the Working Class', *Twentieth Century Literature* 49, no. 4 (2003), pp. 520–46.

the language of the young Marx, we might say that Yank despairs as he 'no longer feels himself to be freely active in any but his animal functions . . . and in his human functions he no longer feels himself to be anything but an animal. What is animal becomes human and what is human becomes animal.'[6] This reading appears to resonate closely with O'Neill's introductory stage direction:

> The treatment of this scene, or of any other scene in the play, should by no means be naturalistic. The effect sought after is a cramped space in the bowels of a ship, imprisoned by white steel. The lines of bunks, the uprights supporting them, cross each other like the steel framework of a cage. The ceiling crushes down upon the men's heads. They cannot stand upright. This accentuates the natural stooping posture which shovelling coal and the resultant over-development of back and shoulder muscles have given them. The men themselves should resemble those pictures in which the appearance of Neanderthal Man is guessed at. All are hairy-chested, with long arms of tremendous power, and low, receding brows above their small, fierce, resentful eyes. All the civilized white races are represented, but except for the slight differentiation in color of hair, skin, eyes, all these men are alike.[7]

The play thus begins in a 'cage' (of the forecastle) only to return to a cage (in the zoo) at its end. Even more significantly for our discussion, the process of dehumanization and stigma is expressed allegorically – the denouncement of naturalism is important here – in the presentation of the workers' bodies: the enforced stooping, the manufactured overdevelopment of their torsos, the absence of physical markers of individuality and postures of intelligence. In fact, the very moment when Yank, prompted by Mildred's exclamation, begins to reflect on his human condition and assumes, according to O'Neill's stage direction, 'the exact attitude of Rodin's "Thinker"', is precisely the moment when he

6 The quote is from Karl Marx's 'Parisian' *Economic and Philosophic Manuscripts of 1844*, cf. Karl Marx and Frederick Engels, *Collected Works*, vol. 3, London: Lawrence & Wishart e-book, 2010, pp. 274f. The close resonance is all the more striking, even uncanny, as this text was unknown at the time of the premiere of O'Neill's play and would be published only decades later.

7 O'Neill, *Early Plays*, p. 358.

recognizes the untenability of his social identity and when his life begins to fall apart.[8]

Yet, even if 'all the men are alike' in their appearance, they are not presented as uniformly dull or monotonous in their views: with the socialist Long we encounter, once again, the precarious, dangerously marginal figure of the 'sea lawyer'. Paddy, moreover, a former deckhand on a sailing vessel who now finds himself condemned to the stokehold, is introduced as the most penetrating mind – more perceptive, at any rate, than any voice to be heard in the play from the upper deck or from New York's Fifth Avenue. It is Paddy who reflects that stokehold work, as opposed to the skilled toil of the sailor, means 'feeding our lives along wid the coal . . . caged in by steel from a sight of the sky like bloody apes in the zoo' and who challenges Yank: 'Is it to belong to that you're wishing? Is it a flesh and blood wheel of the engines you'd be?'[9]

O'Neill wrote his play in a cultural milieu where the image of the human 'ape' or 'gorilla' appeared in various shades oscillating between stigmatizations of race and class: in British and American caricature, simian features had been assigned routinely to lower-class Irish for several decades; [10] Ota Benga, a slave deported from Congo, had been displayed in the monkey house of the Bronx Zoo as late as in 1908, while Frederick Taylor had discovered, a few years later, the 'Pennsylvania Dutchman' 'Schmidt' as the closest approximation to the 'intelligent gorilla' he considered to be the ideal working-class object of 'scientific management'.[11]

O'Neill, on his part, confined the composition of the crew to the so-called 'civilized white races': he kept his 'black gang' all 'white'. Closely associated with the seafaring world, he could not have been unaware of the large proportion of Asian and African (and African American) trimmers and stokers that had been growing for several decades. By excluding them explicitly from the boiler-room crew in his play, O'Neill did not allow his audience to follow the central tenet of racist common

8 Ibid., p. 373.

9 Ibid., p. 364.

10 Lewis P. Curtis, *Apes and Angels: The Irishman in Victorian Caricature*, Newton Abbot: David & Charles, 1971, pp. 58–60; Mary Cowling, *The Artist as Anthropologist: The Representation of Type and Character in Victorian Art*, Cambridge: Cambridge University Press, 1989, pp. 126–30.

11 Cf. Phillips Verner Bradford and Harvey Blume, *Ota Benga: The Pygmy in the Zoo*, New York: St Martin's Press, 1992. Taylor, *The Principles*, pp. 43f and *passim*.

Figure 9.1. Carlotta Monterey as Mildred Douglas and Louis Wolheim as Yank in *The Hairy Ape*, Plymouth Theatre (New York), 1922. Source: Eugene O'Neill Papers, Beinecke Rare Book & Manuscript Library, Yale University. Ten Shots by Abbe Studio (New York) (in Series V).

sense of a time when the Ku Klux Klan re-emerged as one of the US's largest civil society organizations: the particularism of racializing dehumanization was not to be connected to a presumably 'uncivilized' African ethnic essence. The 'filthy beast' was precariously yet unmistakably 'white'. When the play was brought to the stage for the first time in the Plymouth Theatre, the face of Louis Wolheim, who played the role of Yank, was made up to resemble the ape-like representation of the Irish in cartoons that O'Neill, son of Irish immigrants, was certainly aware of (see Figure 9.1).[12]

The play did not foreground dehumanization on account of any specific ethnicity, however. Yank's face was also unevenly blackened by coal work: i.e., by the role assigned to him in the social division of labour or, in other words, by practices of class. The precarity of his 'whiteness' was thus enforced and deepened in a class society and not merely inherited as

12 See also Curtis, *Apes and Angels*, p. 29.

a presumably 'natural' property.[13] Even without the acidic solvent of supposedly inborn racial difference, any presumption of bonds inherent in shared humanity stood revealed as deception when the ruptures of class and the brutality of industrial over-exploitation lost their quotidian anonymity and became, for a brief moment, starkly visible and personal. When the steel heiress Mildred and the stoker Yank encountered each other in the narrow space of the stokehold, the – potentially racializing, but invariably dehumanizing – stigma that nestles in the very universalism of the capital-labour relationship was exposed: the emperor stood naked though, in O'Neill's plot, only the stoker noticed, bothered, and despaired.

A decade later, another US-based writer with a seafaring background, the former marine engineer William McFee, used O'Neill's *Hairy Ape* as a window for reassessing recent developments in maritime work culture. McFee had little patience with O'Neill's tragic anti-capitalism and assumed an attitude, instead, that conformed to the guidelines the P&O had formulated for their chief engineers more than half a century earlier: confident of his nuts-and-bolts knowledge and insistent on his superior station, he also presented himself as having been 'careful to avoid harshness' in his dealings with the boiler-room menials.[14] From this elevated position, he looked back on the fading age of the steamer as a time of manly if back-breaking toil. In McFee's view, O'Neill's play was 'grotesque' and had 'little to do with nautical reality', its main 'fallacy' being the emphasis on the 'immense physical bulk of the chief character, the implication being that only men of enormous strength could keep the ship going'. Instead, he argued:

> As a matter of cold, unvarnished fact, the Hairy Ape had always been the least desired of human beings down below. No vast agglomeration of muscles could ever take the place of skill. We who had the duty of picking firemen for a voyage learned by bitter experience far out on the western ocean in winter time, to pass up the gigantic creatures who thrust forward their jaws and their discharge-books, regarding us menacingly as we read the latest entries in those tragic records. 'Voyage unfinished', 'Master declines to report', 'Failed to join', 'Conduct "Good"',

13 Cf. Nickel, 'Racial Degeneration and "The Hairy Ape"', pp. 34f.

14 NMML, P&O/9/2/1, 'Peninsular & Steam Navigation Company: Instructions for Chief Engineers', London: 1873, p. 9.

> were among the least unfavourable notices we would have of the gentlemen before us. As experience grew we learned to take men who were of normal stature, and even on the small side, if they had the look of knowing their work and if their discharges were in keeping.[15]

In a detailed description of the cumbersome work process 'down below' McFee insisted that a stokehold crew required specific skills and that 'raw' muscle power was quite insufficient. The fireman, he recalled, 'was often much more than a mere shoveller of coal, and could be depended on to give marvellous service in a breakdown and to do his duty in a disaster'.[16] McFee's reference to the discharge books, those 'tragic records', betrays, at the same time, the apprehensions of engineers when dealing with their large 'black gangs'. The limitations of this disciplinary tool, intended to cull out recalcitrant workmen and secure subordination, even 'docility' among the crew, had been a central subject also of the Mercantile Marine Committee's investigations in 1902.[17]

Even in the age of sail, it had been possible to turn the ship into an excessively authoritarian work environment, and, in Britain's highly militarized merchant marine, the climax of such efforts appears to have been reached in the eighteenth and early nineteenth centuries.[18] In this work environment, 'insubordination' was considered a criminal offence and violence was used routinely to assert and reinforce discipline.[19] While the master's largely customary authority to hand out

15 McFee, 'Oil, and the Hairy Ape', *Fortnightly Review*, May 1932, pp. 565–6.

16 Ibid., p. 572.

17 *MMC*, vol. 2, Evidence, pp. 65, 100, 104, 239, 248f, 272–4, 413, 519, 678 and *passim*.

18 Marcus Rediker, *Between the Devil and the Deep Blue Sea: Merchant Seamen, Pirates and the Anglo-American Maritime World, 1700–1750*, Cambridge: Cambridge University Press, 1987, pp. 84, 209–12. For useful correctives to 'technocentric' views arguing that maritime authoritarianism was not an offshoot of the (sailing or steam) ship itself, but the result of social and historically contingent choices between alternative forms of labour management, see Heide Gerstenberger, 'Men Apart: The Concept of "Total Institution" and the Analysis of Seafaring', *International Journal of Maritime History* 8, no. 1 (1996), pp. 173–82; Eric Sager, *Seafaring Labour: The Merchant Marine of Atlantic Canada, 1820–1914*, Kingston: McGill-Queen's University Press, 1989, pp. 6–8.

19 Conrad H. Dixon, 'Seamen and the Law: An Examination of the Impact of Legislation on the British Merchant Seaman's Lot, 1588–1918', doctoral thesis, University College London, 1981, pp. 62f, 300–2; Leon Fink, *Sweatshops at Sea: Merchant Seamen in the World's First Globalized Industry, from 1812 to the Present*, Chapel Hill: University of North Carolina Press, 2011, pp. 43–63. See also Michael Quinlan, 'The Low Rumble

corporal punishment had lost its legitimacy by the 1870s, informal violence did not simply vanish from British merchant vessels in the age of steam.[20] The tense work environment of the engine room may even have provided a new habitat for maritime workplace violence: the 'zone of uncertainty', in which stokehold labour was performed, demanded flexible forms of cooperation, which threw up continuous challenges to the shipboard hierarchy officers were to enforce. As formal chains of command proved fragile, engineers could hope to back up their authority by way of physical coercion. Spokesmen of seamen's unions claimed that assaults on crew by officers and engineers were frequent and that the perpetrators were often not held accountable.[21] Smaller steamers with less formalized structures of authority appear to have seen more informal violence than large liners.[22] And corporal punishment, whether by British officers and engineers or by 'native' foremen, seems to have been inflicted on non-European crews more freely since the assaulted men were less likely to raise a formal complaint.[23]

Violent authoritarianism tended to breed counter-violence, however, among 'white' crews as much as among 'native' seafarers.[24] Pugnacious and 'hot-headed' boss men had been far from unfamiliar – men who would not merely 'thrust forward their jaws' and glare at their superiors

---

of Informal Dissent: Shipboard Protests over Health and Safety in Australian Waters, 1790–1900', *Labour History* 102 (2012), pp. 148–50; Isaac Land, 'Customs of the Sea: Flogging, Empire, and the "True British Seaman", 1770–1870', *Interventions* 3, no. 2 (2001), pp. 169–85; Burton, 'The Making of a Nineteenth-Century Profession', *passim.*

20 Cf. William Senior, 'Master-Mariner's Authority', *Law Quarterly Review* 34, no. 4 (1918), pp. 347–56; Land, 'Customs of the Sea'.

21 *MMC*, vol. 2, Evidence, pp. 203f, 229, 236, 254, 256, 265, 270f, 640. See also Heide Gerstenberger and Ulrich Welke, *Vom Wind zum Dampf. Sozialgeschichte der deutschen Handelsschiffahrt im Zeitalter der Industrialisierung*, Münster: Westfälisches Dampfboot, 1996, pp. 201–3.

22 Cf. Valerie Burton, 'The Work and Home Life of Seafarers with Special Reference to the Port of Southampton 1871–1921', doctoral dissertation, London School of Economics, 1988, p. 129.

23 Cf. Naina Manjrekar, '"Violent and Not Quite Modern?": Lascars and Everyday Resistance across the Sail-Steam Divide', *Labour History* 116 (2019), pp. 29–55.

24 *MMC*, vol. 2, Evidence, pp. 6, 619f, 636, 676; Burton, *The Work and Home Life*, pp. 129f. See also Frank T. Bullen, *The Men of the Merchant Service Being the Polity of the Mercantile Marine for 'Longshore Readers*, London: Smith, Elder & Co., 1900, pp. 138–40. For industrial violence on the part of 'lascars' see Manjrekar, '"Violent and Not Quite Modern?"'. For a contemporary report see, e.g., '40 Rioting Lascars Fell Shipp Officers', *New York Times*, 9 November 1930, p. 28.

'menacingly' but were physically capable of challenging boiler-room hierarchy and of offering resistance. The British *Nautical Magazine* published the following, perhaps tactically over-dramatized 'confession' in 1909: 'A fact which is well known in the Merchant Marine, but which very few engineers will acknowledge, is that they are afraid of their men.'[25] A few years earlier, the general manager of the British Shipping Federation, Cuthbert Laws, had similarly appeared to conjure up the spectre of the 'hairy ape' when quoting to the Mercantile Marine Committee from various logbooks, including that of the steamer *Clinton*, to demonstrate the inadequacy of the instruments officers possessed for disciplining British steamship crews:

> On the 27th of April, 1899, at 11.15 a.m., at sea, Patrick Hughes, fireman, . . . came on the bridge . . . in an abusive and bullying manner, inviting the master to come and try to heave up a basket of ashes, and saying that he was not going to pull his guts out doing it, at same time calling master a damned robber, with other abusive language. The master ordered him off the bridge, telling Hughes that he was paid for the work he had signed to do, which Hughes denied, with more abusive language, at the same time threatening the master that he (the master) was as good as a dead man, that he would go through him, saying that he had done 18 months for one man, and would die for the life of the master . . . Then, on the 27th of April, 1899, . . . a copy of the entry in log against P. Hughes was handed to him by the chief mate. He made answer that he knew it would be a case of logging, and that he did not care a b— . . . On the 19th May, 1899, at Rio de Janeiro, P. Hughes, fireman, discharged; his wages . . . paid to him before the Consul . . . There was no punishment. They were powerless and helpless.[26]

The report from the *Clinton* hints at persistent flashpoints of shipboard conflict to which we shall return in the next chapter. What concerns us here is the tactical use of such logbook entries by the shipowners'

---

25 'Departments. Ashore and Afloat' (by 'Observer'), *The Nautical Magazine: A Technical and Critical Journal for the Officers of the Merchant Marine* LXXXI (1909), January to June, p. 424. For a similar statement by a port missionary see MMC, vol. 2, Evidence, p. 225.

26 *MMC*, vol. 2, Evidence, p. 676.

spokesman: by zooming in on cases of largely unexplained physical violence on the part of firemen – Hughes was reported to have boasted of an earlier conviction for homicide – Laws sought to support the shipowners' claim that 'in the Mercantile Marine . . . there are no means provided of enforcing respect for constituted authority' and, implicitly, that masters could not keep up discipline without autonomous, extra-judicial means of coercion at sea that were either sanctioned or at least tolerated by the state: if 'a Government official [was] thrust between master and man in their most intimate relation,' he argued, 'it is almost impossible to prevent this circumstance from lowering the authority of the captain in the eyes of the crew'.[27]

While the quasi-judicial authority shipmasters had lost in the mid-nineteenth century could not be recovered in the twentieth, British shipowners were more successful in making sure that 'desertion' and insubordination were criminalized in merchant shipping law, until 1970, as offences punishable with imprisonment.[28] The 'intimate relation' between seafarer and shipmaster was thus, as lawyer and historian William Senior put it in 1918, established on a 'peculiar basis [that] has occasionally been disguised by calling it contractual'.[29] Shipowners persisted, nevertheless, in lamenting that their shipmasters were considerably more restricted by Britain's judicial system than, for instance, their US counterparts. The latter, it was said, inflicted extrajudicial violence on recalcitrant crew as a matter of course – in open breach of law but based on 'universal custom' and without having to fear that onshore courts would hold them accountable.[30]

Even in McFee's nostalgically inflected musings, the stokers' stigma did not quite disappear. Despite his distaste for O'Neill's 'grotesque' play, McFee conceded that the violent, insubordinate 'hairy ape' could be considered the 'prototype' of 'firemen in the old days'. Precarious 'whiteness' shone through in his formulations, too: 'The contrast between the

27 Ibid., p. 677.

28 F. J. J. Cadwallader, 'Discipline in British Merchants Ships', *Journal of Maritime Law and Commerce* 2, no. 1 (1970), pp. 147–64; Dixon, *Seamen and the Law*, pp. 221–5, 268, 297. See also *MMC*, vol. 2, Evidence, pp. 395, 399f, 429.

29 Senior, 'Master-Mariner's Authority', p. 351.

30 MMC, vol. 2, Evidence, pp. 81, 619f; 662. See also Bullen, *The Men of the Merchant Service*, pp. 40, 48f, 88f, 268; W. H. Hood, *The Blight of Insubordination: The Lascar Question and Rights and Wrongs of the British Shipmaster*, London: Spottiswoode & Co., 1903, p. 20.

white skin of his nude body and the coal dust that ringed his eyes was a symbol of his vocation.' And, of course, the stoker 'was given to insobriety sometimes, and to missing his passage in a foreign port. There was always something of the buccaneer in his make-up, and "trouble in the fireman's forecastle" was one of those things every engineer took as a matter of course.'[31]

McFee, brought up and trained as an engineer in Britain, had served since 1906 on British and US merchant steamers, rising to the rank of chief engineer before he retired to Connecticut in 1922 to dedicate his time fully to the writing of sea stories, novels, and reviews.[32] In his new oil-producing home country the transformation from coal-fired steamers to either oil-fuelled steamers or vessels propelled by diesel motors was particularly fast during and after the World War.[33] But keeping an oil-fuelled boiler under steam would, for instance, require only a quarter of the amount of labour employed at a corresponding coal-fuelled boiler.[34] Enormous boiler-room crews like that of the *Titanic,* where each of the three watches had comprised as many as eighty-one men, thus became a less common sight in American ports, and the work environment 'down below' changed fundamentally.[35] McFee believed that the new dangers of ships carrying large reservoirs of highly inflammable oil had created a new, submissive, 'unassuming' psychological disposition among the severely downsized crew. The fireman on an oil-fuelled vessel was reduced, he asserted, to a mere 'detached assistant', deskilled and emasculated: a 'high-school girl, with an hour's instruction, could take his place'.[36] However, the hypothesis of a tendential fall of manliness among seafarers as an inevitable corollary of technological transformation was an older idea proposed already when the maritime steam engine rose to dominance. One generation before McFee, another author with a seafaring past, Frank T. Bullen, had reminisced about

31 McFee, 'Oil, and the Hairy Ape', p. 572.

32 Cf. James Norman Leatherby, 'William McFee: Writing Engineer', *Prairie Schooner* 23, no. 2 (1949), pp. 171–80.

33 Max E. Fletcher, 'From Coal to Oil in British Shipping', *Journal of Transport History* 3, no. 1 (1975), p. 7.

34 A. C. Hardy, *Modern Marine Engineering: A Practical Work of Ship Powering and Marine Propulsion Technique* (2nd ed.), vol. 2, London: Caxton Publishing, 1954, p. 2.

35 Richard P. de Kerbrech, *Down amongst the Black Gang: The World and Workplace of RMS Titanic's Stokers*, Stroud: History Press, 2014, p. 67.

36 McFee, 'Oil, and the Hairy Ape', pp. 573, 579.

'those days' of sail when 'men were seamen. In these days [i.e., in the age of steam] they are a kind of male housemaid' busying themselves with scrubbing or painting the deck.[37] The very same idea was resuscitated when coal was replaced with oil and the steam engine with the diesel motor. Yet such fusions of nostalgic masculinism with technological determinism need not detain us further: they tell us little about actual practices of work.

For our purposes, it seems more important to notice that the technological trajectory of merchant shipping followed a chronology in Britain that diverged to some extent from that outlined by McFee. As has been pointed out before, the British dominance in global merchant shipping had rested, for about half a century, not only on an advanced shipbuilding sector but also on the intertwined political economies of coal and empire. Apart from being the preferred fuel of steam ships, British coal was also 'until the Second World War, the single most important internationally traded form of energy' and accordingly one of Britain's key export commodities.[38] Moreover, it had been supplied to a global network of maritime coaling stations that was backed up by the political infrastructure of Britain's colonial empire and connected to powerful capital interests.[39] The P&O Company controlled, for instance, the majority of shares of William Cory & Sons, one of the largest coal bunkering firms.[40] Substituting diesel-fuelled or oil-burning ships for coal-burning steamers was thus not only a question of opting for the most profitable technology of maritime propulsion but had far-reaching economic and political linkage effects.

Furthermore, Britain's major liner companies were no mere shipping concerns, but transnational commercial conglomerates that enjoyed privileged access to the economic resources of the British Empire. Britain's shipping industry thus faced greater obstacles in shifting from coal

---

37 *MMC*, vol. 2, Evidence, p. 618. See also Bullen, *The Men of the Merchant Service*, p. 267. The notion of fading maritime masculinity had been brought up by Joseph Conrad, too, in his *Nigger of the 'Narcissus'*. See above.

38 David Edgerton, *The Rise and Fall of the British Nation: A Twentieth-Century History*, London: Penguin, 2019, p. 82.

39 Christopher James Allen, 'Coal as a Freight, Coal as a Fuel: A Study of the British Coal Trade: 1850–1913', unpublished dissertation, Durham University, 1920, pp. 160–205.

40 Christopher J. Napier, 'Allies or Subsidiaries? Inter-Company Relations in the P&O Group, 1914–39', *Business History* 39, no. 2 (1997), pp. 75f, 81.

to diesel, but also possessed superior, imperial means to compensate for the decreasing competitiveness of their fleet in terms of fuel efficiency – means I have already alluded to in the first chapter of this book. Profits realized in India through various commercial and industrial operations did make up, for instance, for decreasing rates of return of the P&O Company's shipping business.[41] More directly relevant to our discussion, however, is the circumstance that India and other parts of Britain's colonial empire also gave British shipowners means to undercut their competitors in terms of wage expenditure and, more generally, operation costs.

British maritime wages had been considerably lower than those, for instance, paid in the US or Australia even around the turn of the century – a differential that contributed to enormous desertion rates among British seamen once they had crossed the Atlantic or reached Australasia.[42] Lord Thomas Brassey, former secretary to the admiralty and founding director of the Cunard Steamship Company, claimed that 45 per cent of all firemen employed in 1900 on British merchant vessels had violated their contracts through desertion. While this figure was clearly inflated,[43] rates of attrition were sufficiently high to force the British shipping industry to increase the pay for transatlantic voyages.[44] Moreover, desertion rates among British crew also precipitated a change of recruitment patterns, especially in regard to the stokehold, with various companies coming to prefer Asian crews and with 'lascar' employment doubling between 1886 and 1900.[45] The pay of an Indian seafarer was believed to range between a quarter and a third of that of a British seaman – proportions that would not change substantially up

41 Stephanie Jones, *Trade and Shipping: Lord Inchcape, 1952–1932*, Manchester: Manchester University Press, 1989, pp. 121–6. See also Napier, 'Allies or Subsidiaries?'.

42 *MMC*, vol. 2, Evidence, pp. 164, 526, 532, 608.

43 Ibid., p. 281. These figures appear somewhat excessive and may conflate two legally distinct offences, i.e., 'desertion' and 'failing to join'. For an analysis of the relevant data see Dixon, *Seamen and the Law*, pp. 221f, 240–4. See also Tony Lane, *Liverpool: City of the Sea* (2nd ed.), Liverpool: Liverpool University Press, 1997, p. 75.

44 Robert P. Bass and Horace B. Drury, *Marine and Dock Labor: Work, Wages and Industrial Relations during the Period of the War* (Report of the Director of the Marine and Dock Industrial Relations Division, United States Shipping Board), pp. 142f. See also Fink, *Sweatshops at Sea*, p. 102.

45 *MMC*, vol. 2, Evidence, pp. 3, 12, 137, 284, 445, 543, 550.

till the 1980s.[46] Since 'lascar' crews were always considerably larger as well as supplemented by a number of 'skilled' European 'able-bodied seamen' and engine-room mechanics, the overall savings on the wage bill were an issue of contention – British trade union leader Joseph Havelock Wilson believed them to come close to 40 per cent, shipping industrialists asserted they were nearer to 10 per cent and argued that the real economic advantages of 'lascar' employment lay in a reduction of operation costs – an issue we shall discuss in the next chapter.[47] In 1924, the Indian shipping lobbyist S. N. Haji's calculations seemed to be closer to Havelock Wilson's estimate, however.[48]

Be that as it may, between 1914 and 1938, the overall annual employment in the British merchant marine declined from 295,652 to 192,375 (or by 35 per cent), while the annual employment of 'lascars' remained, as we have seen already, constant at about 50,000 (or rose from 17 to 26 per cent).[49] The steady supply of cheap steamship labour from India and other colonies thus provided the beleaguered British shipping industry with a certain competitive edge in terms of labour costs that helped to mitigate, at least in some degree, the demerits of sticking to

46 Ibid., pp. 135, 161. Ravi Ahuja, 'Mobility and Containment: The Voyages of South Asian Seamen, c. 1900–1960', *International Review of Social History* 51 (2006, supplement), p. 112.

47 *MMC*, vol. 2, Evidence, p. 161; see also pp. 243f. Tory MP and shipbuilder John Denny, a member of the Mercantile Marine Committee, deposited a comparative calculation of wage bills for a (predominantly) 'lascar' and (entirely) 'European' crew of a smaller steamer covering the route between Glasgow and Rangoon (or Calcutta). He calculated that the comparative cost advantage of 'lascar' crews amounted to a bit more than 9 per cent if the voyage was between Glasgow and Rangoon (which included transfer costs for the 'lascar' crew from Calcutta to Rangoon) and to about 16 per cent on a voyage between Glasgow and Calcutta. *MMC*, vol. 3, Appendix Q, No. 3, p. 192. See also *MMC*, vol. 2, p. 532.

48 S. N. Haji, a manager of the Scindia Steam Navigation Company and a lobbyist for Indian shipping capital, calculated that the wage and victualling bill for a 7,400 ton steamer with European officers and Indian crew amounted to two-thirds of the costs incurred when employing solely Europeans. S. N. Haji, *Economics of Shipping: A Study in Applied Economics*, Bombay: self-published, 1924, p. 92.

49 Ravi Ahuja, 'Networks of Subordination – Networks of the Subordinated: The Case of South Asian Maritime Labour under British Imperialism (c. 1890–1947)', in Harald Fischer-Tiné and Ashwini Tambe (eds), *Spaces of Disorder: The Limits of British Colonial Control in South Asia and the Indian Ocean*, London: Routledge, 2008, pp. 11–12.

an increasingly obsolete propulsion technology.[50] The availability of vast colonial reservoirs of 'cheap labour' thus did not only contribute to the greater staying power of coal-fuelled merchant shipping in the British Empire, but also prolonged the lifespan of the 'hairy ape'. The stigma attached to the stoker's work persisted, while the racist shades that had always loomed in the background flared up now in garish colours.

Whether racially marked as 'Liverpool-Irish' or of other description, engine-room recruits from British ports had been depicted stereotypically as illiterate, violent, and in need of draconian discipline.[51] In 1902, various witnesses called in front of the Mercantile Marine Committee had characterized British firemen as 'an endless source of trouble', as unsteady drifters and 'bird[s] of passage', as given to drink and thus 'often causing serious delay to the vessel', as being prone to 'uproarious' indiscipline and devoid of skill, with about 10 per cent of them being 'dead-heads' altogether.[52] The 'present day fireman is not a sailor; he goes to sea perhaps because he has misbehaved himself in the neighbourhood, and landed himself in gaol once or twice', claimed Henry Radcliffe, a Cardiff shipowner and self-righteous philanthropist. He quickly added 'some of them', reminding himself, perhaps, of the charitable posture befitting his position. When challenged by Havelock Wilson to give concrete instances and names of such men, Radcliffe refused to go into details, however, and simply retorted 'it is well known, and well known to you': the stoker's depravity, delinquency and degradation could be considered common knowledge, he felt, and did not require specific proof.[53]

Trade union statements of the time correspondingly betray a strong sense of alarm and defensiveness concerning the loss of respectability

---

50 For a concurrent argument focusing more on the compensatory advantages of racially divided crews for increasingly outcompeted British shipowners, see Laura Tabili, *'We Ask for British Justice': Workers and Racial Difference in Late Imperial Britain*, Ithaca, NY: Cornell University Press, 1994, p. 55; Laura Tabili, '"A Maritime Race": Masculinity and the Racial Division of Labor in British Merchant Ships, 1900–1939', in Margaret S. Creighton and Lisa Norling (eds), *Iron Men, Wooden Women: Gender and Seafaring in the Atlantic World, 1700–1920*, Baltimore, MD: Johns Hopkins Press, 1996, p. 187.

51 For an interesting compilation of such stereotypes see de Kerbrech, *Down amongst the Black Gang*, pp. 108–16.

52 *MMC*, vol. 2, Evidence, pp. 130, 137, 164, 531, 538f, 543, 548f, 553, 608.

53 Ibid., p. 477.

(or the *déclassment*) of the seaman's occupation in general and of the stoker's in particular. In expressing the 'respectable seaman's' struggle for social recognition, the language chosen was often one of exclusion – a combination of idioms of craft and, increasingly, of race rather than a language of class. I have quoted already, in an earlier chapter, the *Daily Herald's* complaint, in 1912, that 'Portsmouth and Plymouth drifters, loafers and criminals fresh from prison cells, Chinese and Lascars, the filthy and diseased wrecks of the five continents are recruited to man British boats, whilst British sailors are left to tramp or starve or rot on land'.[54] Across the Atlantic, very similar views could be heard in these years: Andrew Furuseth, powerful trade union leader of US seamen, fumed that maritime employment, by not keeping pace with improving labour conditions on shore, had been turned into the domain 'of the sewage of the Caucasian race and of such of the races of Asia as felt that their conditions could be improved by becoming seamen'.[55] This increasing stigmatization of maritime labour had become attached most visibly – and with distinctly eugenic and racist undertones – to the work of 'Caucasian' stokers who drew, as Eugene O'Neill emphasized, little comfort from their rather brittle 'whiteness'.

However, the expanding employment of 'lascars' or 'natives' did not merely contribute to the crisis of respectability that 'white' seafarers experienced along the North Atlantic rim. The steep command structure of the stokehold was now also underlaid with a more explicit racial hierarchy and a division of labour that was further deepened. This tendency materialized earlier and most comprehensively in the hiring patterns of the shipping concerns with the most privileged access to colonial labour markets: the British India Steam Navigation Company (BISN), which controlled much of the Indian Ocean steamer traffic, and the P&O, which plied the transcontinental routes between Asia and Europe, had relied on 'lascar' labour extensively since the middle decades of the nineteenth century.[56] 'In the P. and 0. service', Liversidge thus informed aspiring engineers,

54 *Daily Herald*, 2 May 1912, p. 1.

55 Andrew Furuseth, 'The Dawn of Another Day', *American Federationist* 22 (1915), p. 718. See also Fink, *Sweatshops at Sea*, p. 106.

56 *MMC*, vol. 2, Evidence, pp. 9, 77, 161, 284.

> these greasers and the firemen are all natives. In the stokehold there is a chief fireman or 'serang', and three leading firemen called 'tindels', one for each watch. The 'serang' keeps no regular watch in the large ships, but in the smaller ships the 'serang' and two 'tindels' keep the three watches and assist the junior engineer of the watch. The engineer directs the 'tindel' to alter the check valves if the water levels are not kept properly; to avoid confusion the actual adjustment is always performed by one man . . . The 'tindel' has nothing to do with the feed pumps, which are managed entirely by the engineer. The winchmen employed on the auxiliary machinery are . . . always Europeans.[57]

This highly centralized, personalized, and racialized structure of command and accountability had two main aspects: firstly, during every watch one 'European' engineer was to supervise the entire labour process in the stokehold with the support of one 'native' intermediary; secondly, 'white' engineers or mechanics were held personally accountable for those elements of the machinery that were considered most sensitive, while 'natives' were explicitly excluded from handling them.

The crew list of the S.S. *Egypt* confirms this pattern. At the time of the accident, the liner's engine-room crew was composed as follows: only twelve of the ninety-five men had British names, eight of them being listed as engineers of various ranks and the other four as skilled mechanics (one each of the following trades: boilermaker, electrician, refrigeration mechanic, and winchman). The remaining eighty-three men all bore Muslim names and appear to have been recruited predominantly from the northwest of the Indian subcontinent. Fifty-five of them were listed as firemen, including one serang (senior foreman or boatswain), two tindals (deputy foremen), six panniwallahs (water tenders) and one storekeeper, lamp-man, and cook each, while twenty-seven coal trimmers were supervised by their own serang.[58] Hence the ship's six boilers were manned during each of the three watches by fourteen firemen and nine coal trimmers on average. Twelve additional Indian crew were employed either in supervisory or ancillary capacities,

57 Liversidge, *Engine-Room Practice*, p. 32.

58 TNA, TS 34/8 '"R.M.S. Egypt": Various Proofs and Documents' ('List of native crew').

but all of them in the stokehold, while no 'native' was allowed to tend to the ship's four triple-expansion engines. On the S.S. *Egypt*, as in other steamers of major British shipping lines, the work of handling coal and stoking the furnaces was thus racially marked out as a job for Indian Muslims.

In effect, the hierarchies in the engine room had become even steeper and the owner's instruction to the engineers of 'not mixing too freely' with the boiler-room crew was even more likely to be implemented. The linguistic and racial partition of the crew reinforced this structure of social bulkheads not only in the engine and boiler rooms but on the steamer as a whole: 'white' sailors would generally communicate in English, while their Indian counterparts would converse not necessarily in the same South Asian language – in the case of the S.S. *Egypt*, Goan stewards spoke Konkani, while Punjabi or Pashto would have been common languages among the firemen. 'Hindustani', as a medium of communication between the segments of the crew and at least some of the British officers, was not the mother tongue of many Indian seafarers, who had to acquire that language as well. This compartmentalization had even received official sanction in the early years of the twentieth century, when the Mercantile Marine Committee recommended that a certain proficiency of English was to be instituted as an employment requirement for 'foreign' (read: non–British European) seamen, but 'that any such provision should not apply to Lascars or other Asiatics or Africans'.[59] A few years earlier, a shipmaster, on being asked by the Board of Trade's Manning Committee whether he would give a command to a 'lascar' directly, responded coolly, 'I should never do so; it would be a very bad practice.'[60]

As a result, the ship's racialized work organization and the linguistic lines of segmentation dividing the crew tended to reinforce each other: as gangs of 'lascars' and other 'native seamen' were recruited to a large extent through competing ethnic networks, the motley crew of the age of sail lost much of its diversity and with it the need for a living and expanding maritime lingua franca, for an experimental, flexible, and

59 *MMC*, vol. 1, Report, p. ix.

60 Interview of Captain William Hogg Hood, 12 December 1894, *Manning Committee*, vol. 2, Minutes of Evidence . . . , p. 581.

self-enriching mode of overcoming impasses in communication.[61] Nor was it, for the same reason, as likely in the 1920s to encounter among the Indian crew of a British merchant vessel 'several men' who spoke 'very good English' as in Herman Melville's time.[62]

61 For a discussion of the nature of these networks see Ahuja, 'Networks of Subordination'.

62 Herman Melville, *Redburn: His First Voyage*, New York: Harper & Brothers, 1855, pp. 216–20.

10

Gains of 'Racial Management': Manning Scales and Liner Schedules

The management of labour in the British merchant marine did not limit itself, however, to maintaining centralized control through steep formal hierarchies on board ship that were reinforced, if convenient, by ethnic and linguistic segmentation. Elizabeth Esch and David Roediger have shown how US management 'experts' practised, in the early years of the twentieth century, an obscurantist kind of racial algebra seeking to express in equations and tables how the presumably divergent physical and intellectual capacities of human 'races' could be harnessed and combined most effectively for the benefit of the employer.[1] One particularly influential propagator of such ideas, who succeeded in building a career on his 'racial management expertise', was the mining engineer and future US president Herbert Hoover, who summed up his calculations in 1909 as follows:

> Much observation and experience in working Asiatics and negroes as well as Americans and Australians in mines, leads the writer to the conclusion that, averaging actual results, one white man equals from two to three of the colored races, even in the simplest forms of mine work such as shoveling or tramming. In the most highly skilled

1 Elizabeth Esch and David R. Roediger, '"One Symptom of Originality": Race and Management of Labor in US History', in D. R. Roediger, *Class, Race and Marxism*, London: Verso, 2017, pp. 138–42.

> branches, such as mechanics, the average ratio is as one to seven, or in extreme cases even eleven.[2]

If a Chinese worker, as Hoover believed, 'required' only a sixth or even a twelfth of the pay of a 'white' worker, optimizing the racial composition of a workforce was thus a mere matter of balancing racially defined wage costs and racial productivity rates.[3] The cultivation of such theories of scientistic racism did not necessarily require the hothouse of US post-slavery society, however, as Esch and Roediger's account might suggest.[4] Very similar ideas proliferated in Britain's Indian Empire, too. The ability to identify and rate the subcontinent's most valuable 'martial', 'seafaring', or 'coolie races', it has been pointed out before, had been held in high esteem as a branch of colonial governance knowledge since the latter half of the nineteenth century, and was further elaborated in the First World War in the light of a growing concern for securing a greater 'efficiency' of labour.[5]

In the shipping industry, rough calculations of how many Indian trimmers and firemen were required to replace a 'European' seaman and speculations about the relative efficiency of 'white' and 'coloured' crews under the climatic conditions of the North Atlantic and the Red Sea respectively had been circulating in British shipping circles for a long time. In the mid-1890s, the Board of Trade's Manning Committee had received starkly diverging responses on questioning British seamen, officers, and shipowners about the relative efficiency of 'lascar' and European crew. While some insisted that three Indian seafarers were required to do the work of one European sailor or fireman, actual manning scales seemed to suggest that 'mixed crews' with a sizeable 'lascar' component were generally about 50 per cent larger than those comprised of 'white crew' only.[6] Witnesses who gave evidence to the Mercantile Marine Committee in 1902 had concurred that a 'native'

2 Herbert C. Hoover, *Principles of Mining: Valuation, Organization and Administration*, London: McGraw-Hill, 1909, p. 163.

3 Esch and Roediger, '"One Symptom of Originality"', pp. 140f.

4 Elizabeth Esch and David Roediger, *The Production of Difference: Race and the Management of Labor in U.S. History*, Oxford: Oxford University Press, 2012, pp. 3–16 and *passim*.

5 Cf. chapter 5, above.

6 *Manning Committee*, vol. 1, Report, p. 20.

stokehold crew should be about twice as large as a 'European' or 'British' 'black gang' while, by strange coincidence, and very conveniently for the shipowners, a 'lascar' trimmer or fireman supposedly required only half the accommodation space deemed necessary to keep up the health and work capacity of a European stoker.[7] These rules of thumb could be turned into formal calculations and staffing formulas such as those to be found in Liversidge's *Engine-Room Practice.* This manual presented detailed (though somewhat inconsistent) computations to the effect that a 'European' fireman could work between 0.71 and 0.729 tons of coal per hour, depending on the size of the respective liner, while 'natives' would move between 0.378 and 0.417 tons.[8]

The positivistic exactitude of these figures reflects the belief that 'race' possessed an objective, measurable quality or *essence*, which allowed taxonomic comparison in terms of work capacity and market value. Yet, if their tabulations displayed precise data with great confidence, the taxonomers of race, Hoover as much as Liversidge, found it characteristically hard to maintain coherence in their calculations. The elusiveness of 'racial essence' as much as the multiple variables of the labour process foiled attempts to calculate crewing requirements solely on the basis of a ship's total indicative horsepower or fire-grate surface.[9] Correspondingly, we have already observed that the figures available for the average work capacities assigned to stokers and trimmers were rather inconsistent.[10] The very messiness of the data indicates that computational exactitude sat uneasily with the actual work organization in the boiler room, with a labour process that defied rigid standardization as it engaged perpetually with a 'zone of uncertainty' contingent upon numerous variables: 'There are many minor causes', admitted the

7 *Manning Committee*, vol. 2, Minutes of Evidence . . . , pp. 149, 161.

8 John G. Liversidge, *Engine-Room Practice: A Handbook for the Royal Navy and Mercantile Marine*, London: Charles Griffin & Co., 1923 (11th ed.), pp. 25–6.

9 Esch and Roediger have pointed out that Hoover, in various statements and publications, pronounced the most divergent ratios of racially defined work capacity – but always with equal confidence. Esch and Roediger, '"One Symptom of Originality"', pp. 138–42. In Liversidge's calculations, inconsistencies are perceivable in regard to the recommended size of engine-room crew: 'native' crews should have been considerably larger if we extrapolate from the figures given for the individual work capacity of a 'native' stoker, which was stated as amounting to about 50 to 60 per cent of that of a 'European' fireman. Liversidge, *Engine-Room Practice*, pp. 25–6.

10 See pp. 127–8.

Manning Committee in 1896, 'for making the work to be done below greater or less.'[11] By 'factoring in' nebulous notions of 'racial essence', this mess was further compounded.

The proposed exactitude of measurements of racially determined work capacity thus reveals itself as an attempt to rationalize an irrational premise. In the age of empire, just as in our own time of 'neoliberal' capitalism, ideological unreason fancied the costume of mathematical reason. Yet such notions of essential, measurable, and manageable difference between 'races' (or, in a present-day identitarian rendering, between nationally defined 'cultures'), have been too persistent in the history of late capitalism to be brushed away on grounds of logical inconsistency alone.[12] For racist (or culturalist) essentialism has served not only – in the sphere of social ideology – as a keystone of counter-enlightenment irrationalism, it has also maintained – in the sphere of labour management – some practical utility for employers that needs to be examined and explained. When Indian seafarers came to be employed in ever larger numbers, essentialized racial difference served as a seemingly self-explanatory shorthand for hierarchies that were steeper and for levels of stigmatization that were higher even than those experienced by the stokehold crews recruited from among the 'Liverpool Irish' in British ports.

For the labour relations of 'lascars' and other 'native seamen' differed substantially from those of 'European' seamen not only with regard to wages and other forms of compensation but, even more importantly, with respect to their level of personal subordination. Legally, these differentials were sanctioned, for Indian workers, not merely in divergent contractual conditions, but in a *bifurcation of the work contract* itself in British-imperial maritime law, i.e., in the creation of a separate category of work contract for 'native seamen' that was referred to as 'lascar (or, Asiatic) articles of agreement'. Ideologically, the reduced formal freedom of 'lascar' contracts (particularly evident in the severely restricted right to terminate contract) was justified by ascribing to these seafarers a

---

11 Cf. footnote 58 on p. 136. *Manning Committee*, vol. 1, Report, p. 27. For a pertinent analysis see Heide Gerstenberger and Ulrich Welke, *Vom Wind zum Dampf. Sozialgeschichte der deutschen Handelsschiffahrt im Zeitalter der Industrialisierung*, Münster: Westfälisches Dampfboot, 1996, pp. 195–7.

12 Cf. Geert Hofstede, *Culture's Consequences: Comparing Values, Behaviors, Institutions, and Organizations across Nations*, 2nd ed., Thousand Oaks, CA: Sage, 2001.

peculiar racial essence that could be harnessed to useful purposes only by specific, skilfully deployed means.[13] If management preferences shaped labour relations of steamship workers in ways that turned racial stigma into a resource for the fortification of steeply hierarchical labour processes, this tendency was given a natural appearance when it was claimed that essential racial difference transformed itself smoothly – *organically* as it were – into contractual difference and, more specifically, into differential entitlements to formal contractual freedom.

Historians like G. Balachandran, Laura Tabili, or myself have examined the work relations of 'native' seafarers that were forged in increasingly racialized maritime labour markets and have done so from various angles, including the specific forms of legal regulation that combined the above-mentioned racialized maritime labour law with harsh and equally racialized immigration restrictions for 'native' seafarers.[14] For, under 'Asiatic Articles', Indian seafarers could be denied shore leave in port while being prevented, by immigration laws, from disembarking in several important shipping destinations that included the US and Australia.[15] Thus, they could be compelled to work continuously even in port, while desertion rates were pushed down, which contributed substantially to the uninterrupted and punctual performance of steamer operations. Moreover, Indian seafarers were not permitted to terminate their contracts in a port outside the Indian subcontinent. Shipowners could 'transfer' seafarers and even entire crews without their consent to any other vessel in any British port in case their services were no longer required on the ship they had originally been

13 OIOC, India Office, E&O, L/E/9/957, 3256 (1926), p. 3: Brief for the International Labour Conference on Seamen's Articles of Agreement. See also Ravi Ahuja, 'Networks of Subordination – Networks of the Subordinated: The Case of South Asian Maritime Labour under British Imperialism (c. 1890–1947)', in Harald Fischer-Tiné and Ashwini Tambe (eds), *Spaces of Disorder: The Limits of British Colonial Control in South Asia and the Indian Ocean*, London: Routledge, 2008, pp. 13f; Ravi Ahuja, 'Mobility and Containment: The Voyages of South Asian Seamen, c. 1900–1960', *International Review of Social History* 51 (2006, supplement), pp. 115–20.

14 Gopalan Balachandran, *Globalizing Labour? Indian Seafaring and World Shipping*, c. 1870–1945, New Delhi: Oxford University Press, 2012, pp. 58–93; Laura Tabili, *'We Ask for British Justice': Workers and Racial Difference in Late Imperial Britain*, Ithaca, NY: Cornell University Press, 1994, pp. 41–57; Ahuja, 'Networks of Subordination'; Ahuja, 'Mobility and Containment'.

15 OIOC, India Office, E&O (Seamen) L/E/9/974: Shore leave for lascar crews. See also Ahuja, 'Mobility and Containment', *passim*.

hired for.[16] At London's Victoria Docks alone, a port facility largely catering to liners, about 8,000 Indian seafarers annually were reported to have been transferred to other ships in the early years of the twentieth century.[17] Maritime newspapers regularly carried advertisements like the following: 'Wanted Lascar Crew of about forty-two hands all told for steamer, not later than 21st inst. Apply, B. J. Sutherland and Co. 38, Sandhill, Newcastle.'[18] If such transfers were far from uncontentious and sometimes openly resisted by Indian crew, shipowners insisted on them in order to avoid temporary but costly labour shortages as well as the expenses for the repatriation of crew with expired contracts.[19]

While studies examining such practices remain useful and relevant, they address merely one side of the racialization of maritime labour in the age of the steamship: they emphasize the labour market rather than the work site, study labour *relations* rather than the labour *process*, or, in other words, they examine the *sale* of labour power, not its *extraction*. In what follows, we shift the focus to the organization of work, and since a comprehensive analysis of the interdependent labour processes in a steamship liner's three departments would require a book of its own, we can merely discuss, pars pro toto, the engine room – the department below decks where the increase in the employment of Indian seafarers had been most dynamic.[20] We will ask what the managerial advantages of racializing stokehold labour might have been on steamers and particularly on liners like the S.S. *Egypt*. The question is, in other words: Can we trace any managerial compulsions and needs in the organization of shipping operations that nurtured the shift from the proverbial 'motley crew' of the sailing vessel to the increasing racial segmentation

16 See the instructions for Lascar Transfer Officers in OIOC, India Office Records, Commercial & Revenue Papers, L/E/7/1120, File 1495 (1922).

17 *MMC*, vol. 2, Evidence, p. 107.

18 *Lloyd's List*, 11 December 1906, p. 9.

19 Ravi Ahuja, 'A Freedom Still Enmeshed in Servitude: The Unruly "Lascars" of the S.S. City of Manila or, a Micro-History of the "Free Labour" Problem', in Ravi Ahuja (ed.), *Working Lives and Worker Militancy: The Politics of Labour in Colonial India*, Delhi: Tulika, 2013, pp. 101–7, contains a detailed account and analysis of once such contentious transfer.

20 As early as in 1892, when the proportion of 'lascar' employment in the British merchant marine did not exceed 12.6 per cent, they were reported to have accounted for almost a third of the firemen and trimmers engaged on steamers in the foreign trade. *Manning Committee*, vol. 1, Report, p. 19.

of the steamer (and specifically the liner) crew? To approach this question, we need to step back for a moment to ask whether there were any fundamental differences in the requirements and options of management for the operation of sailing vessels, on the one hand, and those for the operation of steamers, on the other?

Two key differences appear to have been conducive to modalities of 'racial management' in steam shipping: Firstly, the division of labour on steam vessels was, as we have seen already, much more compartmentalized than on sailing ships. On a steamer, labour processes were sharply divided between the two or three departments, each of them with a separate chain of command headed respectively by the chief officer, the chief engineer, and, on passenger liners, the purser.[21] Further compartmentalization took effect within the engine department between the engine-room and stokehold crews and also between engineers, specialized mechanics, stokers, and trimmers. While the latter two occupations were considered unskilled, their work navigated a complex 'zone of uncertainty' nevertheless, which required the autonomous, flexible, and knowledgeable cooperation of workers thereby potentially subverting officers' authority.[22] To supervise this elastic, inherently instable process of cooperation was a highly laborious management task, which, to some extent, could be delegated, however, to foremen like the serangs and tindals. This layer of intermediaries curbed the 'black gang's' autonomy in organizing their work while simultaneously reducing the need for – potentially contentious – end-to-end communication along the chain of command. 'No leading fireman or engine-room petty officer of an ordinary British steamer can compete', wrote Captain W. H. Hood, 'with the engine-room serang in keeping control of the black squad.'[23] In short, the compartmentalized division of labour on a steam vessel created the desire and the means for a partial 'outsourcing' of management tasks. Direct communication was conversely, at least under

21 See p. 12.

22 Cf. Gerstenberger and Welke, *Vom Wind zum Dampf*, p. 199; Valerie Burton, 'The Work and Home Life of Seafarers with Special Reference to the Port of Southampton 1871–1921', doctoral dissertation, London School of Economics, 1988, p. 140. For a narrative account of a perhaps typical conflict between an engineer and the 'black gang', see Karl Helbig, *Seefahrt vor den Feuern. Erinnerungen eines Schiffsheizers*, Hamburg: Hans Georg Prager Verlag, 1987, pp. 275–8.

23 W. H. Hood, *The Blight of Insubordination: The Lascar Question and Rights and Wrongs of the British Shipmaster*, London: Spottiswoode & Co., 1903, p. 50.

standard conditions, less necessary, which permitted and facilitated an 'ethnic' segmentation of the crew.[24]

The second key difference favouring modalities of 'racial management' was grounded both in the technology and in the economics of steam shipping, which exerted a much more rigorous compulsion to secure continuous operation and reduce unavoidable interruptions to a minimum. In navigational terms, a steam vessel's manoeuvrability ceased when the pressure dropped in its boilers. Failing to keep up the pressure while at sea thus put at risk the ship as well as the lives of crew and passengers.[25] Interruptions of the labour process were, therefore, to be avoided at sea under all circumstances. In economic terms, moreover, the much higher capital intensity of steamships as compared to sailing vessels meant that they could not be allowed to lie idle in port, and the decline of maritime freight rates in the late nineteenth century further increased the pressure to cut down on demurrage. To sustain work intensity in ports of call and reduce lay days, fluctuations in labour supply on account of land leave, 'failure to join' or 'desertion' needed to be curbed.[26] Moreover, maintenance work could neither be neglected nor taken care of only in port without risking extended and expensive periods of repair. Much of this work, therefore, had to be dealt with at sea implying a further intensification of work.[27]

The requirement of continuous operation both at sea and in port was perhaps somewhat less compelling in the case of so-called 'tramp steamers' that had longer amortization periods, delivered goods to a port to take up new cargo, and needed more lay days in harbour for this purpose. Crucially, as the profitability of 'tramp' businesses hinged on low shipment costs for bulk commodities, fuel saving often took priority

---

24 For a similar argument emphasizing 'divide and rule' tactics see Laura Tabili, '"A Maritime Race": Masculinity and the Racial Division of Labor in British Merchant Ships, 1900–1939', in Margaret S. Creighton and Lisa Norling (eds), *Iron Men, Wooden Women: Gender and Seafaring in the Atlantic World, 1700–1920*, Baltimore, MD: Johns Hopkins Press, 1996, pp. 181f.

25 Cf. Frank T. Bullen, *The Men of the Merchant Service Being the Polity of the Mercantile Marine for 'Longshore Readers*, London: Smith, Elder & Co., 1900, pp. 308–10.

26 Cf. *MMC*, vol. 2, Evidence, pp. 77, 98.

27 Cf. Gerstenberger and Welke, *Vom Wind zum Dampf*, pp. 190–2; Alston Kennerley, 'Stoking the Boilers: Firemen and Trimmers in British Merchant Ships, 1850–1950', *International Journal of Maritime History* 20, no. 1 (2008), pp. 208–10.

over speed. No loss of time at all could be allowed, however, in the case of the ocean liners that were more costly while having a shorter period of usage as they competed perpetually for size as well as speed. For liners, as opposed to tramps, were running on tight and inflexible schedules, which were determined by the needs of passenger and postal services.[28] In 1898, the P&O Company was, for instance, contractually bound to provide a weekly mail steamer service between London and Bombay within 14.5 days, which meant a reduction of travel time by more than 60 per cent in comparison to the 23 days required twenty-five years earlier.[29]

These key traits of the steamship's (and particularly the liner's) economy heightened the importance of issues of authority and discipline – and they did so in particular ways. In the stokehold, that 'zone of uncertainty', the actual expenditure of labour power required to 'keep up the pressure' was fairly unpredictable. We have heard already that the machinery was proverbially fault-prone and that different qualities of coal varied in caloric value as well as in the proportion of ashes and clinker they would yield. These were, however, only two of the numerous variables that implied strong fluctuations in labour demand.[30] Chronic undermanning on British merchant vessels – a state conceded only reluctantly by the report of the Manning Committee in 1896 – exacerbated the situation, triggered conflicts in the stokehold, or, from the perspective of management, raised problems of safety and discipline.[31]

---

28 Cf. S. G. Sturmey, *British Shipping and World Competition*, London: Athlone Press, 1962, pp. 88, 239f, 249–52. Liners were almost exclusively passenger vessels (which often carried mail and cargo also) before the 1930s when cargo liners became more prevalent. See also Liam Campling and Alejandro Colás, *Capitalism and the Sea: The Maritime Factor in the Modern World*, London: Verso, 2021, pp. 217, 228 and *passim*.

29 House of Commons, *Report from the Select Committee on Shipping Subsidies: Minutes of Evidence*, London: H.M.'s Stationery Office, 1901 (statement by Sir Thomas Sutherland), p. 233 (question 4232).

30 Cf. Kennerley, 'Stoking the Boilers', pp. 208–10; Gerstenberger and Welke, *Vom Wind zum Dampf*, pp. 204–10. For a descriptive account of an incident requiring repair of boilers while at sea, see Helbig, *Seefahrt vor den Feuern*, pp. 275–8.

31 The report stated that the committee had not attempted to 'press charges' of undermanning and insisted that the 'large majority of British ships' was manned adequately, but admitted 'that in certain classes of ships there is a tendency to reduce the number of men, out of proportion to the adoption of improvements in the rig or

Let us return, for a moment, to the logbook entries of the shipmaster of the S.S. *Clinton* regarding the disorderly fireman, Patrick Hughes.[32] The conflict arose, it appears, over unpaid overtime enforced (or, from Hughes's perspective, over wages 'robbed') for the removal of ashes. We can see immediately how 'racial management', namely the employment of Indian firemen on Asiatic Articles, might have made a difference. While working hours remained legally unregulated in British merchant shipping in general,[33] informal work-time arrangements – two four-hour shifts per day in the case of stokers – were considered a customary entitlement by European seafarers and, in principle, even by the shipping industry, though overtime and infringement on rest periods were common.[34] The much-quoted and equally informal 'khalasi watch' system, by contrast, explicitly required 'lascars' to be available whenever needed and was officially acknowledged in 1896.[35] Valentini's 'lascari' dictionary for P&O steamers provided a command formula for this practice: '*Yih log, hamesha taiyar hona, rat-ko, dinko*' ('These people are to be always ready, day and night').[36] In practice, Indian stokers appear to have been often employed in *three* four-hour watches,[37] though the Government of India reported to the ILO in 1929 that *two* four-hour watches were customary as much as for 'white' firemen.[38] In sum, and as

labour-saving appliances of the vessels, and that many vessels which have been referred to in evidence, or reported on by courts of inquiry, have not been so manned as to conduce either to the safety or the well-being of the crews'. *Manning Committee*, vol. 1, Report, p. 6. See also 'Seafarers Under Steam: "Each Task Has Its Man, and Each Man His Place"', Maritime History Archive, More Than a List of Crew, mha.mun.ca.

32 See p. 148.

33 Conrad H. Dixon, 'Seamen and the Law: An Examination of the Impact of Legislation on the British Merchant Seaman's Lot, 1588–1918', doctoral thesis, University College London, 1981, p. 203; Burton, *The Work and Home Life*, pp. 116f; 'Hours of Labour in the Mercantile Marine: Labour Conditions', *International Labour Review* 5, no. 2 (February 1922), pp. 321f (322–8).

34 Cf. *MMC*, vol. 2, Evidence, p. 194. See also Burton, *Work and Home Life*, pp. 116f.

35 *Manning Committee*, vol. 1, Report, p. 20; Hood, *Blight of Subordination*, pp. 48f; *MMC*, vol. 2, Evidence, p. 200.

36 A. I. Valentini, *Lascari-Bât: A Collection of Sentences Used in the Daily Routine of Modern Passenger Steamers, Where Lascars Are Carried as the Deck Crew; Also a Copious English-Lascari Vocabulary*, London: Miller & Sons, 1896 (2nd ed.), p. 15.

37 See, e.g., Liversidge, *Engine-Room Practice*, pp. 23, 30.

38 International Labour Office, International Labour Conference, Thirteenth Session: The Regulation of Hours of Work on Board Ship, ILO: Geneva, 1929, pp. 202–10.

in more openly 'unfree' labour relations, working time was not separated from off time by legal regulation, while 'custom' appears to have been a particularly elastic concept in this case. In conflicts over the length of the working day, the shipmaster would also have had less occasion to feel 'powerless': the exercise of sharp and coercive disciplinary action against a recalcitrant 'lascar' was less likely to be contested in court and, unlike Patrick Hughes, an Indian seafarer would not have been able to sign off in Rio de Janeiro or withdraw legally from the master's authority in any other port outside India.

Yet difference was not merely held up by law and custom. 'Native' firemen were bound into an even steeper and, crucially, *mediated* structure of shipboard hierarchy that reduced (though it did not rule out) the likeliness of direct conflict with the shipmaster on his bridge or the chief engineer down below. For the serangs and tindals, the intermediaries used by British shipping companies to recruit as well as supervise the work of Indian seafarers functioned as a buffer between the 'white' officers and the 'native' crew.[39] 'In a British ship which carries an Indian crew,' wrote Amir Haider Khan in his memoirs, 'it is a sarang through whom the authorities make man [sic] work for unlimited hours' – whose mediation made, in other words, 'khalasi watches' possible.[40] This hierarchical arrangement encumbered an egalitarian tendency emerging, as Valerie Burton has argued, among European stokehold crews that 'worked as gangs, organized and disciplined by their own rules': a need for close cooperation at work the flip side of which was a

39 Balachandran has cautioned that the central role of the serang as a disciplinary agent existed more in the reifying, essentializing minds of British colonizers than in actual practice, which he perceived to be more ambivalent. See esp. Balachandran, *Globalizing Labour?*, pp. 68–78; Gopalan Balachandran, 'Searching for the Sardar: The State, Pre-capitalist Institutions and Human Agency in the Maritime Labour Market, Calcutta, 1880–1935', in B. Stein and S. Subrahmanyam (eds), *Institutions and Economic Change in South Asia*, Delhi: Oxford University Press, 1996, pp. 206–36. I agree that the power of intermediaries was never absolute or uncontested and that recruitment networks were far from all-encompassing and possessed relative stability only. However, my evidence suggests that intermediaries were sufficiently effective to be of practical utility for European shipping companies and that their networks were sufficiently durable to persist for generations and adapt to changing conditions. See esp. Ahuja, 'Networks of Subordination'.

40 Amir Haider Khan, 'I Break with the Old World' (Part I: Nasik manuscript 1939–1942, typed copy with editorial markings by Hasan Gardezi, Pakistan Study Centre, University of Karachi), p. 225. See also p. 228.

tendency towards industrial militancy or, in the employers' dictionary, 'insubordination'.[41] It is not as if relations between 'lascars' and these middlemen were harmonious or free of tension – we do have various accounts of conflict and at times of open confrontation, including an unusually detailed sequential narrative by Amir Haider Khan, which I have analysed closely elsewhere.[42] But serangs possessed means of control over their men that were not available to 'white' officers including, crucially, systematic indebtedness – a contractual bond that was not infrequently reinforced and secured by ties of village or kinship networks.[43]

Family links between Indian crew members appear to have been common even among the lower ratings of the stokehold.[44] Shipping concerns like the P&O favoured such continuity – their nautical inspector reported with some pride that the 'natives' 'stick by the Company. There are men there almost for generations.' The P&O's 'lascars', he added, were 'almost an institution of the company'.[45] A retired shipmaster of the British India Steam Navigation Company (BISN) confirmed that the 'lascar' took 'a greater interest in a ship than the British seaman'.[46] Such statements were repeated time and again but clearly need to be taken with a pinch of salt. For the shipping industry, it was surely easier to keep the moral high ground by conjuring up paternalistic bonds with the 'lascar' while deploring the depravity of British seafarers than by admitting that considerations of cost played a role in the increasing displacement of the latter by the former. And yet, other evidence, including the memoirs and reminiscences of seafarers, corroborate a certain stability of maritime village links in areas as far apart as interior Goa, coastal Gujarat, northern Punjab, and Sylhet in

41 Burton, *The Work and Home Life*, p. 140.

42 Ahuja, 'A Freedom Still Enmeshed'.

43 Cf. Ahuja, 'Networks of Subordination'.

44 The importance of such links for accessing the maritime labour market, for coping with periods of illness and unemployment, as well as for opening up new opportunities of subsistence are discussed repeatedly and at length, for instance, in Amir Haider Khan's autobiographical text 'I Break with the Old World'. See also chapter 13, below.

45 Examination of John Charles Almond, *Manning Committee*, vol. 2, Minutes of Evidence . . . , pp. 582f.

46 Examination of William Cosens, *Manning Committee*, vol. 2, Minutes of Evidence . . . , p. 781.

Eastern Bengal as well as the importance of family links for gaining access to the maritime labour market.[47]

There is also evidence for the fact that the age range of Indian trimmers and firemen was somewhat wider than that of their European colleagues and competitors who were usually younger adults. Between 1891 and 1911, less than a third of all British seamen on foreign-going ships were older than thirty-five, while up to half of the stokehold crew was below thirty.[48] A study of a sample of crew lists even found that, between 1850 and 1950, the average age of British workers in the fire-room was just over thirty.[49] Indian shipping law as well as ILO conventions digressed from European legislation, however, in that they permitted well into the 1930s the employment of Indian adolescents as trimmers and stokers. This was justified by British officials with the fantastic claim that 'in a tropical climate a boy reaches maturity much earlier than in Europe'.[50] Among Indian crews, the recruitment of trimmers in their late teens, at times even at the age of ten or twelve, appears to have been rather common.[51] 'A young man who intends to qualify for employment in the engine-room', an official letter from Bengal stated in 1911, 'usually commences his career as a coal trimmer at about 16 years of age; he seldom goes away in a vessel by himself, but is almost invariably accompanied by a relative holding some post in the engine-room.'[52] At the same time, it was also known that middle-aged men continued to

47 I have explored some of these links in some detail in my 'Networks of Subordination'. See also Yousuf Choudhury, *The Roots and Tales of Bangladeshi Settlers*, Birmingham: Sylheti Social History Group, 1993, pp. 42, 57–9.

48 Valerie Burton, 'Counting Seafarers: The Published Records of the Registry of Merchant Seamen', *Mariner's Mirror* 71, no. 3 (1985), p. 316.

49 Kennerley, 'Stoking the Boilers', p. 202.

50 League of Nations, *International Labour Conference, 2nd Session, Genova 1920*, International Labour Office: Geneva, 1920, p. 146 (Captain Duncan Vines, delegate of the Government of India). See also OIOC, BoMP P/8587, A205–8, A393–95; ibid., P/8838, A49–50 (February 1911): Despatch from Government of India to Secretary of State, 20 October 1910; ibid., P/11535, A35–36 (27 January 1926); R. K. Das, *History of Indian Labour Legislation*, Calcutta: University of Calcutta, 1941, pp. 126–9; E. C. Tsandis, 'International Maritime Labour Law: A Case Study of the ILO's Attempts to Develop Aspects Thereof', doctoral thesis, London School of Economics, 1992, pp. 120–5.

51 See, e.g., Minutes of the Evidence recorded by the Indian Mercantile Marine Committee, n.l., n.d., p. 643.

52 OIOC, BoMP P/8587, A319–20 (July 1911): Letter from the Government of Bengal to the Government of India, Department Commerce & Industry, 29 March 1911.

be recruited by serangs even when their physical strength was beginning to ebb: 'There have been instances of grandfather, father, and son in the same ship', reported the P&O Company's nautical inspector.[53] This permitted a skill transfer that could begin at an earlier age while the experience of seasoned stokers was preserved in the workforce for a longer period and could be utilized for purposes of supervision and on-the-job training. Those in their twenties and thirties could be relied upon for full performance, while Indian village boys were groomed for future service besides taking care of auxiliary tasks. 'Racial management' thus also provided means for the *maintenance of uncertified skill*: a certain stabilization (or, in the nautical inspector's words, 'institutionalization') of the workforce and the harnessing of inter-generational modes of supervision and skill transfer held substantial advantages for managing the 'zone of uncertainty' in the stokehold.

The wider generational scope certainly contributed to the larger size of 'lascar' boiler-room crews exceeding European 'black gangs', as we have seen, often by 50 per cent and sometimes more. If the report of the Manning Committee had conceded in 1896 that undermanning and a 'tendency to reduce the number of men' was endemic in 'certain classes' of British merchant vessels, the simultaneously expanding practice of hiring considerably larger 'lascar' crews begs explanation: at a time when freight rates dropped and shipowners sought to reduce the wage bill, how do we account for what appears to be, at first sight, a case of inadvertent 'excess employment'?[54] Spokesmen of the shipping industry often repeated the above-mentioned and presumably 'scientific' calculations of comparative racial efficiency to justify this unevenness of manning scales, though some also mentioned that the larger size of 'native' crews meant that ships 'are better worked, kept in better order, and generally more efficient as mail and passenger ships than they would be with European crews'.[55]

When official commissions interviewed British seafarers, the respondents would often use a language of white supremacism that denied their

53 Examination of John Charles Almond, *Manning Committee*, vol. 2, Minutes of Evidence . . . , pp. 582f.

54 *Manning Committee*, vol. 1, Report, p. 6.

55 The quote is from the testimony of J. C. Almond, Nautical Inspector of the P&O Company to the Board of Trade's Manning Committee in 1894: *Manning Committee*, vol. 2, Minutes of Evidence . . . , p. 582; see also p. 771, and vol. 1, *Report*, p. 20.

competitors any physical prowess or skill, any efficiency or courage. 'Lascars' were inept in the stokehold, declared, for instance, fireman James Coyle before the Mercantile Martine Committee: 'They could not do the work; they were not strong enough, and absolutely no use. It took four of them to do one Britisher's work.'[56] Thomas Alty, another stoker, appeared less inclined to racial stereotyping, however, as he hinted at uneven relations of power and issues of labour management. He believed that British officers preferred 'foreign' crew because 'they seem to do as they like with them; they think we can speak our mind too freely'. As for numerical proportions, he observed that work in the stokehold was 'very trying, but there are a couple of them ["lascars"] to do the work of only one of our men, *and that makes a lot of difference down in a stokehold*'.[57] Unfortunately, Alty was not questioned any further by the committee on how exactly the employment of more men made 'a lot of difference', but we can find some clues in the statements of other witnesses. Hence several testimonies of shipowners and officials asserted that steam pressure could be kept up more evenly and that coal consumption could be reduced when employing 'native' firemen. The spokesman of the Liverpool Shipowners' Association stated, for instance, that

> the inferiority of the Lascar firemen in physique is an advantage, as he cannot put on a great deal of coal at a time, and he is, therefore, constantly stoking putting on small quantities of coal, so that the steam pressure is evenly maintained. The European fireman, on the other hand, will put on a great deal, and have a rest, and the consequence is loss of pressure, and the result is that ships which employ Lascars are able to keep better time than ships employing European firemen.[58]

The Superintendent of Liverpool's Mercantile Marine Office held the same view:

> A European fireman exposed to the radiant heat of the furnace when opening doors to coal, naturally threw as much coal as possible on the

56 *MMC*, vol. 2, Evidence, pp. 347f.
57 Ibid., pp. 333f. Emphasis added.
58 Ibid., p. 531.

> fires, shut the doors, and rushed away, sometimes on deck to cool – result: reduction of pressure followed by excess. The Asiatic did not care so much for the heat, and was only capable of putting or throwing on a moderate supply, and repeating the operation when necessary – result: uniform pressure and less consumption.[59]

The Board of Trade's principal Marine Department official for London joined the chorus by informing the committee that 'since the introduction of Lascars I am told that the consumption of coal has decreased, and the speed of ships has increased'.[60] If such claims were generally substantiated in the jargon of 'racial management' by referring to the 'lascar's' presumed 'inferior physique' and lesser sensitivity to heat, another more plausible (but for shipowners also somewhat less comfortable) explanation was clearly that less restrictive manning scales enabled the stokehold crew to tend to the fires more efficiently, i.e., to feed them more frequently and regularly with smaller quantities of coal rather than tossing in heavy shovelfuls at longer intervals.

More men made 'a lot of difference', too, with regards to those unending and crucial ancillary tasks like preventing an accumulation of clinker and ashes next to the furnace, which jeopardized the quick repairs of the machinery that could become necessary at any time and had to be seen to, while at sea, without letting off in the production of steam. Certainly, at least some of these maintenance tasks could be taken care of while the ship was in port and when reduced boiler pressure did not pose any danger for the security of the vessel. But, even then, the compulsion to continuity did not cease to matter, since the capital intensity of large steamers and the speed requirements of mail contracts forced their owners to reduce lay days and keep them in perpetual motion.[61]

However, issues of discipline played out quite differently at sea and in port: while at sea, the physical seclusion of the ship made it much harder to break the chains of command that had been forged to

59 Ibid., p. 21.

60 Ibid., p. 137.

61 See footnote 29 of this chapter, above. See also Freda Harcourt, 'British Oceanic Mail Contracts in the Age of Steam, 1838–1914', *Journal of Transport History* 9, no. 1 (1988), p. 15.

impose a rigid hierarchy upon its work processes.[62] For absconding (or 'desertion' in the militarized language of merchant shipping) as a historically widespread means to escape individually from oppressive labour relations was impossible, of course, for as long as the ship was at sea.[63] Moreover, the fact that the safety of vessel, passengers, and crew depended on the continuous production of steam pressure embedded a disciplinarian mechanism in the labour process itself while reinforcing the legitimacy of the ship's structures of authority.[64] In ports of call, the situation was quite different, however. Here, it was considerably easier to evade the authority of ship's officers and engineers by signing off, by overstaying land leave, or by 'jumping ship', which could cause unexpected labour shortages and costly delays.[65]

The steam shipping industry comprised several segments and business models, however, which were not in the same way affected by such shortages and delays. Tramp shipping was less dependent on high speed and punctuality. 'Tramps' could, therefore, put up more easily with underpaid, undermanned, contractually 'freer', radically casualized, and consequently highly unstable crews.[66] As long as proletarian neighbourhoods in port cities like Liverpool or Cardiff

62 I agree with Heide Gerstenberger's argument that the tendency of historians to frame the ship as a 'total institution' is misleading if it suggests that maritime authoritarianism is a direct consequence of shipping technology rather than the result of social choices, negotiations, and conflicts. At the same time, the peculiar position of the ship in social space – mobile *and* secluded when in operation – enables forms of discipline that are more difficult to implement elsewhere. Cf. Heide Gerstenberger, 'Men Apart: The Concept of "Total Institution" and the Analysis of Seafaring', *International Journal of Maritime History* 8, no. 1 (1996).

63 On desertion of workers see Matthias van Rossum and Jeanette Kamp (eds), *Desertion in the Early Modern World: A Comparative History*, London: Bloomsbury, 2016; Marcus Rediker, Titas Chakraborty, and Matthias van Rossum (eds), *A Global History of Runaways: Workers, Mobility, and Capitalism 1600–1850*, Oakland: University of California Press, 2019.

64 Cf. Ahuja, 'A Freedom Still Enmeshed', pp. 109–11.

65 See p. 152.

66 An engineer surveyor of the Board of Trade, extensively quoted in the report of the Manning Committee, described in graphic detail how a process of work intensification had led to serious undermanning and to a decline of maintenance work particularly in the stokeholds of 'cargo steamers' (most of which would have been categorized as 'tramps'). *Manning Committee*, vol. 1, Report, pp. 24f. See also *MMC*, vol. 2, Evidence, pp. 35, 164, 613.

supplied an overabundance of poorly paid and precariously employable firemen, mostly poor 'whites' but also African or Yemeni crew, they were readily hired for tramp stokeholds.[67] Owners seemed to be less concerned about the reputation of these men for drink, for insubordination, and for 'backing out' on contracts after one voyage – a reputation that was partly an expression of class prejudice and partly, as Tony Lane observed, a reflection of behavioural patterns rooted in a culture of casual employment.[68] The situation was different, however, in the upper segment of the industry. 'A liner', aspiring engineers were thus informed by Liversidge's variously reprinted manual,

> steams almost continuously at full speed; stopping for a period of a few hours to coal at ports of call, she steams to her destination, where she may stay from ten to fourteen days. On her return to the home port, after an interval of from one to five weeks, she starts on another voyage. Consequently there is very little time or opportunity for repairs to be made between the terminal ports.[69]

One such schedule was described in more detail:

> The Routine in the P. and O. Service. – The following outline sketch of this routine is given as an example of the general conditions under which a mail steamer is worked. The longest voyage is from London to Sydney, and is about 12,500 miles . . . The principal ports of call and the lengths of stoppages are as follows: Gibraltar; Malta, 8 hours; Brindisi, 14 hours; Port Said, 3 hours; Aden, 6 to 12 hours; Colombo, 18 to 24 hours; King George's Sound, 6 to 8 hours; Adelaide, 12 hours; Melbourne, 36 hours; Sydney, nearly a fortnight.
>
> The tubes of the boilers are swept as far as possible, and all fires are cleaned at each port of call. This requires considerable management

67 For the link between casual employment patterns and the business model of the 'tramp' steamer, see Burton, *Work and Home Life*, esp. pp. 70–4. See also Tabili, '"A Maritime Race"', pp. 177f.

68 Cf. Tony Lane, *Liverpool: City of the Sea* (2nd ed.), Liverpool: Liverpool University Press, 1997, pp. 59–82.

69 Liversidge, *Engine-Room Practice*, p. 29.

> as steam is required for working the cargo, and it is not advisable to light up the auxiliary boiler for short stoppages.[70]

The port time of a liner was thus measured in hours rather than days, and this tight schedule implied that the boilers could not be allowed to cool down in most ports of call. Amir Haider Khan thus remembered from his own childhood days in the early 1910s that he, along with a gang of other Bombay street urchins, was regularly hired by a contractor to clean the smokestacks, flues, and boilers of British steamers. 'The worst of all jobs', he wrote in his memoirs,

> was cleaning the inside of steam boilers. At first they would put out the fire and then hot water and steam pressure were let out. After that an engineer from a ship would open the man-hole cover by loosening the nuts. Thereafter the contractor's men would force small boys into the hot boiler through the manhole, which, due to about two or three months continuous steaming, would not cool down at once. In fact we were forced to get in often when vapours were still coming out, causing burns and suffocation. If our bare skin came into contact with the surface of the metal, we used to get horrible blisters.[71]

If Liversidge believed that cleaning duties in port required 'considerable management', this was mainly a question of coordinating a variety of work tasks and of ensuring the availability of the required workforce.[72] This was, of course, much facilitated if the liner's own crew could be prevented from taking shore leave or even signing off and if they could be deployed to work tasks continuously even during the short stays in port. Accordingly, in the opinion of the superintendent of the Mercantile Marine Office in Liverpool, the fact that 'Lascar and other Asiatic seamen' were 'not given to going on shore at every port' was one of the reasons why it was 'not difficult to understand how they soon were preferred in regular lines'.[73] His Cardiff counterpart added that 'lascars'

70 Ibid., pp. 30–1.
71 Khan, 'I Break with the Old World', part I, p. 151.
72 Liversidge, *Engine-Room Practice*, p. 31.
73 *MMC*, vol. 2, Evidence, p. 21.

remained 'by the ship during her stay in port, and work on board during that period'.[74] The representative of the Liverpool Steamship Owners' Association stated that 'in port all necessary work can be done by Lascars; whilst if you have a European crew, native labour would have to be employed ashore', and his trade union opponent from Birkenhead concurred:[75] 'Where the Lascars are employed no shore gang is employed.'[76] These statements contained some exaggeration: contract workers, including juvenile 'scorfers' or 'scalers' like the ones described for Bombay by Amir Haider Khan, were regularly employed in British ports as well.[77] If a liner was worked by an Indian crew, this merely meant that casual port labour had to be hired in smaller proportions, as a reinforcement for specific tasks and not as a replacement for crew on land leave.

However, if continuous, uninterrupted operation was the crucial problem of labour management on steam-powered ocean liners, no single, inescapable solution for this problem sprang up by itself from either the technology or the economy of the liner. Multiple responses to the problem could emerge from processes of political and social contestation and, in the case of British liner companies, at least two alternative strategies appear to have been found: Valerie Burton has shown that liner companies using Southampton as a home port sought to regularise their liner workforces by increasing their pay and reducing turnover. Average wages of British stokers employed in the liners of Cunard, the American Line, or the White Line thus appear to have been about 20 per cent higher than those paid to firemen serving on tramp steamers. In order to 'counter-balance the attractions of wages in the American mercantile marine and ashore in the United States and Canada', the highest wages were paid in the North Atlantic liner service. The typical stoker serving on these British ocean liners was 'white' and English, a family man settled in Southampton or

74 Ibid., p. 61.

75 Ibid., p. 531. For a similar statement by Captain W. H. Hood, see *Manning Committee*, vol. 2, Minutes of Evidence . . . , p. 581.

76 *MMC*, vol. 2, Evidence, p. 244.

77 James Lynch, a fireman examined by the Manning Committee in 1894 stated that 'the better part of the firemen have been scorfers' and regarded this a kind of 'apprenticeship' period for work in the stokehold. *Manning Committee*, vol. 2, Minutes of Evidence . . . , p. 581. For a graphic description of the employment of older children and adolescents as 'scalers' in early twentieth-century Liverpool, see James Hanley, *Boy*, Bury St. Edmonds: André Deutsch, 1990 (1st ed. 1931), pp. 28–60.

thereabouts and in long-term employment, while Liverpool stokers of often Irish descent were avoided on account of their reputation for carelessness and truculence. Local men were believed to be more likely to remain 'with their ships for the duration of the round voyage' and 'particular preference was given to men who had sailed with the company before'. Labour turnover was much lower accordingly on Southampton liners than on tramp steamers and the desertion rate appears to have been negligible.[78] At the same time, as Burton emphasizes, the 'foreign going passenger liner was, perhaps, the most authoritarian of civilian workplaces and the liner crews the most tightly controlled of all workforces'.[79]

From the mid-nineteenth century onwards, the British India and P&O companies, however, pioneered an alternative approach replacing British crew, and particularly stokers, with Indian seafarers. Even though this process of replacement was in full swing long before the Suez Canal was opened in 1869, P&O chairman and managing director, Sir Thomas Sutherland, strongly linked it to this event when questioned by the House of Commons Shipping Subsidies Committee in 1901.[80] 'When our ships first went through the Suez Canal,' he said, 'we endeavoured to work them entirely by Europeans, but found it impossible to do so owing to intemperance and insubordination.' He conceded that he could 'quite believe that a vessel going at a slow rate of speed, and not being tied down to time, might employ Europeans quite as well in the tropics' but insisted that a mail steamer could not do that. On being questioned whether firing was not 'as hard on a tramp steamer as it is on a regular liner' he retorted that 'a liner, and by that I mean a mail steamer, has to be at each point at a given date, and we found our European crews would not bring us to those given points at those given dates'. Sutherland revealed that – despite the much lower pay of Indian seafarers – about a third of the P&O's annual wage bill was spent on 'natives' by the turn of the century.[81] The Manning Committee observed correspondingly that

78 Burton, *Work and Home Life*, pp. 80–101.

79 Ibid., p. 130.

80 In 1902, the Mercantile Marine Committee assumed that the P&O Company had been manning their ships with 'lascars' for about sixty years. *MMC*, vol. 2, Evidence, p. 296; see also Hood, *The Blight of Insubordination*, p. 13.

81 House of Commons, *Report from the Select Committee on Shipping Subsidies: Minutes of Evidence*, London: H.M.'s Stationery Office, 1901 (statement by Sir Thomas Sutherland), pp. 252, 254 (questions 4598, 4619, 4621).

'Lascar crews' were 'carried principally in the P. & O., British India, and other large liners', which included the Liverpool-based Hall Line as well as the Glaswegian City Line.[82]

If Sutherland emphasized issues of endemic insubordination among British seafarers as well as the climatic conditions of the 'tropics' as the main reasons for his preference for 'native' crews, deeper causes thus seem to lurk behind. Asian stokehold crews could facilitate uninterrupted operation at sea because their size could be augmented, as we have seen, to comprise an internal labour reserve without increasing labour costs. This internal labour reserve permitted a levelling out of the typical fluctuations of workload in the stokehold and the high incidence of sickness in this work environment. It also enabled the employment of an additional layer of subordinate intermediaries to supervise the labour process more closely. Further, this labour reserve allowed for a wider range of age groups among trimmers and firemen than was usual among 'white' British liner crews, thereby preserving skill and providing for its transfer to very young Indian village boys. In sum, the existence of this internal labour reserve explains the repeated insistence of shipping spokesmen that liners could be kept in better shape and that tight schedules were fulfilled more reliably with a 'lascar' crew.[83]

Indian seafarers were quite aware of this management model. Hence Amir Haider Khan, remembering his first attempt to gain seafaring employment with a 'lascar' crew in early 1915, observed that in 'those days in most of the big coal-burning ships were employed some extra men who were signed on as firemen or coal passers' but were in fact deployed to cleaning tasks in the 'engine room or other auxiliary work', and also served as substitutes when regular stokers and trimmers were taken ill.[84] If 'extra men' were recruited in Bombay and Calcutta while 'undermanning' was the rule in British ports, this may well explain

82 *Manning Committee*, vol. 1, Report, p. 20. One of the most vocal public advocates of 'lascar' employment, William Hogg Hood, was a ship master in the service of the Hall Line. *Manning Committee*, vol. 2, Minutes of Evidence, p. 576; for the City Line see p. 52; Hood, *The Blight of Insubordination*, p. 17; *MMC*, vol. 2, Evidence, p. 48. Both companies were eventually absorbed into the Ellerman group.

83 *Manning Committee*, vol. 1, Report, p. 20; vol. 2, Minutes of Evidence . . . , pp. 582, 771, 775; *MMC*, vol. 2, Evidence, pp. 531, 543.

84 Khan, 'I Break with the Old World', part I, p. 156.

why an overseer for the Liverpool shipping company Gillison & Chadwick claimed that one engineer had told him 'he would sooner go for less wages if we would give him Lascars'.[85] The racist stereotypes commonly used to vindicate the larger size of these crews were thus condensed and ideologically supercharged verbalizations of perfectly workable and cost-saving management practices.

If the internal labour reserve of 'lascar' crews facilitated the uninterrupted operation at full capacity of the steamer's power plant at sea, the peculiar combination of immigration law, of the 'Asiatic Articles', and of informal modalities of control through intermediaries served the same purpose while simultaneously tying Indian crews more tightly to their ships even in ports of call. The practice of 'khalasi watches' thus undercut customary work-time arrangements on steamers by asserting the claim to unlimited availability during the voyage. A racialized form of maritime labour contract and anti-Asian immigration restrictions combined to keep the workforce available even in ports of call, push down the rate of attrition, and stabilize the workforce without raising the costs of employment. If similar elements of contractual unfreedom remained, in the twentieth century, justifiable for 'white' wage workers under circumstances of exceptional crisis or war, 'racial management' offered a route of circumvention available at all times: the structural tension between the compulsion to continuity in the labour-intensive work processes of the steamship, on the one hand, and the disruptive potentials of formally 'free' wage labour, on the other, could be resolved, without raising labour costs, through the racialization of labour relations and labour process.[86]

The intricacies of such calculations were rarely spelled out as they were generally presented in those rickety frames of racial taxonomy. Yet, when oil replaced coal and maritime labour relations were, for the second time since the invention of the steamer, fundamentally transformed in other parts of the shipping world, 'racial management' and the privileged access of British shipping companies like the P&O to apparently unlimited reservoirs of colonial labour gave the stokehold stigma of the 'hairy ape' a second if brief span of life.

---

85 *Manning Committee*, vol. 2, Minutes of Evidence . . . , p. 692.

86 Cf. Alessandro Stanziani, *Sailors, Slaves, and Immigrants: Bondage in the Indian Ocean World, 1750–1914*, Basingstoke: Palgrave Macmillan, 2014, pp. 125–33.

11

The Break-Up: Findings, Rulings, and the Limits of 'Racial Management'

In order to understand the daily routines in a steamer's stokehold we moved away, for a while, from the events and narratives surrounding the loss of the S.S. *Egypt*. We had to turn to more generic material like service regulations, engineering manuals, or evidence gathered by government committees to retrace patterns of the everyday, while having no illusions that these texts, despite their authors' ambition to afford comprehensive examination and regulation, succeeded in illuminating the 'zones of uncertainty' in the workings of the stokehold and the other departments of the steamer. Memoirs and visual material have helped us, to some extent, grasp moments of the daily labour process when contingency punctured routine, when experiential skill stood in for failing standard procedure, and when, consequently, cooperation overrode hierarchy. We sought recourse, moreover, to literary sources to recuperate notions of social status and stigma that were forged in the excruciating heat of the stokehold. However, it is in situations of emergency and break-up that the absolute limits of everyday management, including the management of work processes, are fully revealed. Trying to locate the breaking point of 'racial management' in British steam shipping in the early twentieth century, we retrace our steps, therefore, to the files of the *Egypt* inquiry.

The spectre of emergency, and specifically the all-too-real possibility of deadly shipping disasters, had provided legitimacy, more than anything else, to the steep hierarchies imposed on the maritime world of labour since the eighteenth century:[1] 'Democracy in the abstract is all very well *on shore*', wrote a former shipmaster and widely read author on maritime matters around the turn of the century, 'but at sea *the life of all on board often depends on instant, unquestioning obedience*; a ship must be ruled conservative – the competent must govern, not the multitude.'[2] The need to react swiftly and efficiently in moments of peril thus seemed to suggest the inevitability of steep hierarchies and well-oiled chains of command. Lifeboat procedures were, therefore, at least in principle, highly regulated by shipping companies like the P&O and, to some extent, by state authorities, though tight steamer schedules and competition for passengers and mail contracts between rivalling companies precipitated a tendency to cut corners.[3] This had clearly been the case on the S.S. *Egypt*, where Chief Officer Cartwright, who was in charge of lifeboat operations, had dealt with the procedure rather casually, defending himself before the court by asserting that the tight schedule had not permitted him to prepare the 'Collision and Boat Stations Bill' before departure from Tilbury.[4]

The P&O Company provided a standardized, printed form for this mandatory document, which was to be displayed on deck throughout the voyage. While this obligation had been flouted on the *Egypt*'s final

1 For the increasingly disciplinarian tendency in the British merchant marine, see Conrad H. Dixon, 'Seamen and the Law: An Examination of the Impact of Legislation on the British Merchant Seaman's Lot, 1588–1918', doctoral thesis, University College London, 1981, p. 300.

2 Alan Oscar (pseud. of Captain W. B. Whall), *School and Sea Days*, London: Thomas Burleigh, 1901 (quoted in W. H. Hood, *The Blight of Insubordination: The Lascar Question and Rights and Wrongs of the British Shipmaster*, London: Spottiswoode & Co., 1903, p. 19). For a similar denunciation of democracy at sea and a propagation of a 'nautical aristocracy' from the *Sunday Times* in 1912, see Lucy Delap, '"Thus Does Man Prove His Fitness to Be the Master of Things": Shipwrecks, Chivalry and Masculinities in Nineteenth- and Twentieth-Century Britain', *Cultural and Social History* 3, no. 1 (2006), p. 61.

3 For an anonymous shipmaster's critical reflections on the usually slack execution of boat drills on steamers, see 'Ships' Boats and Boat Drill', *Manchester Guardian*, 9 May 1912, p. 16. For the pressures inducing officers to neglect boat drills and the need to scale up safety procedures on passenger steamers see 'The "Egypt" Finding' (letter to the editor by an anonymous officer), *Lloyd's List*, 6 September 1922; 'Our London Correspondence', *Manchester Guardian*, 5 September 1922, p. 6.

4 TNA, TS 34/10 'R.M.S. Egypt: Transcript of Court Proceedings', Eighth Day: 2 August 1922, pp. 121f (Re-examination of Charles Walter Cartwright, Chief Officer, by Mr Darby); 'The "Egypt" Inquiry', *Lloyd's List*, 5 September 1922, p. 11.

voyage, even the Boat Stations Bill prepared for the previous passage merely assigned the British crew members as well as the Goan stewards to a specific lifeboat and station by name and rank, while the spaces for 'Serang', 'Tindal', 'Lascar', 'Coal Trimmer' and other Indian deck and engine-room crew were left void. When this list was submitted to the Court of Inquiry, a note was pinned to it stating that 'the Native Crew, other than the Goanese Stewards, are allotted to boats at Boat Stations Drill and not by this List'.[5]

According to the P&O Company's own rules, lifeboat operations were to be practiced regularly at such 'Boat Stations Drills' to test the chain of command, check on the crew's performance and on the equipment, and familiarize the passengers with the procedure. Crew members were to stand by the boat they had been assigned to; the boats were to be swung out then and lowered into the water.[6] However, after the ship took up passengers as well as new crew for her return voyage to Bombay, a boat drill had been performed in Tilbury on 18 May, as mentioned before, only in the most superficial manner. The Indian crew was simply made to stand in one line when 'boat stations' were exercised while the lifeboats were not lowered, and their life jackets were nowhere to be found. Crucially, the seventy-eight Indian firemen and deckhands who had been 'transferred' to the *Egypt* from another ship before its departure from Tilbury had not been assigned to any specific boat and even those of them who dared to inquire could not get an answer.[7]

Board of Trade regulations stipulated, moreover, that each member of a lifeboat crew was to be 'supplied with a numbered badge corresponding with the number of his boat', but testimonies on whether this regulation was implemented on P&O ships were vague and contradictory.[8]

---

5 TNA, TS 34/9 'R.M.S. Egypt: Exhibits'.

6 TNA, TS 34/8 '"R.M.S. Egypt": Various Proofs and Documents' ('The British Steamship "Egypt" of Greenock, Official No. 105581. Formal Investigation ordered by the Board of Trade . . .', n. d.), detailed brief for the legal counsel of the Board of Trade, pp. 12–14; BL: OIOC, IOR/L/E/7/1123, F. 1989, Commerce & Revenue Department, Loss of the S.S. Egypt (Report of Court on the loss of the S.S. Egypt, 4 September 1922 with Annex, p. 2).

7 See p. 103.

8 TNA, TS 34/8 '"R.M.S. Egypt": various proofs and documents' ('The British Steamship "Egypt" of Greenock, Official No. 105581. Formal Investigation ordered by the Board of Trade . . .', n. d.), detailed brief for the legal counsel of the Board of Trade, p. 15; deposition of Andrew Collyer (Master), p. 2; deposition of Sidney Herbert French (Supernumerary

Moreover, Chief Officer Cartwright's statements leave no doubt that he had never followed the procedure while serving on the S.S. *Egypt.*[9] Further, when questioned by one of the court's assessors why the names of 'native' 'lascars' and firemen were not entered into the Fire and Boat Stations Bill, he responded that 'we found it was useless putting in their names at all': it was 'unnecessary trouble' because 'natives' were solely dealt with through the serang and would, in any case and in distinction to 'Europeans', not know what boat their names were attached to.[10] He alleged that the 'native' stokers would not 'understand' tokens with boat numbers as they were unable to 'decipher the numerals' and was doubtful whether providing 'lascars' 'with some symbol that is equivalent to our numerals' would serve a purpose.[11] That the fireman tindal, Sabdin Fazuldin, had insisted in his deposition and again during his examination that he had not been supplied with a boat *number* did not induce the court to question Cartwright's statements.[12] As a result of such attitudes and practices, a significant part of the crew had received no instructions on what to do in the event of an accident. In a moment of danger, this was to unsettle the ship's state of authority: if the imposition of maritime hierarchy implied a promise of protection in the event of calamity for the entire company of the ship, the neglectful exclusion of 'native' seafarers from generally known safety procedures had put this promise – and thereby hierarchy itself – into question.

The testimonies of British and Indian crew reveal, at least to some degree and despite their inconsistency, where chains of command endured and where they broke in the twenty minutes before the *Egypt* went down. For this purpose, I need to elaborate on some of my earlier

---

Second Mate), p. 19. TNA, TS 34/10 'R.M.S. Egypt: Transcript of Court Proceedings', Second Day: 25 July 1922, p. 5 (Examination of Andrew Collyer, Master); TNA, BT 239/2 '"Egypt" in Collision with "Seine"' (deposition by Mahomed Adam, 2 June 1922).

9 TNA, TS 34/8 '"R.M.S. Egypt": Various Proofs and Documents' ('The British Steamship "Egypt" of Greenock, Official No. 105581. Formal Investigation ordered by the Board of Trade . . ,', n. d.), (second) deposition of Charles Walter Cartwright.

10 TNA, TS 34/10 'R.M.S. Egypt: Transcript of Court Proceedings', Second Day: 25 July 1922, p. 100 (Examination of Charles Walter Cartwright, Chief Officer).

11 Ibid., p. 74.

12 TNA, BT 239/2 '"Egypt" in Collision with "Seine"' (deposition by Sabdeen Fazuldeen, fireman tindal, p. 1); TNA, TS 34/10 'R.M.S. Egypt: Transcript of Court Proceedings', Fifth Day: 28 July 1922, (examination of Sabdeen Fazuldeen, pp. 71, 81). For a corroborating statement, see TNA, BT 239/2 '"Egypt" in Collision with "Seine"' (deposition by Barrum Mustapha, 2 June 1922, p. 1).

findings on the conduct of the rescue operations.[13] Evidently, the chains of command connecting the ship's British officers and Indian crew, especially in the engine room, did not collapse entirely under the impact of the collision. Thomas Whyte, the second engineer who oversaw the engine room at the time, could communicate directly with his Punjabi crew. He was informed immediately after the accident by fireman tindal Sabdin Fazuldin that water was rushing into the stokehold, while Baram Mustafa, another court witness and fireman, recalled telling the engineer that the ship was 'finished'. Fazuldin also assisted Whyte and a couple of British engine-room workers in their attempt to close a bulkhead door.[14] When the engine-room hold had to be given up to the inrushing water and the 'black gang' retreated to the deck, the second engineer reportedly still established his authority over part of his crew, ordering several out of unlaunched lifeboats in which they had sought refuge and involving about twenty of them in various attempts to set boats afloat.[15]

Among the deck crew, however, the chain of command does not seem to have extended beyond the British workforce during these crucial twenty minutes. The steam-operated whistle, we need to remember, could not be used to give the signal for 'boat stations' as the engines were extinguished almost immediately after the collision.[16] Instead Chief Officer Cartwright claimed in court to have sung out the command to launch the boats – an assertion confirmed by British deck crew, but not by any of the Indian seafarers.[17] But Cartwright also made clear, in regard to the latter,

13 See pp. 105–13.

14 TNA, BT 239/2 '"Egypt" in Collision with "Seine"' (depositions by Sabdeen Fazuldeen, fireman tindal, and Barrum Mustapha, fireman, 2 June 1922); Caird Library, P&O Collections, 65/3, f. 303 ('draft statement' of Sabdeen Fazuldeen, p. 4); TNA, TS 34/10 'R.M.S. Egypt: Transcript of Court Proceedings', Fifth Day: 28 July 1922, (examinations and cross-examinations of Sabdeen Fazuldeen, pp. 74, 78; Barrum Mustapha, p. 83).

15 TNA, TS 34/10 'R.M.S. Egypt: Transcript of Court Proceedings' (answers of Thomas Whyte to questions by the British Consul in Brest, n.d.); BL: OIOC, IOR/L/E/7/1123, F. 1989, Commerce & Revenue Department, Loss of the S.S. Egypt (Report of Court on the loss of the S.S. Egypt, 4 September 1922, with Annex), p. 4.

16 TNA, TS 34/8 'R.M.S. Egypt' (deposition by Gordon Dixon Brown, Third Officer, p. 81).

17 TNA, TS 34/8 'R.M.S. Egypt' (deposition of Chief Officer Charles Walter Cartwright, p. 8; depositions by crew and passengers: Sidney Herbert French, Supernumerary Second Mate, p. 15; Donald Gates, boatswain, p. 39; Edward W. Ruskin, quartermaster, pp. 47, 49); NMM, Caird Library, P&O Collections, 65/3 (draft statements of Mohammed Adam, f. 261; Moossa Fackeer, f. 278); TNA, BT 239/2 '"Egypt" in Collision with "Seine"' (deposition by Mahomed Adam, 2 June 1922); TNA, TS 34/10 'R.M.S. Egypt:

that 'personally I do not have any individual dealings at all. I deal through the serang only with the natives.'[18] However, the 'khalasi serang', the sole conduit between the British officers and the Indian deck crew, had been ordered by the second mate to join him in the first useable lifeboat (no. 18) and clear away from the ship before the efforts had even started to swing out and lower the other boats.[19]

Thereafter, apparently, all 'dealings' ended and communication stalled: Cartwright, in his detailed deposition of the last minutes of the *Egypt*, mentioned the 'natives' only to repudiate statements of Indian witnesses that they had asked him for life jackets.[20] When examined in court, he insisted he had not noticed any 'lascars' at all on the boat deck during the rescue operations, despite contrary evidence.[21] If he could not remember the whereabouts of the Indian members of his department, their presence or absence had not been a major concern apparently. The chain of command thus broke – a situation clearly perceived by the Indian crew: we saw that the deck tindal Mohammed Adam, the khalasi Musa Faqir, and the fireman Baram Mustafa testified unequivocally that they had been unable to get clear instructions even after approaching the officers on the bridge.[22]

The S.S. *Egypt* was equipped with eighteen lifeboats, each of them with a capacity of carrying between forty and fifty passengers and crew.[23] The P&O Company's safety instructions directed that boats were to be 'secured outboard at sea whenever practicable'.[24] In fact, only four of the

---

Transcript of Court Proceedings', Fifth Day: 28 July 1922 (examination and cross-examination of Barrum Mustapha, p. 86).

18 TNA, TS 34/10 'R.M.S. Egypt: Transcript of Court Proceedings', Second Day: 25 July 1922, p. 100 (Examination of Charles Walter Cartwright, Chief Officer).

19 Cf. BL: OIOC, IOR/L/E/7/1123, F. 1989, Commerce & Revenue Department, Loss of the S.S. Egypt (Report of Court on the loss of the S.S. Egypt, 4 September 1922, with Annex), p. 3.

20 TNA, TS 34/8 'R.M.S. Egypt' (deposition of Chief Officer Charles Walter Cartwright, p. 7).

21 TNA, TS 34/10 'R.M.S. Egypt: Transcript of Court Proceedings', Second Day: 25 July 1922 (examination of Charles W. Cartwright), pp. 62–4, 67.

22 See p. 103.

23 TNA, TS 34/8 '"R.M.S. Egypt": Various Proofs and Documents' ('The British Steamship "Egypt" of Greenock, Official No. 105581. Formal Investigation ordered by the Board of Trade . . ,', n. d.), detailed brief for the legal counsel of the Board of Trade, p. 17; BL: OIOC, IOR/L/E/7/1123, F. 1989, Commerce & Revenue Department, Loss of the S.S. Egypt (Report of Court on the loss of the S.S. Egypt, 4 September 1922, with Annex), p. 1.

24 TNA, TS 34/8 '"R.M.S. Egypt": Various Proofs and Documents' ('The British Steamship "Egypt" of Greenock, Official No. 105581. Formal Investigation ordered by the Board of Trade . . ,', n. d.), detailed brief for the legal counsel of the Board of Trade, p. 13.

boats had been swung out before the collision, while the remaining fourteen, except a mere two, were jammed in the davits as the ship listed heavily within minutes. Hence altogether only six of the boats could be lowered into the water to receive passengers and crew, though one (no. 4) too late to escape the suction of the sinking ship. Of the remaining twelve boats three were merely cut adrift with the hope they might float off when the ship sank, while the remaining nine were still on their chocks and lashed to the davits when the *Egypt* turned turtle.[25] Captain Collyer, defending himself in court, pointed out that different opinions were held among shipmasters about the wisdom of swinging out lifeboats especially under the conditions of rough weather that had been forecast for the day when the *Egypt* capsized.[26]

This was indeed a moot point in the maritime safety procedures followed at the time.[27] In the case of the *Egypt*, however, chances to swing out and launch the lifeboats evaporated within minutes after the collision as the ship tilted quickly and steeply to the heavily damaged port side. That most boats were 'turned in' thus hampered coordinated rescue operations, but things were made even worse by the fact that large parts of the crew as well as the passengers had not participated in a thorough boat drill and were not aware of the numbers of the boats they were to turn to in the event of emergency. As the court noticed: '*In no case* did the allotted Officer and his crew go to their appropriate boat.'[28] Passengers and crew appear to have approached mainly and randomly the boats on the

25 See Figure 11.1. See also BL: OIOC, IOR/L/E/7/1123, F. 1989, Commerce & Revenue Department, Loss of the S.S. Egypt (Report of Court on the loss of the S.S. Egypt, 4 September 1922, with Annex), pp. 3f; TNA, TS 34/8 '"R.M.S. Egypt": Various Proofs and Documents' ('The British Steamship "Egypt" of Greenock, Official No. 105581. Formal Investigation ordered by the Board of Trade . . .', n. d.), detailed brief for the legal counsel of the Board of Trade, pp. 39–41; TNA, TS 34/9 'R.M.S. Egypt: Exhibits' (tabular summary of lifeboat launching operations).

26 TNA, TS 34/10 'R.M.S. Egypt: Transcript of Court Proceedings', Second Day: 25 July 1922, pp. 32f; BL: OIOC, IOR/L/E/7/1123, F. 1989, Commerce & Revenue Department, Loss of the S.S. Egypt (Report of Court on the loss of the S.S. Egypt, 4 September 1922, with Annex), p. 4.

27 For a technical discussion of the controversial views on the matter of swinging out lifeboats, see John Todd and W. B. Whall, *Practical Seamanship for the Use in the Merchant Service*, London: George Philip & Son, 1905 (5th ed.), pp. 170–4.

28 BL: OIOC, IOR/L/E/7/1123, F. 1989, Commerce & Revenue Department, Loss of the S.S. Egypt (Report of Court on the loss of the S.S. Egypt, 4 September 1922, with Annex), p. 4. Emphasis added.

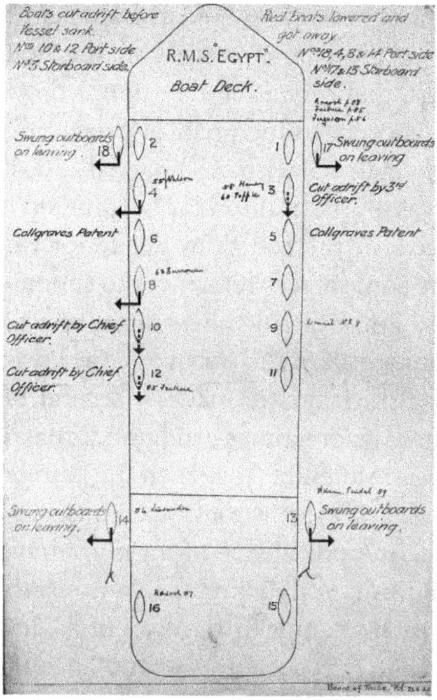

Figure 11.1. Diagram of the eighteen lifeboats of S.S. *Egypt*, drawn up for the court (with arrows added)[30] ↵ ↳ boats swung out and lowered (18, 4, 8, 14, 17, 13) ↓ boats cut loose (10, 12, 3). Source: The National Archives (UK), TS 34/9 'R.M.S. Egypt: Exhibits'.

foredeck and particularly on the starboard side where the lifeboats, with the exception of those swung out already, were hopelessly jammed. At the same time, the boats launched from the afterdeck got away with small numbers of crew and without passengers. Hence boat 17 (starboard foredeck), where the shooting incident occurred, was overcrowded with about seventy-five passengers and crew, while boat 14 (port afterdeck) appears to have rowed away with a mere six members of the crew.[29] Structures of command thus also proved incapable of distributing effectively the available spaces even in those lifeboats that could be launched.[30]

However, when the chain of command disintegrated and hierarchical communication collapsed on board a sinking ship, it may still be asked whether a quick mobilization of lateral, informal modes of

29 Ibid., p. 4; TNA, TS 34/8 '"R.M.S. Egypt": Various Proofs and Documents' (deposition by passengers and crew: Donald Gates, boatswain, p. 40; Horace Lissenden, quartermaster, p. 53).

30 TNA, TS 34/8 '"R.M.S. Egypt": Various Proofs and Documents'.

communication might not have served as a partial substitute? After all, in our discussion of the labour process in the boiler room we have encountered the fact that even everyday labour processes could not be subjected in their entirety to hierarchical procedures. Here, trust and collegial bonds among the 'black gang' enabled a flexible, self-organized cooperation that was a precondition for keeping up the pressure in the boilers. And, indeed, in the court's evidence for the S.S. *Egypt*'s final twenty minutes, we come across references to spontaneous cooperation between Indian and European members of the crew: lifeboat no. 17 that gave refuge to about a fifth of the survivors was lowered by Musa Faqir together with two British quartermasters; several of the 'white' deck-hands acknowledged, if sometimes grudgingly, that 'lascars' had joined them in their desperate attempts to launch the jammed lifeboats.[31] At an even more basic level, if most witness accounts, whether European or Indian, corroborate the prevalence of a rigorous racial dichotomy on board ship, this did not entirely preclude a nonverbal, basic acknowledgement of shared humanity in the way of saving each other from drowning: instances were reported when Indian seafarers pulled 'white' passengers and crew into lifeboats and vice versa.[32]

Nonetheless, the testimonies also show how tenuous the social bonds and how narrow the channels of communication were between the racially defined segments of the crew. They were, I argue, too tenuous and narrow to enable swift, flexible action in self-organized teams in order to improvise rescue operations. Shared work experience did permit, as we have just seen, the distribution of work tasks, but bonds of trust and easy communication were not available as lubricants to speed up work. The limits of communication are indicated by the fact, for instance, that the testimonies of European crew hardly ever distinguished individuals from the 'mass' of Indian workers who were dealt with almost always in the plural, either as a whole or according to their occupational

31 NMM, Caird Library, P&O Collections, 65/3, f. 278 (draft statement of Moossa Fackeer). TNA, TS 34/8 '"R.M.S. Egypt": Various Proofs and Documents' (depositions by passengers and crew: Donald Gates, boatswain, p. 40; David Ferguson, quartermaster, p. 56).

32 See, e.g., TNA, TS 34/8 '"R.M.S. Egypt": Various Proofs and Documents' (depositions by passengers and crew: Walter Frederick Randall, second-class passenger, p. 17; Albert Sheppard, bed-room steward, p. 77); NMM, Caird Library, P&O Collections, 65/3, f. 315 ('draft statement' of Antonio Phillip de Silva, n. d.).

status or ethnicity: they were referred to as 'lascars' or 'coolies', as 'firemen' or 'Goanese'. The 'natives' did not seem to have personal names that could be called out to attract attention at a moment of crisis. Nor did they have to, for everyday purposes: lateral and personalized communication between British and Indian crew was not encouraged as the structures of the ship's hierarchy channelled communication flows through serangs and tindals with longer years of service and often some ability to communicate in English. The same held true between the different segments of the Indian crew. When First Mate Cartwright was asked in court whether 'your lascars have the duty of communicating any orders to the Goanese stewards and the engine room crew', he responded curtly: 'No. They have nothing to do whatever with another.'[33]

No need was perceived, as we have seen, to take the trouble of entering the 'lascars' and stokers' names in the *Egypt*'s Boat Stations Bill.[34] The reduced importance assigned to the Indian seafarer as an individual is also reflected in the official crew list of the S.S. *Egypt*: the pages referring to Indian crew provide us with the names, the date and place of joining the ship, as well as the 'capacity' the respective seafarer was engaged for; further information was not transcribed from agreements or discharge certificates. For European sailors, we find more detailed and personalized data: their age, nationality – and in the case they were British even their birthplace – the ship they had served on previously, the year they had been discharged, and the date when they had signed the current agreement.[35] Indian witnesses, in turn, did distinguish 'white' individuals only by rank or capacity and not by name: Musa Faqir, for instance, recalled that he had served on a previous voyage on the *Macedonia* along with one of the British quartermasters he had joined in lowering lifeboat no. 17. He could even remember that this man had been employed as a baggage master at that time, but he did not know his name.[36]

If British sailors rarely referred to Indian seafarers as individuals, it is evident that they were also unlikely to perceive them as shipmates

33 TNA, TS 34/10 'R.M.S. Egypt: Transcript of Court Proceedings', Second Day: 25 July 1922 (examination of Charles W. Cartwright), p. 52.

34 See p. 184.

35 TNA, TS 34/9 'R.M.S. Egypt: Exhibits' (crew list).

36 NMM, Caird Library, P&O Collections, 65/3, f. 278 (draft statement of Moossa Fackeer).

deserving solidarity. In British testimonies concerning the frantic attempts to launch the *Egypt*'s jammed lifeboats, the cooperation of Indian seafarers was at best mentioned in passing. Even those British crewmen who refrained from accusations and racist slurs did not frame such cooperation, in their testimonies to the court, in terms of a joint collegial effort.[37] When Musa Faqir was shot at by the trigger-happy Captain Carr, the two British sailors whom he had helped to lower the boat did not intervene or testify later in his support. Openly hostile men like the ship's joiner Arthur Popple insisted on referring to Indian crew members as 'coolies', implying an unbridgeable gulf separating these men from 'free' and skilled British sailors.[38]

There appears to have been a hegemonic sense of maritime 'whiteness': an imaginary racial bond that could, at times, even eclipse the stark divisions of class on board a British merchant vessel: Captain Collyer who insisted repeatedly, on being questioned in court, that there was not much to choose between a British and a 'native' crew if they were 'led properly' and that the panic on the foundering *Egypt* had not been confined to Indians, would nevertheless revert to the routinely abusive registers of British shipboard racism when he described direct physical interaction with the latter: on being asked by the solicitor general how many 'natives' had been in his lifeboat, he responded: 'I suppose there were 40 niggers there.'[39]

Both phrases, 'coolie' and 'nigger', were historically charged, of course, with meanings of unfreedom and unrestrained personal subordination under 'white' masters. These meanings translated easily into a sense of entitlement to inflict extrajudicial violence: this was evident in the various testimonies of 'white' passengers and crew on Captain Carr's use of his pistol against Indian seafarers.[40] This was also evident when quartermaster James Henry testified that the 'Third Officer and myself

37 TNA, TS 34/8 '"R.M.S. Egypt": Various Proofs and Documents' (depositions by passengers and crew: Donald Gates, boatswain, p. 40; David Ferguson, quartermaster, p. 56).

38 TNA, TS 34/8 '"R.M.S. Egypt": Various Proofs and Documents' (depositions by passengers and crew: Arthur Popple, joiner, p. 60).

39 TNA, TS 34/10 'R.M.S. Egypt: Transcript of Court Proceedings', Second Day: 25 July 1922 (examination and cross-examination of Captain Andrew Collyer, p. 9).

40 See, e.g., TNA, TS 34/8 '"R.M.S. Egypt": Various Proofs and Documents' (depositions by passengers and crew: Alison Joyce Moore, first-class passenger, p. 12; Mrs Enid Corbould Southby, first-class passenger, p. 13; Harry Scott, quartermaster, p. 44).

succeeded in stopping a few of the Lascars by hitting them with a lump of wood' and when Harry Scott, another quartermaster, boasted in his deposition that he was 'a big man' and that, encountering 'native firemen and Goanese stewards' at the boats he 'simply slung them out of the way'.[41]

The crew was thus deeply divided along the 'colour line' by an employment system amounting to shipboard apartheid. Suspicion, fear, and violence stood in the way of easy and swift cooperation, which could have made a difference when time ran out on a sinking ship. How much difference exactly a more effective work organization would have made was a matter of debate at the time and must remain a matter of speculation, of course.[42] It is evident, however, that the excessive hierarchical stratification and racial segregation of the crew became not just impractical but positively dysfunctional and irrational when the daily work schedule of a steamer was shattered by an accident. Such moments of crisis marked, in other words, the limits of 'racial management' – and did so even more starkly if emergency routines had been neglected as in the case of the S.S. *Egypt*.

Considerations of operational speed, profitability, and managerial efficiency clashed with the communication needs in a moment of crisis: the multiple communication gaps and blockages between the segments of a steamship crew may not have mattered much, and may have even had advantages under everyday conditions from a managerial point of view. On the foundering *Egypt*, however, these gaps and blockages certainly did not facilitate or expedite rescue operations. In this sense, British seamen's unions hit a raw nerve when they brought up the issue of language, even if the communication blockages had deeper causes rooted in a system of racial discrimination, which they chose not to question, and even though their exclusionary deductions oozed with white supremacism and narrowly conceived self-interest.

41 TNA, TS 34/8 '"R.M.S. Egypt": Various Proofs and Documents' (depositions by passengers and crew: James Morris Henry, quartermaster, p. 56; Harry Scott, quartermaster, p. 43).

42 While the court obviously perceived the loss of lives as partly avoidable, Captain Collyer defended himself by stating that the conditions of the accident were 'absolutely abnormal' and that 'the same thing would have happened in any liner on the high seas under the same circumstances'. 'Captain of the Egypt Defends Himself', *Hull Daily Mail*, 6 September 1922, p. 3.

Figure 11.2. Court sketch published in the *Sphere*, 5 August 1922, p. 136. © Illustrated London News Ltd / Mary Evans.

The evidence presented to the court thus points to the limitations of the British shipping industry's variety of 'management by race' – a set of practices that further enhanced the rigidity and deepened the fault lines of one of the historically more extreme regimes of shipboard hierarchy.[43] However, when the court, consisting of the wreck commissioner and four assessors, presented their report on 4 September 1922 after nine days of court hearings in July and the perusal of numerous deposits, their conclusions strongly endorsed the general need for high levels of shipboard hierarchy while emphasizing the specificity of the circumstances of the accident and of the conditions prevailing on the S.S. *Egypt.* The existence of a more fundamental problem was inadvertently acknowledged when they stated, in their analysis of the reasons for the heavy loss of lives, that 'the system failed'.[44] Yet the court's main verdict was comprised in the following sentences:

43 Even though I agree with Heide Gerstenberger's assessment that the ship was not a 'total institution' per se and that excessive hierarchization was no historically persistent trait of shipboard organization, there seems to be a consensus among historians that hierarchies were sharpened on British (and other) ships in the eighteenth century as evidenced in the prevalence of penal contracts in merchant shipping well into the second half of the twentieth century. Cf. Heide Gerstenberger, 'Men Apart: The Concept of "Total Institution" and the Analysis of Seafaring', *International Journal of Maritime History* 8, no. 1 (1996); Dixon, 'Seamen and the Law', p. 300.

44 BL: OIOC, IOR/L/E/7/1123, F. 1989, Commerce & Revenue Department, Loss of the S.S. Egypt (Report of Court on the loss of the S.S. Egypt, 4 September 1922, with Annex), p. 4.

> The loss of life was mainly due to default on the part of the Master and the Chief Officer in failing to take proper measures to safe life; default on their part in failing to exercise their authority to ensure good order and discipline at the time of the casualty; default on their part in failing to make the crew efficient in collision and boat drill; and failure on the part of the owners through their officials and servants to take proper and effective measures to ensure good compliance with their regulations and to exact good discipline on the ship.[45]

The court thus believed that the non-implementation of time-tested standards of hierarchical order and procedure was at the heart of the matter: 'In the case of the "Egypt" there seems to have been a slackness and lack of discipline, which when the hour of trial came prevented proper use being made of the boats.' The court also deplored the decision to send off the serang with the first boat and expressed their doubts as to the officers' ability to converse in 'lascari bat'. They admonished that 'a great Company like the P. and O. Company . . . would do well to take lesson from this unhappy disaster and set for themselves the highest standard of care and efficiency in the future'.[46]

Yet if the court, composed of 'white' men exclusively, were keen to quickly 'get rid' of the few Indian witnesses that had been imposed on them for political reasons by the India Office and the Board of Trade, they were also reluctant to rely for their conclusions on the evidence provided by these unwanted witnesses.[47] The court's bias coloured (or rather 'whitened') their judgment, which repeated and endorsed the formula that 'these men, if properly led, discharge their duties with efficiency and a ready obedience to orders' but stated that 'on this occasion many of them were panic-stricken'. The judgment thus did not fully refute the press campaign of disparagement against the Indian crew and speculated instead that the 'non-European members of the crew would have been kept under effective control, and probably assisted instead of hindering in the saving of life' if only the 'European members of the crew had shown more alacrity . . . in going

45 Ibid., p. 1.
46 Ibid., pp. 4f.
47 See p. 73.

to their allotted boats'.[48] 'The sting is in the tail', commented the nationalist *Bombay Chronicle* pointing out that the court's findings were 'bolstering up with a vengeance, the long-exploded shibboleth about the superiority of the European whether in sea-faring or any other business'.[49] They also 'bolstered up', I may add, the core doctrine of 'racial management', that competent and firm 'white' leadership was indispensable for an efficient utilization of the 'native' capacity for work.

The British press perceived the court's findings as 'sensational', the general tone being that the judgment was 'a stern verdict' but not 'too stern'.[50] While parts of the British public, and particularly the associations of mercantile marine officers, felt that Captain Collyer and First Officer Cartwright had been sacrificed as scapegoats, many papers seemed to agree that the P&O Company had been justly reprimanded.[51] 'If that company has been lulled into a false security by its comparatively clear record of disasters, it is evident that its system of protection for those whom it carries requires a very drastic revision', commented the *Pall Mall Gazette*.[52] The *Economist* chose more guarded language in their otherwise similar comment:

> The judgment reflects on the P. and O. Company, which has a great record for the safe carriage of passengers . . . The judgment recommends an increase of Board of Trade regulations, but it is permissible to doubt whether this would avail much. The great shipping companies are bound, for the preservation of their good name, to take all possible precautions. Probably boat-drill will now be more seriously regarded.[53]

---

48 BL: OIOC, IOR/L/E/7/1123, F. 1989, Commerce & Revenue Department, Loss of the S.S. Egypt (Report of Court on the loss of the S.S. Egypt, 4 September 1922, with Annex), p. 5.

49 'Notes of the Day', *Bombay Chronicle*, 7 September 1922.

50 'Egypt Wreck Sensation', *Pall Mall Gazette*, 4 September 1922, p. 1. See, e.g., 'A Stern Verdict', *Westminster Gazette*, 5 September 1922, p. 6.

51 See, e.g., 'Egypt's Captain. Strong Appeal for His Reinstatement', *Westminster Gazette*, 23 September 1922, p. 3; 'Sequel to Egypt Findings', *Hull Daily Mail*, 8 September 1922, p. 3.

52 'Safety Last!', *Pall Mall Gazette*, 5 September 1922, p. 6.

53 'The "Egypt" Inquiry', *Economist*, 9 September 1922, p. 426. For similar comments see 'Lessons of the Egypt', *The Times*, 5 September 1922, p. 11.

Even before the publication of the court's verdict, the India Office in London had informed the Commerce Department of the Government of India that, according to the press, 'the P&O have come very badly out of the enquiry' and that it seemed 'that they are distinctly uneasy about his findings'.[54] When the court hearings had been concluded, the India Office's legal adviser who had closely followed the proceedings wrote down the following assessment in an internal memorandum:

> In his address to the Court at the close of the inquiry the Solicitor General (Sir Leslie Scott) put the blame on the Company rather than on the crew. The representative of the Amalgamated Marine Workers Union of course attacked the Indian crew and also the P&O Company for employing them. His address was too violent to be effective. The Board of Trade certainly did not attempt to press the case against the Indian crew.[55]

If a reference to the unseemly 'violence' of Joseph Cotter's language sufficed to signify the inability of the trade unionist to retrieve a 'racial dividend' from his investment in imperial social partnership, less proletarian parts of the British public joined his efforts nevertheless to use the *Egypt* inquiry as a lever for the exclusion of Indian seafarers from employment on British ships.

The crudest statement, perhaps, could be found in the widely circulated *John Bull* magazine, which brushed away the court's findings by quoting 'an old saying among sea-captains the world over . . . that "the more tar-brush, the less of the sailor"'. The author felt the need to spell out for his readers 'that a seaman's incompetence increases with the depth of his colour'. The 'lascar's' panic was 'an ineradicable racial characteristic, as much a component part of his atomic structure as is the Britisher's stolidness under similar conditions'. It was, therefore, 'more than time that Government stepped in and cast these unstable

54 NAI, Commerce Department, Lascar Seamen, October 1922, F.Nos. 48–70, f. 31 (F. Noyce, Indian Trade Commissioner, to H. A. F. Lindsay, Secretary to the Government of India, Commerce Department, 17 and 24 August 1922, ff. 30f).

55 BL: OIOC, IOR/L/E/7/1123, F. 1989, Commerce & Revenue Department, Loss of the S.S. Egypt (letter from Edward Chamier, legal adviser, to Arthur Hirtzel, Under-Secretary of State, India Office, 8 August 1922).

wretches out of all good British ships'.[56] A stylistic variant was offered by Lieutenant A. E. Spry, organizing secretary to the British and Foreign Sailors' Society, in his address to the Rotarians of Leicester. Among gentlemanly humanitarians the required idiom was only moderately milder it appears: 'So far as the Lascar was concerned,' the pious philanthropist was quoted by the *Leicester Chronicle*, 'they had only to consider the recent disaster of the Egypt to know what he was worth. It should be made compulsory by legislation that none but British subjects should be employed on British owned ships.'[57] Similarly and one day after the publication of the *Egypt* verdict, an unfazed *Liverpool Echo* insisted that 'Lascar seamen are excellent fine-weather shipmates' but that 'white crews . . . give a better account of themselves when trouble comes along than any other sailors that were ever created'.[58] The *Morning Post*, on the same day, commented that the court's suspension of the captain's certificate and the censure of the first officer had been too harsh while imperial considerations prevented the real issues from being addressed:

> It is unquestionable that the loss of life would have been much smaller with a perfectly disciplined crew. The employment of Lascars and Goanese is not a question for the officers, but for the Company. To discuss it takes one straight into politics of an unprofitable kind, any reflection of the seamanship of Lascars being fiercely resented by Brahmins in India who have never been on a ship and never intend to go. The court has carefully refrained from embarking on this thorny question, and we may follow their example.[59]

In trade union circles, the response to the court's judgment appears to have been rather mixed, suggesting that the seamen's unions' strategic aim of a racially exclusive cross-class alliance with the shipowners was far from uncontroversial. On 6 September 1922, the *Daily Herald*'s editorial thus emphasized that the effort 'made in certain quarters to throw all the blame for the confusion at the boats on to the "panic-stricken

56 'Those – Lascars: Seamen Who Never Were', *John Bull*, 12 August 1922, p. 13.

57 'Plea for British Crews', *Leicester Chronicle*, 2 September 1922, p. 12.

58 'Fine Weather Shipmates', *Liverpool Echo*, 6 September 1922, p. 4. They quoted this from an article by D. H. Bernard previously published in the *Nautical Magazine*.

59 'The Loss of the Egypt', *Morning Post*, 5 September 1922.

Lascars" receives no sort of help from the Court of Enquiry' and expressed the hope in the event of future accidents that 'sapient critics will not immediately start to hurl abuse exclusively and unjustifiably at the lower-paid workers'.[60] Only a page later, however, the *Daily Herald* made space for the opinion of Robert Williams, secretary of the National Transport Workers' Federation, who asserted in an interview with the paper, despite all evidence to the contrary and without qualification, that the Court of Inquiry's findings 'showed, beyond the shadow of a doubt that the accident was due to the P. and O. Co.'s desire for cheapness, employing Lascar crews and throwing white British seamen out of work, on the dole and on the Guardians'.[61] Three weeks later, 'a crowded meeting of seamen and transport workers' in London's borough of Poplar 'expressed admiration of the stand taken by the Marine Workers' Union in connection with the Egypt inquiry'.[62] Yet, as we have seen already, entreating appeals to British 'whiteness' would continue to cut little ice, both with the shipowners and within government circles.

What were the consequences then, if any, of this highly conspicuous shipping disaster and the subsequent closely observed inquiry? British liner companies may indeed have been concerned, after the publication of the court's findings, that their reputation for providing safe passenger services had suffered, and that the employment of Indian seafarers required public justification. A few weeks later, some papers reported that the participation of passengers in boat drills had been made obligatory on liners departing from Southampton, but it turned out that no formal regulation had been passed: the Cunard Company's management had merely urged their shipmasters and the passengers 'to bring forward the boat drill'.[63] When the *Mauretania* departed for New York, the only indication of reform was apparently that 'along the deck the numbers of the boat stations had been freshly painted in large letters'.[64] Liner companies thus sought to reassure the public that they were

60 'The Egypt', *Daily Herald*, 6 September 1922, p. 4. For a similar if ambivalent view see also F. Tanner, 'The Sea Wolves', *The Communist*, 16 September 1922, p. 8.

61 'The Egypt', *Daily Herald*, 6 September 192, p. 5.

62 'Seamen Show Fight', *Daily Herald*, 27 September 1922, p. 6. The representative of that union was Joseph Cotter, who has been mentioned frequently in this book.

63 See, e.g., 'No One Need to Assert Independence', *Dundee Courier*, 16 September 1922, p. 3.

64 'Passengers and Liner Boat Drills', *The Times*, 18 September 1922, p. 7.

LASCARS AT BOAT DRILL.

The Lascar crews of the City liners, City of Exeter and City of Marseilles went through their boat drill and lifeboat races yesterday on the Firth of Clyde, for which prizes were awarded. An officer instructing Lascars to lower a boat.

Figure 11.3. 'Lascars at Boat Drill', *Birmingham Gazette*, 16 September 1922, p. 3. Source: British Newspaper Archives.

tightening their safety procedures and made sure that newspapers were provided with photographs of boat drills – the City Line had pictures printed specifically of 'lascars' releasing and lowering lifeboats (see Figure 11.3).[65]

The P&O Company's management, on their part, were keen to put the accident behind them as quickly and quietly as possible. A campaign sponsored by officers' associations for the reinstatement of Captain Collyer into the company's service was passed over, but the elderly shipmaster was promptly retired on a full pension ahead of schedule,

65 See Figure 11.3: 'Lascars at Boat Drill', *Birmingham Gazette*, 16 September 1922, p. 3. See also *Daily Mirror*, 16 September 1922, pp. 8f. A photo of a boat drill with passengers on a Cunard liner was published for instance in the *Belfast Telegraph*, 28 September 1922, p. 8.

even though his entreaty for a compensation of his income losses was turned down rather impatiently.[66] When, a year later, the British Consul in Brest suggested the erection of a monument to commemorate the victims of the *Egypt* disaster, an internal memorandum for the P&O chairman advised that this suggestion be shelved, 'the circumstances attending the loss of the "Egypt" not being creditable to the Company'.[67]

If the *Egypt* inquiry's impact was insignificant on recruitment policy and superficial on safety procedures, newspaper coverage of shipping accidents continued to follow the entrenched discursive ruts.[68] On 10 September 1922, less than a week after the publication of the results of the *Egypt* inquiry, the foundering of another passenger steamer, the German Hamburg-Amerika Line's *Hammonia*, hit the headlines. The *Hammonia*, carrying 365 passengers, mainly Spanish labour migrants on their way to Cuba, and 192 crew was damaged in a heavy gale off the coast of Portugal and went down eight hours after the accident. The circumstances were thus quite different: there was ample time to launch the lifeboats, and several British merchant vessels responded to the SOS call of the *Hammonia* and assisted in rescue operations. Most lives were saved, though fifteen passengers and four crew went missing. This loss was later ascribed, by the Court of Inquiry in Hamburg, to the circumstance that 'several boats were hastily launched and capsized' due to 'the excitement among the passengers and part of the crew'.

But the emphasis of British newspaper reports lay on the success of the rescue operation and particularly on the fact that British merchant vessels had rushed to help a German ship in distress only a few years after the war. Unsurprisingly, 'British pluck and resource' were celebrated once again, with much emphasis on Captain Day, the shipmaster of the first vessel reaching the damaged *Hammonia*, and on the single

---

66 'Captain of the Egypt. Powerful Plea for His Reinstatement', *Portsmouth Evening News*, 23 September 1922, p. 12. NMM, Caird Library, P&O Collections, 65/2, f. 137f (correspondence between Directors and Captain Andrew Collyer, 14 and 15 September 1922).

67 NMM, Caird Library, P&O Collections, 65/5 (Memorandum for Chairman, writer not stated, 28 August 1923).

68 On a campaign on familiar lines targeting 'negro stokers' after the shipwreck of the *Vestris* in 1928, see Laura Tabili, '"A Maritime Race": Masculinity and the Racial Division of Labor in British Merchant Ships, 1900–1939', in Margaret S. Creighton and Lisa Norling (eds), *Iron Men, Wooden Women: Gender and Seafaring in the Atlantic World, 1700–1920*, Baltimore, MD: Johns Hopkins Press, 1996, pp. 169f and *passim*.

British passenger of the foundering ship. Moreover, in one newspaper report at least, a German passenger, named as 'Erick Huebner', was quoted to have drawn a direct comparison with the *Egypt* disaster: 'It was the Egypt over again, perhaps not quite so bad, but Spaniards excited and in a state of frenzy instead of Lascars.' As might be expected, the racist cliché of the 'Dago' could be easily substituted for that of the 'coolie'.

However, there was a curious twist in this later tale of maritime disaster, which never reached the printing press. British support for a German ship in distress, a mere four years after the armistice, seemed a potent symbolic gesture towards rebuilding the relations between the two countries. Germany's President Friedrich Ebert decided, accordingly, to decorate with bronze or iron plaques the crews of all ships involved in the rescue operation, and the British press reported solemnly on the conferral of these plaques to Captain Day and other British crew members. One of the involved ships, however, the S.S. *City of Valencia*, had been manned with a crew recruited, in part, from districts of Eastern Bengal. Based on the crew lists, the German Reichspräsident thus conferred 'iron plaques' on twelve Indian seafarers. The British Board of Trade and the Foreign Office, in late 1923, requested that the India Office ensure the awards were forwarded, which set off a sluggish bureaucratic process that was concluded only in 1929 – some seven years after the accident and four after Friedrich Ebert's demise. The correspondence file ends with the confirmation that an 'iron plaque' had been 'made over' in the presence of a sub-divisional officer to 'Sahid (son of Ofazoody)' in Narail, Jessore District, Bengal. The India Office's file contains a list of twelve corrected names of 'lascars' with their respective home addresses – crew of a ship that took on board some of the rescued passengers of the *Hammonia*.[69]

If the involvement of Indian seafarers in a peacetime shipping accident resulted, in this case, in a documentation of their personal names, this list never made it into the British press. As with the *Egypt* inquiry: the name of the 'native' might be recorded for bureaucratic purposes, was rarely used in the interactions of a hierarchical labour process, and

69 BL: OIOC, IOR/L/E/7/1355, F. 3469, Economic and Overseas Department, Seamen: Award by German President of Iron Plaques to certain Lascar seamen. I thank Svenja von Jan for alerting me to this case and file.

seemed to be unmentionable in public discourse. This fugaciousness and frequent evaporation of the 'native seafarer's' name is evident, too, in the confidential records of the *Egypt* case: we will never be able to establish conclusively whether that ship carried a fireman known to his mates by the name 'Kara' and whether he was killed, as Baram Mustafa asserted, by a British officer who was clearly identifiable as Captain Douglas G. Carr of the 120th Prince of Wales's Rajputana Infantry. For the court did not try to ascertain how many Indian seafarers had been injured with the army man's revolver, nor does the issue of personal compensation for these injuries crop up anywhere in the diverse material on the loss of the *Egypt*.

The anonymity of the 'native seafarer', I argue, was not merely a discursive convention: it was an essential component of the excessively hierarchical and segregated structures of 'racial management' – a historically specific modality of organizing the labour process that was sufficiently profitable at the time to be adopted by major players of the British shipping industry. The reverse side of 'racial management' was a racially radicalized alienation and dehumanization of the worker, one concrete expression of which was that 'lascars' were even more likely than precarious European seamen to be represented as nameless elements of a 'mass'. This namelessness of the 'native seafarer' pointed simultaneously to the limitations of this management model and did so specifically, as we have seen, in situations of emergency. 'Racial management' on a merchant steamer was profitable only at the cost of being socially wasteful of human energy at the best of times and of being positively dysfunctional under strain. The *Egypt* disaster turned the glossy appearance of capitalist rationality limpid to reveal, for a brief moment, the underlying patterns of capitalist irrationality – irrationality both in the practices of labour management and in the racist discourses that tried to make sense of these practices.

12

Course Adjustment: The Names of the 'Native'

This is where the drama of the 'natives' of the S.S. *Egypt* ends. In its final act, I have emphasized the constraints encountered by the various actors that entered the stage as the drama unfolded. This book could, too, be concluded at this point: explanations have been offered both for the prevalence and for the limitations of 'racial management' in early twentieth-century merchant shipping. But, if we left off here, an argumentative paradox would be left unresolved: I have proposed that strategies of management-by-ethnicity had a practical utility for British shipowners and helped them to withstand, for some time, the heightened competition in the global shipping industry and compensate for the growing technological obsolescence of the British merchant fleet after the First World War. For the 'native seafarer', this implied conversely a process of racially radicalized alienation, of depersonalization, and of silencing. But, and here comes the catch, if the voices of these seafarers were thus muted, if only scraps of their interjections can be heard, if their pleas were muffled by thick filters of legal proceedings and translations, how can we be sure that the efficacy of these strategies of 'racial management' was not merely claimed by their proponents, not just wishful thinking on the part of shipping industrialists and officers of the merchant marine, but actually ingrained in everyday management practices?

The point is sure to be raised by today's historians, historians shaped by an intellectual climate where the labour of emancipating history from the grip of the victors – Walter Benjamin's conception of history – tends to be replaced by a reluctance to present subalterns as victims.[1] And yes, if the historian focused exclusively on structures of subjection and victimization, this was surely problematic as it would endorse the workers' reduction to mere objects of management. The implication would be that they were comprehensively incapacitated to express their subjective will or 'agency'. Such a perspective would be not only implausible and historically untenable but would present as inescapable the very structures it undertook to critique. It would thereby unwittingly endow these structures with the justification of being without alternative. However, the critique of 'victimologies' can be equally unsatisfactory on methodological and equally suspect on political grounds, if such critique is accompanied, as is often the case, with a rather cavalier approach to the analysis of concrete labour relations and processes, i.e., of regimes of exploitation, control, and, yes, of victimization. For, if the fortifications of social power remain unreconnoitered and uncharted – the fortifications that the subordinated are up against in their attempts to make the best of their lives and those of their children – narratives of 'appropriation' and 'agency' may, again unwittingly, blend into a belittlement and twisted apology of capitalist regimes of exploitation, of domination, and of victimization.

If this book was a boat, one might say that after making some leeway towards the Scylla of 'victimology' it was now high time for us to steer clear of that sea monster's tentacles, adjust the course, and bear down, for a moment at least, on the Charybdis of 'agenciology'. Yet this tacking manoeuvre requires, in the final chapter of this book, a change of gear and a conscious break in the narrative: I now need to abandon the wreck of the S.S. *Egypt* and reshelve the newspaper reports, official letters, and judicial records covering the sinking of that ship. Instead, I must turn to material that allows us to perceive how Indian seafarers strained against the limits of possibility at that time, and to what extent they succeeded in expanding them. For this purpose, I will now take a closer look at some

1 See esp. paragraph VII of Walter Benjamin's 'On the Concept of History', in *Selected Writings*, vol. 4, *1938–1940*, ed. Howard Eiland and Michael W. Jennings, Cambridge, MA: Belknap Press, 2003, p. 391f.

Figure 12.1 Amir Haider Khan (1900–1989). Photograph taken in Bombay in 1939. Source: Communist Party of India Archives, Ajoy Bhawan, New Delhi.

incidents remembered in an unusual autobiographical account of an Indian stoker's seafaring career.[2]

Amir Haider Khan (1900–1989) was the youngest son of a smallholding peasant family in the hills of Northwest Punjab – a family whose hold over their land and social position began to slip after the early death

2 Hasan Gardezi, in a commendable labour of love, edited Amir Haider Khan's autobiographical writings, merged the most substantial ones into a single autobiography, and summarized the remainder in his postscript. This important edition was published as *Chains to Lose: Life and Struggles of a Revolutionary: Memoirs of Dada Amir Haider Khan*, Karachi: Pakistan Study Centre, 2007. The preserved typescripts, on which this edition was based, consist, however, of an extensive text of 953 pages that was written in Nasik Central Jail (India) between 1940 and 1942, and of several smaller manuscripts that were written in the early half of the 1970s in Pakistan. In this book, I have used the typescripts of these various manuscripts, the originals of which are preserved at the Pakistan Study Centre at the University of Karachi. I have generally disregarded the edits and abridgements, which Hasan Gardezi considered necessary to enhance readability.

of Khan's father. With little schooling and after a period of casual employment as a child labourer in the port of Bombay, his seafaring life began at the age of fifteen, when he joined the Indian stokehold crew of a hospital ship sent out to Basra to serve the British imperial troops in Mesopotamia. For about three years, until the beginning of the year 1918, he was variously employed on British hospital ships and merchant steamers as a coal passer, a fireman, and eventually as an oiler.[3] His detailed accounts of labour-intensive, life-draining management practices in British shipping, of shipboard hierarchies, and the denial of physical and social mobility have been referred to in earlier chapters. Yet his memoirs are more unusual in that they permit a close-up view of the causes, modalities, and dynamics of shipboard conflict.[4] And it is in this context that experiences of racial subordination in the British merchant marine were deeply engraved in his memory.

Two such instances occurred within the space of a few days in early 1916 after he reached London from Colombo on a freighter of the City and Ellerman Line. Amir Haider Khan recalled having been 'transferred', along with a group of Punjabi trimmers and firemen, to a large cargo steamer of the same shipping concern, which was being readied for its maiden voyage around the world from West Hartlepool. The first incident took place when the Indian stokehold crew was disembarked for the transfer:

> Hence 20 of us were ordered to get ready immediately. Indeed there was nothing for us to get ready except to wash off some black and dirt of the flues and boilers with which our whole bodies were covered from top to toe. However we were ready within two hours after bathing and changing into some clean cotton overall or ordinary linen clothes which are used by poor Punjabis in streets of Bombay. Unfortunately it was not Bombay, but it was London; that too, in the earlier spring when still there was cold. But it could not

3 Amir Haider Khan, 'I Break with the Old World' (Part I: Nasik manuscript 1939–1942, typed copy with editorial markings by Hasan Gardezi, Pakistan Study Centre, University of Karachi), pp. 159–279.

4 I have analysed his accounts of such conflicts on a British steamer at length in 'A Freedom Still Enmeshed in Servitude: The Unruly "Lascars" of the S.S. City of Manila or, a Micro-History of the "Free Labour" Problem', in Ravi Ahuja (ed.), *Working Lives and Worker Militancy: The Politics of Labour in Colonial India*, Delhi: Tulika, 2013.

> be helped since we had nothing else to put on. In the meantime, there came near the ship down in the dock an open horse waggon in which we had to load all our dirty beddings, mats, the ugly looking wooden boxes and all other paraphernalia. Shortly we were ordered off from the ship down into the dock. From there we had to follow behind the horsewaggon, which was loaded with our belongings, through some of the London streets without knowing as to where we were going. But in the olden days the galley slaves were never told about their destination. In the eyes of our civilized British masters we were not any better.
>
> With our troubled, starved and clumsy appearance, with our heterogeneous cotton clothes, and with the dissimilar footwear and head gears, with our bed-bug-ridden beddings, mats, boxes and other things on the waggon (and behind it our procession!) we were an awful scene.
>
> But we appeared very amusing to the civilized Londoners, who grinned and some even openly laughed at us, as if we were an object of ridicule and fun-making and some street urchins even followed us some distance as if we were a circus or a carnival.[5]

If this scene was etched into Amir Haider Khan's memory in photographic detail, this may well indicate the degree of humiliation he felt at the time. Racist behaviour always sets the 'foreigner' apart for being 'different', of course, but this incident had more specific features: the 'native' stokers were 'laughing stock' in the original meaning of the phrase: they were deemed ridiculous because they had been forcibly locked into a shameful, demeaning position. They were paraded through the streets of London as a group whose 'strange' and miserable appearance was not of their own choosing and making. If Amir Haider Khan used the analogy of the 'galley slave' – as he did repeatedly in his manuscript – this was surely coloured by political views he embraced several years later, and more specifically by his espousal of the long-established labour movement denouncement of 'wage slavery'.[6] Yet that analogy was deployed here not merely as a polemical standard phrase: it resonated strongly and concretely with the lived experience of degrading coercion.

---

5 Khan, 'I Break with the Old World', part I, pp. 212f.

6 Cf. ibid., pp. 750, 810, 823.

Soon after, a second incident occurred, which Amir Haider Khan recalled, too, in lively detail. On reaching their new workplace and after joining a 'black gang' newly assembled by way of transfer from various vessels, a conflict arose between Amir Haider Khan's group of stokers and the engine-room serang who had been recruited along with another segment of the crew. While the serang had some standing as well as family connections among the latter group of stokers, his authority was challenged when he demanded from Amir Haider Khan's party the payment of dues that appeared to exceed the *dasturi* (or customary) fees usually collected by such intermediaries and foremen. The conflict escalated and eventually the larger part of the stokehold crew forced their way off the ship, pushing aside the British officers and quartermasters who attempted to block the gangway.[7] When the protesting Punjabi stokers made their way to the shipping master to lodge a complaint and demand the dismissal of the serang, British workers looked on. 'There were many other workmen,' remembered Amir Haider Khan,

> mechanics and engineers from the shipyard who were on board. Some workmen were working on the deck and round about there. They also had their eyes on us. They were talking to each other. We could not understand it but it seemed from their faces that all these white-skinned people were discussing among themselves with great amusement about our walking off from the ship at an English port. It was something new and strange to them. They never expected such unanimous and spontaneous protest from the galley slaves like us. Nevertheless, they all were watching everything with mischievous curiosity.
>
> I called their watching us mischievous curiosity because they knew that at that time there was no labour union or labour movement in India while in England the labour movement had already a long history. They all were members of various labour and trade union organizations. But no one from amongst them approached us as a worker to advise us[,] the other workers who were on strike, or to give us any help. They watched us as any other indifferent spectators [*sic*] would watch a play or tamasha.

7 Ibid., pp. 216–25. See also Ahuja, 'A Freedom Still Enmeshed', pp. 103–7.

> They might have been workers in relation to their employers. But in their relation to us they behaved and acted so indifferently as if they were the members of the same ruling class who ruled our country.[8]

Amir Haider Khan's reflections on this incident imply his awareness, when writing these lines more than two decades later as a political prisoner in colonial India, that this scene might have played out differently in other circumstances: the Indian stokers might have been perceived as 'the other workers who were on strike' and at least one of the unionized British labourers might have 'approached us as a worker'. But they did not, and the humiliating memory stuck of having been perceived collectively as an outlandish travesty, as a ludicrous *tamasha*. In the first incident, the Punjabi stokers had been paraded past jeering British bystanders, while in the second their collective entry on the stage was a self-willed act of insubordination. Yet, if the segmentation – rather than diversity – of the maritime workforce of imperial Britain allowed for a parade in tatters that turned hard-working stokers into racially stigmatized laughing stock, the second incident showed that even industrial action was no safe method for overcoming segregation and stigma.

The encapsulation of 'native' crews in a British imperial setting appeared at other levels, too, during this conflict. An elementary problem faced by the crew when approaching the harbour authorities in West Hartlepool was the issue of how to even make their grievances and demands understood. Apart, perhaps, from his reckless youthfulness, the reason sixteen-year-old Amir Haider Khan was elected the crew's single spokesman was that he was the only one among them with the reputation of knowing some English. In fact, he recalled, his comprehension of that language was very limited at the time, while he could utter barely a handful of words. But even this rudimentary level of linguistic skill had neither been acquired on account of his work in the port of Bombay, the commercial hub of 'British India', nor while toiling in the boiler rooms of British steamers. Rather, it had been the extraordinary, war-related circumstance of being confronted with numerous British soldiers in Basra that had given him occasion to pick up some stray words and phrases.[9]

---

8 Khan, 'I Break with the Old World', part I, pp. 218f.

9 Ibid., p. 220.

We may well ask ourselves at this point why Amir Haider Khan bothered, on this background, to write his memoirs. And indeed, the very first sentence of his earliest and most extensive manuscript reads: 'It is almost impossible to write or narrate about something in which one never has taken any interest.'[10] This sentence, edited out of the published version of the autobiography, should give us some pause. Across the globe, working-class memoirs are, of course, less likely to be written and preserved not only because working people have less favourable conditions for producing them, but also because the sense of entitlement to having one's life history read and passed down to posterity is more prevalent among the privileged few: presumably 'common people' or, as the equally telltale North Indian phrase has it, *chote log* ('small people') do not often believe they have grand life histories to tell nor are they expected to do so. Indian seafarers, too, were unlikely autobiographers though several efforts have been made, since the 1970s, by academics and community activists to record life histories of 'lascars' who had worked on British vessels in the 1930s and 1940s.[11]

Yet even these accounts focus on memories of recruitment, of port leave, or of times when seafaring careers were left for more promising avenues towards social respectability: 'jumping ship' in Britain or North America is often the beginning rather than the end of their story. The experiences of ship-work rarely figure or are touched upon only in passing – dramatic wartime events giving occasion for exceptions.[12] Amir Haider Khan's memoirs, exceptional as they are, offer some explanation for these glaring 'memory gaps': accounts of exploitation and humiliation, of racially radicalized alienation and depersonalization were hardly a source of pride. Moreover, and as for the everyday experience of work itself, the requirement of uncertified

---

10 Ibid., p. 1.

11 For Britain see esp. Caroline Adams (ed.), *Across Seven Seas and Thirteen Rivers: Life Histories of Pioneer Sylheti Settlers in Britain*, London: Eastside Books, 1994 (1987); Yousuf Choudhury, *The Roots and Tales of Bangladeshi Settlers*, Birmingham: Sylheti Social History Group, 1993. For North America see Vivek Bald, *Bengali Harlem and the Lost Histories of South Asian America*, Cambridge, MA: Harvard University Press, 2013.

12 Cf. Yousuf Choudhury, *Sons of the Empire: Oral History from the Bangladeshi Seamen Who Served on British Ships during the 1939–45 War*, Birmingham: Sylheti Social History Group, 1995. See also Tony Lane, *The Merchant Seamen's War*, Manchester: Manchester University Press, 1990, pp. 187f (fn 88).

skills and very high levels of labour intensity did not preclude a grating repetitiveness and sheer boredom, which Amir Haider Khan pointed out time and again.[13] Stokehold yarns were thus unlikely to hold the attention even of one's own close kin let alone enhance one's recognition within the community. Why, then, should they attract a wider audience?

And yet, Amir Haider Khan did write his memoirs. In part, this was certainly a consequence of his later life as a communist militant. Most immediately, the largest part of his autobiographical writings, dealing with his childhood, youth, and young adulthood until 1926, were drafted during his third term of political imprisonment in 'British India' from 1940 to 1942.[14] He responded to these years of confinement with a strong urge to discipline his mind by way of systematic remembrance to withstand the psychological strain and keep up his mental health.[15] Intellectual influences were no less important: in the Soviet Union, he had observed that proletarian memoirs were encouraged, with Maksim Gorky's autobiographical novels providing a model for writings that undertook to expose the narrowness of life and the human devastations imminent to class societies.[16] This, too, was the political justification, which Amir Haider Khan offered in retrospect, for writing down his early life history: he saw his task in 'expos[ing] everything bad in society, no matter how ugly it may be; those who do not like it, let them work for ending the same'.[17] While Khan's early autobiographical writings are indeed replete with such memories of 'ugliness' and include, like Gorky's novel *My Childhood*, vicious instances of social brutalization among the lower classes, they cannot

13 Khan, 'I Break with the Old World', part I, pp. 182, 227, 335, 341, 362, 549.

14 See footnote 2 of this chapter.

15 Amir Haider Khan, 'A Little Poison' (handwritten eight-page manuscript, undated but written c. 1974, continuation of manuscript 'My Discovery of South India', Pakistan Study Centre, University of Karachi), pp. 98–102; Khan, 'I Break with the Old World', part I, preface.

16 Maksim Gorky, *My Childhood*, transl. Ronald Wilks, Baltimore: Penguin, 1977, p. 25. See also Georg Lukács, 'Maxim Gorki: Die menschliche Komödie des vorrevolutionären Russland', in *Probleme des Realismus II* (Georg Lukács Werke, vol. 5), Berlin: Luchterhand, 1964, p. 299.

17 Amir Haider Khan, 'My Experiences with Preventive Detention' (handwritten introductory letter to the manuscript, dated 11 October 1974, Rawalpindi, Pakistan Study Centre, University of Karachi), p. 4.

be reduced to any presumably uniform pattern of the communist working-class autobiography.[18]

The space he gives to work routines, labour processes, workplace relations, and work accidents seems excessive for the standards of this genre also. Even the manuscript's attentive and sympathetic editor felt that some abridgement of 'overly exhaustive' sections was called for to increase the text's readability.[19] Yet to me the memoirs' consistent focus on minute details of stokehold and engine-room work does not appear as the awkward meandering of an unpractised writer. Rather, they were central to the image the author wished to convey of his younger self and of the influences that had shaped his thinking and his approach to life. As Antonio Gramsci observed, the worker's adaptation to the repetitive rhythms of industrial machinery 'leaves his brain free and unencumbered for other occupations': 'not only does the worker think, but the fact that he gets no immediate satisfaction from his work and realises that they are trying to reduce him to a trained gorilla, *can* lead him to a train of thought that is far from conformist.'[20] That Amir Haider Khan could realize this nonconformist potential for himself, that he could turn industrial work experience into a source of confident self-assertion (rather than silent shame or a desperate sense of 'non-belonging') was more easily possible because this experience *changed* over time.[21] He could compare different industrial work regimes, which thereby became perceivable to him not as an immutable given, but as a configuration of socially shaped and *changeable* practices. Even though 'wage slavery' persisted as a hard limiting frame ('I had to do it, but I never liked it'), the transformation of his work experience permitted to develop self-confidence and pride in growing technical skills and enabled him to anticipate even the possibility of unalienated work.[22]

So, what happened? Early in 1918, Amir Haider Khan, together with another Indian stoker, 'jumped ship' in New York City on a cold winter

---

18 See, for instance, James R. Barrett, 'Was the Personal Political? Reading the Autobiography of American Communism', *International Review of Social History* 53, no. 3, pp. 395–423.

19 Hasan N. Gardezi (ed.), *Chains to Lose: Life and Struggles of a Revolutionary. Memoirs of Dada Amir Haider Khan*, Karachi: Pakistan Study Centre, 2007, vol. I, p. xvi.

20 Antonio Gramsci, *Selections from Prison Notebooks*, ed. Q. Hoare and G. Nowell Smith, London: Lawrence & Wishart, 1991 (1st ed. 1971), pp. 309f. Emphasis added.

21 Cf. my discussion of Eugene O'Neill's 'hairy ape' in chapter 9, above.

22 Khan, 'I Break with the Old World', part I, p. 823.

day. They had thus prised open, in an illegal act, the 'capsule' of racial segregation that had shaped and delimited, to a large extent, their working lives in a British imperial labour force. That this 'capsule' had burst is reflected by an immediate though probably unconscious shift in the autobiographical narrative: so far, non-Indian individuals had only cropped up in Amir Haider Khan's life history as figures of authority or enmity, such as the shipmaster who sought to restore discipline 'in his funny Hindustani with great seriousness' or the 'husky' British engineer who indulged in thrashing Gulam Haider, a 'small frail' oiler.[23] As on the S.S. *Egypt*, even such direct confrontations did not imply that the name of the other person was revealed and communicated. The act of 'desertion', however, set off interpersonal encounters that were not entirely or not at all governed by considerations of self-interest:[24] the Jewish shopkeeper in the dock area who suggested that they jump ship and helped them find their feet in an alien environment, the African American landlady who opened her house to those tattered foreigners at midnight and took care they could keep out of sight for as long as their ship was in port, even a young British seaman who shared his knowledge on how to use wartime decrees for securing legal employment status in the US.[25]

These were the United States of Jim Crow laws and Chinese Exclusion Acts, of course, and racism was absent neither in maritime employment relations nor in Amir Haider Khan's own work experiences on US steamers in the following four years. If he encountered, before the end of the war, racist hostility from 'white' fellow workers who refused to work alongside 'coloured' stokers, he associated these men with the retrograde atmosphere of the US South.[26] But the decline of post-war maritime employment, he felt, brought exclusionary racism up to New York, the city he had come to regard his cosmopolitan 'home port'. Here, in 1922, the very year when trade union leader Andrew Furuseth used the commotion around the *Egypt* shipwreck to renew the case for an exclusion of Asian seafarers from employment on US merchant vessels, he met twice over with

23 Ibid., pp. 223, 269.

24 This shift has been pointed out by Vivek Bald in his fine analysis of Amir Haider Khan's account of his American years. Bald, *Bengali Harlem*, p. 152.

25 Khan, 'I Break with the Old World', part I, pp. 278f, 283f, 281–3, 285.

26 Ibid., pp. 368, 440f, 445.

the outright refusal of unabashedly racist chief engineers to work with him in open disregard of the contracts issued by the port's shipping office.[27] Deeply offended, he turned away from the waterfront to look for industrial employment in mainland North America.[28] And yet, contrasting his life on British ships with the conditions on US steamers, Amir Haider Khan concluded:

> Apart from equal treatment with others in every respect I was at times even more assertive than some of the Americans themselves. In every respect there was a World of difference. I attributed all these things, at that time to the glorious U.S. of America[,] 'the sweet land of liberty'[,] which was [the] dominant spirit of the American people.[29]

If, in hindsight, he smiled at his youthful adoration of American 'spirit', he notably did not question his having found indeed 'a World of difference' in the stokeholds of US steamers. And if he capitalized 'World', he underlined thereby that he was not using the phrase lightly. Recalling the day of his departure from India on the ship he would soon 'jump' in New York, he had stated already that it marked his 'entirely parting with [the] Hindustani outlook on life'.[30] 'I Break with the Old World' was, significantly, the title he gave to the *entire* manuscript, which he began to write in 1940 with the intention of covering his life history from his early childhood up to his third internment at the beginning of the Second World War.[31] In the United States he believed, for the first time and for several years, to have entered 'a new world', a land of liberty and freedom of contract: this was his first 'break with the old world' with momentous consequences at various levels and most immediately for his working life.

When recalling 'equal treatment with others in every respect', however, he was clearly not suggesting the absence of racist discrimination, but

27 'Furuseth Warns Americans of Sea Danger from Cheap Labor', *Labor World*, 3 June 1922, p. 2.

28 Khan, 'I Break with the Old World', part I, pp. 590–3, 666–70.

29 Ibid., p. 493; see also p. 550.

30 Ibid., p. 273.

31 Ibid., p. 1; Khan, 'I Break with the Old World' (Part II: Rawalpindi manuscript 1970s, typed copy with editorial markings by Hasan Gardezi, Pakistan Study Centre, University of Karachi), p. 1.

merely, regarding his own work contracts, the absence of racialized categories of employment status and compensation entitlements. After 'backing out' from his employment on British ships on 'Asiatic Articles', he found himself in stokeholds of the US merchant marine that were no havens of racial harmony and internationalism either but were more likely to be ethnically diverse than segmented. On most voyages, he was the only Indian in the engine room and worked side by side with anglophone 'whites' (including numerous Irish) as well as with Spaniards, Eastern Europeans, Latin Americans, and Egyptians.[32] Racial segregation was far from unknown on US steamers, but less likely to be met with in the early decades of the twentieth century when African Americans were largely excluded from deck and stokehold crews and confined to the purser's (or mess) department.[33] Yet when Amir Haider Khan once encountered African Americans in the stokehold of a ramshackle coal-fuelled steamer, they comprised the entire hard-worked gang of trimmers and firemen, while the 'petty officers' (oilers and water tenders) were ethnically diverse (without including African Americans) and the engineers exclusively 'white'.[34] Moreover, he repeatedly mentioned the refusal of 'white' stokers from the US South to work alongside African Americans.[35] For Amir Haider Khan, however, the escape from racial encapsulation was real enough and made much of a difference.

Amir Haider Khan recounted various incidents when these changes unlocked new opportunities for self-assertion and even for upward mobility. The first incident occurred during the last weeks of the First World War, when he was employed on a supply ship for the American Corps in France where all other stokers were either Irish or Irish

32 Khan, 'I Break with the Old World', part I, pp. 299, 335, 357.

33 Most studies on African American seafarers appear to focus on the nineteenth century and often the decades preceding the civil war, while the early decades of the twentieth century appear to be less researched. For references to the exclusion of black seafarers from the deck and engine departments of US merchant steamers see, however, Bruce Nelson, *Workers on the Waterfront: Seamen, Longshoremen, and Unionism in the 1930s*, Urbana: University of Illinois Press, 1988, pp. 32, 8, 246. In the US Navy, an earlier 'mixed crew' policy, too, was increasingly replaced by segregation towards the late nineteenth century – a process that reached its climax during the First World War. Cf. Michael Shawn Davis, '"Many of Them Are Among My Best Men": The United States Navy Looks at Its African American Crewmen, 1755–1955', doctoral dissertation, Kansas State University, 2011, pp. 52–5.

34 Khan, 'I Break with the Old World', part I, p. 381.

35 Ibid., pp. 367, 440, 591, 667–9.

American. When a shipboard conflict arose in Brest with the rest of the stokehold crew demanding the full payment of their dues and refusing to accept the partial advance offered by the shipmaster, Amir Haider Khan also declined to receive his money even though he had not been involved in the controversy. 'The firemen', he remembered,

> very much appreciated my spontaneous solidarity with them. My name was strange and too long for them to pronounce from the very beginning of my joining the ship. I was given the nick-name 'Dublin'. Thus every body called me 'Dublin'. But from the day I refused to take my pay unless the firemen's demand was satisfied 'Dublin' became the subject matter of discussion.[36]

If a limited 'ethnic' diversity was thus more likely on American vessels than racial segmentation and segregation, this went along with a need for mutual addressability among the crew – a need that did not arise on the S.S. *Egypt* and on British steamers in general. On the US Army supply ship, this need had been satisfied initially by way of impersonal naming: 'Dublin' was entirely unrelated to Amir Haider Khan's actual name or place of origin and erased his life history as much as if he had been named 'Friday' like the 'native' manservant in Defoe's novel. The incident, however, had charged the appellation 'Dublin' with connotations of reputable personal behaviour. It had gained Amir Haider Khan a meaningful name, as it were: he had succeeded in breaking down the depersonalization and racial reductionism that marked, for instance, the testimonies of all 'white' witnesses of the *Egypt* disaster.[37] And 'Dublin' would only be the first of a series of names that Amir Haider Khan acquired in his American employment history: 'Jimmy' would be less impersonal though still generic, while 'Tonny' would 'promote' him, who had previously been referred to as the 'little Hindoo', to the barely less ambivalent racial status of a southern Italian.[38]

A second set of reminiscences concerns Amir Haider Khan's employment as an oiler on the S.S. *Merry Mount,* a state-of-the art oil-fuelled steamer, in 1920. The chapter dwelling on his experiences on board that

36 Ibid., p. 324.
37 See chapters 3 and 11 above.
38 Khan, 'I Break with the Old World', part I, pp. 395, 691.

ship begins with the observation that he was highly 'conspicuous' as the 'only dark-skinned one among the whole crew'. On this backdrop, he recalled an encounter with the first assistant engineer James J. Miller:

> The main engine of the ship was the General Electric turbine. It was closed in the casings. He told me to go to the centrifugal pump, which was by the reciprocating engine, to see whether the bearings and other things were alright. I went there where I put my hand into the crank to feel the crank bearing, whether it was hot, dry or otherwise. Mr. Miller stealthily followed me to see whether I knew the tricks of the trade. He saw me attending to the job and he became quite free with me and took me round other parts of the engine room to acquaint me with everything which would subsequently require my attention.[39]

In a racially segregated crew, chances to compensate for one's racial 'conspicuousness' with a demonstration of skill would have been significantly lower: we saw that racial hierarchy also regulated, on British merchant steamers like the S.S. *Egypt*, the division of labour and the access to technical skill.[40] Moreover, he was now working on oil- rather than coal-fuelled steamers, where the predominant work task of the much smaller stokehold crews was to attend to the machinery, and skill requirements were less fragmented.[41] As the acquaintance deepened between Amir Haider Khan and James Miller on the S.S. *Merry Mount*, such divisions became increasingly blurred: on the engineer's recommendation and encouragement, the former 'scorfer' enrolled for a correspondence course for marine engineering, where he eventually gained the certificate of a second assistant marine engineer.[42]

When Amir Haider Khan signed off from that ship eventually and received a contract in the port office for the S.S. *Zaca*, a smaller, technically inferior but equally oil-fuelled steamer, Miller's letter of recommendation eventually helped him to avert racial exclusion.[43] 'The minute I climbed on the ship with my luggage,' he recalled, however,

39 Ibid., pp. 404f.
40 See chapter 9 above.
41 Khan, 'I Break with the Old World', part I, pp. 405, 409.
42 Ibid., pp. 414f, 663–5.
43 Ibid., p. 442.

> there was standing on the deck an oiler from the Southern part of the U.S.A. He, after seeing me, immediately ran down below to inform his other colleagues about me. They jointly went to the chief engineer and told him that a negro or a coloured water tender had come on the ship and that they were not willing to work or sail with me.[44]

The Danish chief engineer initially attempted to discourage Amir Haider Khan from insisting on the fulfilment of his contract, but after some back and forth he was eventually sent down for his watch despite the continuing boycott on the part of other stokers:

> the other water tender instead of giving me the charge and showing round the different valves, manifolds, the pumps, the water and oil tanks . . . which is usually done to acquaint a new comer [sic] in a ship, at once went on top without speaking a single word to me.[45]

Amir Haider Khan was sufficiently skilled to hold his own and succeeded even in making himself indispensable to the engineers during a voyage marred by numerous technical faults. His experiences of US steamers thus seemed to suggest that 'colour prejudice' was widespread but not insurmountable: 'When once I was allowed to work,' he wrote in his memoirs, 'I was able to melt their hardened race-hatred by my working ability, personal conduct and social behaviour towards others.'[46] This experience appeared to confirm the libertarian and potentially depoliticizing individualism that Amir Haider Khan had imbibed since his arrival in a purportedly 'new world' (as have, perhaps, some of the academic 'agenciologists' of the neoliberal present): the ideology of every person being the architect of their own future.[47]

Even so, the four years of employment amid ethnically diverse crews had also spurred a process of political radicalization. This process had commenced early, when Khan was serving on a hospital ship in Basra where the numerous Indian Muslim soldiers of the British forces often

44 Ibid., p. 440.
45 Ibid., pp. 441f.
46 Ibid., p. 591.
47 For a similar argument, see Bald, *Bengali Harlem*, p. 152.

resented having to fight their co-religionists. He remembered that the anti-British atmosphere he imbibed resulted in 'vague pan-Islamic sentiments'.[48] Three years later, on a US military supply ship, among a predominantly Spanish-speaking stokehold crew, he struck up a friendship with an Irish American fireman, Joseph Mulkane. Their endless conversations, conducted 'side by side, in two bunks', improved Amir Haider Khan's English. Mulkane was also Khan's 'first and foremost source of political knowledge', making him aware of Irish nationalism and opposition against British imperialism outside the Indian subcontinent while buttressing his admiration for the US as a political alternative.[49] In his remaining seafaring years, he met Indian nationalist exiles and their American supporters in New York, being impressed particularly by Agnes Smedley. He was strongly attracted by the plebeian anti-imperialism of the Ghadar (or, Revolution) Party whose pamphlets he smuggled on board to distribute them among Punjabi immigrants in various Asian ports.[50] Put off by the racist exclusionism of the American Federation of Labor he also joined the Industrial Workers of the World (IWW) in 1922, at the time still a force to reckon with.[51]

However, if the experience of shipboard conflict and racial discrimination had rendered him susceptive for militant and internationalist labourism, he still recalled having been, at the time, 'a vague I.W.W. in outlook but sceptical of everything'.[52] One source of this 'vagueness' or ambivalence was that, until confronted with the hard exclusion from stokehold work in 1922, he had been rather successful in navigating a maritime labour market that was no less marked by racial hierarchies than that of the British Empire, but not in quite the same way. If he had been able to counter the racist resentment of 'white' stokers and officers by demonstrating his individual 'working ability, personal conduct and social behaviour', this was only possible because his position within the racial hierarchy was negotiable, to some extent, and not fixed at the very bottom. And, in response to these conditions of 'agency', he strove, like so many immigrants before and after him, to distance himself from that

48 Khan, 'I Break with the Old World', part I, pp. 178–86.
49 Ibid., pp. 344–6.
50 Ibid., pp. 471–89, 492f, 496f, 510, 515–19, 521–38.
51 Ibid., pp. 618f.
52 Ibid., p. 649.

bottom of the local racial hierarchy. Twice he absolutely refused to be put up in the 'Negro ward' of marine hospitals when he was taken ill as a seaman.[53] Being an Indian, he recalled, 'I would never allow anybody to call me a coloured man or a negro'.[54] His ambivalent social position made him receptive to a 'Negro-phobia', which he described as

> such a contagious disease that it even affects immediately the new arrived . . . Even I whose skin was not fairer than an average American Negro, had unconsciously developed the superiority complex within a few months of my landing in the U.S.A. when absolutely I did not know anything about the country or even its language to converse properly.[55]

Vivek Bald, in his otherwise superb discussion of Amir Haider Khan's American years, has perceived the use of the naturalizing metaphor of 'disease' as a lack of reflection on the social foundations of racism, which Khan would eventually overcome.[56] But the use of this metaphor was the result already of later reflection: it conveyed his enduring bewilderment not of the presence or the social causes of racism in the US, but of the ways in which racist ideas proliferated and had affected him also. He struggled to understand the person he had been: 'I have tried to analyse myself as to what I was then signifying. But I confess that I cannot explain anything definitely.'[57] In doing so, however, he had found words that anticipated and confirmed, from the converse, self-reflective perspective, James Baldwin's acerbic observation three decades later: 'I had my fill', recalled the African American writer, 'of seeing people come down the gangplank on Wednesday, let us say, speaking not a word of English, and by Friday discovering that I was working for them and they were calling me nigger like everybody else.'[58]

Like so many others, Amir Haider Khan might have continued to search for a corner of individual comfort and a route towards personal

---

53 Ibid., pp. 322, 400f.

54 Ibid., p. 896.

55 Ibid., pp. 321f.

56 Bald, *Bengali Harlem*, p. 152.

57 Khan, 'I Break with the Old World', part I, p. 650.

58 James Baldwin and Margaret Mead, *A Rap on Race*, New York: J. B. Lippincott, 1971, p. 71.

advancement within a racially layered hierarchy. But he ceased to deploy his 'agency' in this plausible direction. When, in New York, two chief engineers successively denied him stokehold employment, when he failed to defeat racist exclusion individually by insisting on the performance of contractual obligations, when the door towards negotiating his racial status was thus shut in his face, and when the precarious substance of his recently found American liberty evaporated before his eyes, Amir Haider Khan ventured a road that only few would take of those who made similar experiences: it spurred him on to less 'vague' and more radical political views and choices.[59]

Detroit offered him employment as an auto worker in the Packard Plant, but also immersed him in diverse social and political movements that would change his understanding of the world in fundamental as well as very specific ways.[60] When the IWW was crushed and forced into decline in the mid-1920s, the Communist Party filled the vacuum in the US labour movement as an internationalist force reaching out to 'coloured' workers. Amir Haider Khan's acquaintance with Detroit communists resulted in his being sent to Moscow in 1926 to study at the Communist University of the Toilers of the East (KUTV) along with other Punjabi immigrant workers, most of whom were associated with the Ghadar Party.[61]

Back in India in 1928, he established a clandestine courier link with the Comintern, was elected a member of the Bombay Provincial Committee of the Indian National Congress, and was the only accused in the Meerut Conspiracy Case against militant trade unionists who succeeded in escaping detention by going underground.[62] During the final years of British rule in India and in the successor state of Pakistan, where his party sent him after the partition of the country, he paid a heavy price, in terms of individual liberty, for his choice of asserting 'agency': almost nine years in colonial jails followed by four prison sentences in Pakistan and three banishments to the remote mountain

59 Khan, 'I Break with the Old World', part I, pp. 590–3, 666–70.

60 Ibid., p. 824.

61 Ibid., pp. 937f.

62 Khan, 'I Break with the Old World', part II, pp. 152–4, 181–8; BL: OIOC, IOR/L/P&J/12/419 (Indian Police Intelligence File on Amir Haider Khan, 1932–1936). Amir Haider Khan, 'My Experiences with Preventive Detention' (handwritten introductory letter to the manuscript, dated 11 October 1974), p. 1.

hamlet where he had been born.[63] He defied, nonetheless, the depersonalization experienced during his seafaring years by acquiring a succession of new if unlikely noms de guerre: his student alias, 'Sakorov', in Moscow, 'Francisco Fernandez' when impersonating a citizen of Goa to escape from police persecution in Bombay, or the cover name 'Shanker' as he feigned to be a 'North Indian Brahmin' when organizing a 'Young Workers' League' in Madras.[64] In Pakistan, eventually, he would be addressed respectfully as 'Dada' (grandfather) Amir Haider by his young activist admirers.[65]

Amir Haider Khan remembered his encounter with communism in Detroit, for all the momentous consequences it had for his future life and outlook on the world, as the exploration of merely one of several avenues of political dissent he felt drawn to at the time. Eventually and without even having joined the Communist Party, he turned his back on the country, which he considered his 'adopted home' and of which he was, by that time, a 'naturalized citizen' to make the clandestine voyage to Soviet Russia. His disillusionment with the United States and his urge to search for another radically 'new world' had been decisive for his departure rather than firm communist convictions, which he was to develop only subsequently.[66]

In Detroit, he was deeply moved and impressed by his engagement with the African American community, growing rapidly at the time through Southern migration and as a base for vibrant social mobilization against racial discrimination.[67] When he 'scribbled', as he put it, his memoirs in Nashik Road Central Jail fifteen years later he

63 Amir Haider Khan, typed letter to Hasan Gardezi, 9 February 1980 (Pakistan Study Centre, University of Karachi), p. 1; Khan, 'My Experiences with Preventive Detention' (handwritten introductory letter to the manuscript, dated 11 October 1974), p. 4.

64 Khan, 'I Break with the Old World', part II, p. 10 (Khan used the spelling 'Sukharoff'); Harry Haywood, *Black Bolshevik: Autobiography of an Afro-American Communist*, Chicago: Liberator Press, 1978, pp. 164f. Amir Haider Khan, 'My Struggle, part II' (typed manuscript, retitled 'Mission Abroad' with editorial markings, Pakistan Study Centre, University of Karachi), p. 1. Amir Haider Khan, 'My Discovery of South India' (handwritten manuscript with extensive editorial markings, Pakistan Study Centre, University of Karachi), p. 33.

65 Gardezi, *Chains to Lose*, vol. 1, p. v.

66 Khan, 'I Break with the Old World', part I, pp. 820–2, 887–92, 916, 920, 949–53.

67 Ibid., pp. 854–82. For an excellent analysis of these encounters, see Bald, *Bengali Harlem*, pp. 154–8.

remembered in graphic detail a civil rights meeting in the Second Baptist Church of Detroit. By now he was an experienced communist organizer but would still emphasize that he had never seen, before and after, the audience of a meeting 'in such a grave mood'. The speakers, he recalled, 'were not the usual type of public orators or demagogues but they were grieved men, who fully were aware of the wrongs that had been done to their race'.[68] Subsequently he made acquaintance with various strands of radical African American movements in Detroit, including followers of Marcus Garvey and more militant circles pondering over violent retribution.[69]

Breaking down, in this way, another capsule of racial segregation made again a 'World of difference': it made Khan reflect critically on his own susceptibility to 'Negro-phobia' in his American years, and these reflections would have a lasting effect. In his memoirs, he recalled visiting neighbourhoods where African Americans 'led a segregated life as untouchables have to do in South India': his cathartic experiences in Detroit had sensitized him more to caste oppression and 'untouchability' than was usual among Indian communists of his generation.[70] And even the septuagenarian Amir Haider Khan had still remarkably lively and fresh memories of the heated debates on the 'negro question' among young communists in late 1920s Moscow – debates that nurtured enduring feelings of friendship with 'black Bolshevik' Harry Haywood, who would remain a powerful voice of the African American radical left for more than half a century.[71] Haywood was a vocal advocate of a right to national self-determination for the African Americans of the 'black belt' in the US South. If this view was unlikely to gain strategic traction, it served to foreground 'race' as a social and political issue that revolutionary labour movements could not evade or reduce to a mere appendix of the class question.[72] Amir

---

68 Khan, 'I Break with the Old World', part I, p. 873.

69 Cf. Bald, *Bengali Harlem*, pp. 154–8.

70 Khan, 'I Break with the Old World', part I, p. 865. See also ibid., p. 433, and Khan, 'My Discovery of South India' (handwritten manuscript with extensive editorial markings, Pakistan Study Centre, University of Karachi), pp. 13–15 and *passim*.

71 Amir Haider Khan, Untitled and undated addition to part II of 'I Break with the Old World', to be inserted after p. 106 (Pakistan Study Centre, University of Karachi).

72 Harry Haywood (1898–1985) was a key figure of the CPUSA's 'Negro Department' in the 1930s and 1940s. He was expelled in the 1950s but continued to advocate until his death among the African American far left the 'Southern negroes'' right to

Haider Khan's exposure to and involvement in these debates may well have further heightened his awareness of 'caste' as a fundamental problem of social emancipation in South Asia.

In this postscript, in our search for the 'native' seafarers' ability to shape their own lives, we have travelled far from the coast of Brittany where the wreck of the S.S. *Egypt* lies. 'Jumping ship' in New York or elsewhere, escaping British imperial forms of maritime 'racial management', and enabling oneself to embrace new opportunities of wartime labour scarcity and transformed maritime labour processes could make a 'World of difference' to a South Asian seafarer. The margin for manoeuvre – or 'agency' – was widened under these changed circumstances and the sense of disempowerment alleviated. Consequently, the 'native' seafarer's depersonalization, muteness, and elusiveness in the historical record was less inevitable, and there were windows of opportunity that rendered more likely the preservation of an Indian stoker's life history.

Yet even if autobiographical accounts, like Amir Haider Khan's memoirs, may illuminate such windows in bright colours, we should not lose the sense of proportion and forget that openings were few and far between in a wide expanse of sooty brick. We need to recall that most life histories vanished unrecorded and that most names of working people, 'native seafarers' included, were and continue to be erased from memory: the shooting and even the sheer physical existence of 'Kara' on the S.S. *Egypt* will remain unconfirmed. Among the numerous newspaper reports on the shipwreck of the *Egypt*, replete with

national self-determination. Cf. Oscar Berland, 'The Emergence of the Communist Perspective on the "Negro Question" in America: 1919–1931. Part One', *Science and Society* 63, no. 4 (1999–2000), pp. 411–32; Oscar Berland, 'The Emergence of the Communist Perspective on the "Negro Question" in America: 1919–1931. Part Two', *Science and Society* 64, no. 2 (2000), pp. 194–217; Beverly Tomek, 'The Communist International and the Dilemma of the American "Negro Problem": Limitations of the Black Belt Self-Determination Thesis', *Working USA: The Journal of Labor and Society* 15, no. 4 (2012), pp. 549–76. Haywood was one of Amir Haider Khan's most trusted friends to whom he gave a copy of his memoirs after his release from prison when they met again in Bombay for a few days in 1943 or 1944. Amir Haider Khan, Handwritten letter to Hasan Gardezi, 21 October 1979 (Pakistan Study Centre, University of Karachi), p. 1. Haywood, too, recalled his friendship with Khan (or 'Sakorov') in his own memoirs: Haywood, *Black Bolshevik*, pp. 164f, 509.

'human interest' vignettes, I have not found the name of even one of the forty-nine Indian seafarers who perished in the *Egypt* shipwreck. As for those who were crushed under more quotidian circumstances in the gruelling, super-exploitative labour process of the stokehold and could not find a window of opportunity for themselves, it is even less likely that we can trace their names: according to official figures, 'lascar' suicides on board British ships reached a peak in 1931 – a year when more than thirty Indian seafarers – mostly stokehold crew – had been officially reported to have taken their own lives or to have 'disappeared' from the ship while at sea.[73] The names of suicidal 'lascars' entered newspaper reports and even official documents only in rare cases; most were swallowed up by the sea together with their bearers.

Certainly, few 'native' seafarers took the desperate decision to regain control over their lives by terminating it. Windows of opportunity were scarce but visible as a hopeful proposition and in reach as a real if slim possibility. Racially managed steamships in late imperial Britain were no 'totalitarian' workspaces in the sense of a comprehensively regulated and hermetically closed system. There were numerous rifts in the net that permitted individual escape, even though these rifts were never large enough to jeopardize the functioning of the regime of racial labour management in its entirety. The net remained sufficiently robust and small-meshed, as it were, to ensure profitability: the nexus of racist immigration laws, racialized labour contracts, and racialized labour process management could afford numerous gaps and considerable incoherence without ceasing to guarantee an attractive and economically viable business environment for maritime employers. For 'native' seafarers, however, these gaps and this incoherence opened up spaces for the renegotiation of their position – mostly at the level of the individual or of an ethnically defined section of the workforce while the racialized wage labour regime was rarely questioned in its entirety.

The scope and the limitations of such spaces for negotiation are indicated, for instance, by the very different levels of employment security among steamship workers. Those in the lower echelons of the tramp shipping labour market, whether 'white' or 'coloured', could be marked by the extreme precariousness of an existence alternating

73 Cf. Stephen E. Roberts et al., 'Suicides among Seafarers in UK Merchant Shipping, 1919–2005', *Occupational Medicine* 60 (2010), p. 59.

between long periods of beachcombing and occasional periods of super-exploitative employment in the stokehold that would (and could) generally only last for one voyage. Such precariousness has been described for Liverpool by Tony Lane, denounced or celebrated in novels by B. Traven and Claude McKay, and referred to disdainfully in Amir Haider Khan's autobiography.[74] The more regularly employed and sedentary family men stoking the Southampton transatlantic liners were an altogether different category of workers in an infinitely stronger position.[75] Even among the racially subordinated 'lascar' crews of British steamers there were significant differentiations: most of the Indian witnesses the P&O Company had handpicked for the *Egypt* inquiry belonged to a core of long-term employees who ranged at the upper end of the pay scale and enjoyed a greater level of security in India's packed maritime labour market where four to five seafarers were believed to compete for a single job.[76]

Some could rise to be serangs or other labour intermediaries and partake in a chain of informal payments and small-scale money-lending, which could augment their employment compensations with narrow profit margins.[77] Small savings could facilitate an upwardly mobile life after seafaring: some would run coffee houses, portside shops, or boarding houses, or engage in petty trade and contraband; others would return to inland villages to consolidate their family's land holdings and social reputation.[78] Amir Haider Khan sought to escape

74 Cf. Tony Lane, *Liverpool: City of the Sea* (2nd ed.), Liverpool: Liverpool University Press, 1997, pp. 59–82; B. Traven, *The Death Ship: The Story of an American Sailor*, New York: Lawrence Hill, 1991 (1934); Claude McKay, *Banjo: A Story without a Plot*, San Diego: Harcourt Brace, 1957 (1929); Khan, 'I Break with the Old World', part I, pp. 285, 407, 665f.

75 Valerie Burton, 'The Work and Home Life of Seafarers with Special Reference to the Port of Southampton 1871–1921', doctoral dissertation, London School of Economics, 1988.

76 See chapter 6, above.

77 Cf. Ahuja, 'Networks of Subordination', p. 27.

78 For Sylheti seafarers, such life histories (as well as less upwardly mobile trajectories) are documented in Adams, *Across Seven Seas*, and Choudhury, *The Roots and Tales*. Katy Gardner, focussing too on Sylheti labour migrants, has explored the differential long-term consequences for social status from an anthropological perspective; see esp. Katy Gardner, 'Keeping Connected: Security, Place, and Social Capital in a "Londoni" Village in Sylhet', *Journal of the Royal Anthropological Institute* 14, no. 3 (2008), pp. 477–95.

'wage slavery' – unsuccessfully as so many others – by investing most of his savings from seafaring, 750 US dollars, in a dry cleaning shop in New York City.[79] Such strivings for upward mobility were often precarious as well as contentious: a serang's exaction of informal payments from the crew could result in violent shipboard conflict but was unavoidable if he wished to sustain his intermediary position by paying bribes, in turn, to port officials and the ship's officers.[80] Making use of the inconsistencies and loopholes of immigration and maritime labour law could be a successful strategy for individual upward mobility but implied the risk of serious setbacks. Small-scale businesses often had to navigate closely on either side of the limits of legality.[81] 'Agency' in the way of 'playing the system' thus always came at a cost and implied perpetual risk.

One price to be paid for rising within the racialized labour hierarchy of US merchant shipping dawned slowly on Amir Haider Khan only during his 'American years': the flipside of working to prove one's individual 'ability, personal conduct and social behaviour' was to distinguish oneself from those of presumably lesser skill and respectability. And if socially prevalent notions of 'skill' and 'respectability' were heavily racialized and excluded African Americans, embracing racist prejudice while claiming a place in the upper echelons of the labour market seemed to suggest itself as a perfectly respectable, common-sensical and therefore *quasi-natural* attitude – an 'infectious' attitude, as it were, that could be fought back only by way of a consciously political and determined effort. Amir Haider Khan, after his first 'break with the old world' and when serving as an oiler on US steamers, was sufficiently alert to notice the discrimination against African Americans in military and civil maritime employment, but he did so as a distant observer and made every effort not to be identified with them.[82] Effectively, his stance mirrored the 'mischievous' attitude British workers had displayed

79 Khan, 'I Break with the Old World', part I, pp. 603–16.

80 Cf. Ahuja, 'Networks of Subordination', p. 27. See also Khan, 'I Break with the Old World', part I, p. 161.

81 For a close-up analysis of the precarious life histories of small-scale Indian entrepreneurs in European port towns during the interwar period, see Svenja von Jan's unpunblished doctoral dissertation, 'Exploring Migrant Lives'.

82 Khan, 'I Break with the Old World', part I, pp. 317, 320–3, 339. See also Bald, *Bengali Harlem*, p. 151.

towards him and his striking colleagues in West Hartlepool: he did not approach African American seafarers as 'the other workers' and watched them instead 'as any other indifferent spectator'.

How was it possible that Amir Haider Khan, despite his passionate aversion against discrimination and domination, assumed an attitude that had left himself deeply offended? This is the question that lingers behind his comparison of racism with an infectious disease that befalls the unaware. Arguably, the susceptibility to racist ideology was more than merely an issue of individual disposition and experience – these were instances of a behavioural pattern that was rooted in the very foundations of capitalist society: if workers came to perceive themselves, in their everyday struggle for subsistence, as owners of a capacity to perform labour that could be separated from their living being and sold in the market as any other *object*, they acknowledged thereby a severe restriction of their ability to shape their own lives as *subjects* of history. For Georg Lukács, the comprehensive commodification of society under capitalism implied a 'splitting up of man into an element of the movement of commodities and an (objective and impotent) observer of that movement'.[83]

Lukács's words resonate strongly with Khan's bitter memories of West Hartlepool port workers as 'indifferent spectators' of the travails of Indian firemen: if labour power, a human individual's physical and mental capacity for work, was conceived of, in everyday practice, as a 'thing', as a quantifiable and exchangeable commodity competing for a market with other commodities, and if the taxonomies of commodified labour and measurements of market value were radically racialized in ways this book has examined, it was at least as likely to perceive protesting 'native' seafarers as another 'element of the movement of commodities' as it was to look upon them as 'the other workers' in need of solidarity. Amir Haider Khan's experiences in the 'new world' across the Atlantic confirmed this pattern. He recalled that 'hell with you Jack, I got mine' was 'the commonest catchword of the Americans' during his seafaring years in the US merchant marine.[84] This sense of atomistic

83 Georg Lukács, *History and Class Consciousness: Studies in Marxist Dialectics*, Cambridge, MA: MIT Press, 1971, p. 166.

84 Khan, 'I Break with the Old World', part I, p. 360. Amir Haider Khan clearly considered this phrase significant: in a clean typed copy of his memoirs, held in Ajoy Bhavan, the Communist Party of India's head office in New Delhi, he used it also as a

individualism was premised on the lived experience that every worker was exposed to the anonymous forces of the market and as powerless as any other to control these forces. They appeared to be stripped, in other words, of any subjectivity or 'agency' that sought to transcend the iron cage of the commodity market. The scope for shaping their own lives was a severely curtailed, depoliticized 'agency' that allowed a minority to secure a more comfortable place for themselves in that cage at the cost of other 'elements' of commodified labour. Such 'agency' thus implied individual elbowing or, at an extended level, the forging of inherently inconstant alliances among a particular section of labour market competitors for the purpose of excluding others.

Seeking to sustain one's market value by asserting racial superiority over any section of 'the other workers' thus provided only a semblance of empowerment as it implied, in essence, the acceptance of a logic of commodification that assigned *all* ethnicities a place in racialized taxonomies of labour power. These taxonomies were never coherent, as we have seen, and historically unstable, which meant that they could be turned in time against any group of workers even though the recently immigrated and those categorized as 'non-white' were targeted most consistently. Claiming superiority within this structurally disempowering, reifying 'old world' of wage labour and its racialized taxonomies thus came at a price, and implied unceasing insecurity and inescapable anxiety. Amir Haider Khan became fully aware of this price eventually: 'I always had felt a sort of inferiority complex and a mental inhibition', he recalled, 'while I was in the United States'.[85]

Amir Haider Khan's autobiography also shows, however, that the vantage point of the impassive, inert, insecure, and only purportedly superior observer could be left behind. The horizons of possibility that were visible to workers at that time did not inevitably end when one accommodated oneself to more spacious and comfortable niches within one or the other ethnically segmented labour market. 'Agency', loosely defined, could blend into acquiescent complicity and chances were that it did, for as long as it remained fragmented and

heading for one of the chapters on his seafaring years in the US. Amir Haider Khan, 'I Break with the Old World: Testament of a Hindoo', typed manuscript of 645 pp. with glossary, preserved in Ajoy Bhavan, New Delhi, p. 216.

85 Ibid., part II, p. 119.

depoliticized. But if the everyday experience of waged work was shaped by competition and fragmentation, it was not so entirely: labour processes always required the cooperation of workers, emphasized the social character of work, and generated, thereby, material foundations for self-organization and solidarity. Amir Haider Khan's experience of racialized wage labour prepared him for the search of another 'World of difference' as much as his experience of stokehold cooperation and shipboard solidarity.

His search for a 'new world' became conceivable and urgent, however, only once this experience was worked over politically through his engagement with African American radicalism and communist internationalism. It was possible – imaginable as well as doable – to 'break with the old world' more than once, perhaps even time and time again. It was possible to defy the odds and push against the hard historical limits of a society that continues to thrive on the subordination of fragmented and often racially divided labour. If the anger and the protest of the S.S. *Egypt*'s surviving 'native' seamen erupted but briefly in Brest to be soon subdued and hushed up, mounting experience of such encounters could result, when shored up by organized political reflection, in more sustained, organized, and radical forms of resistance. Many who took to this dangerous road were broken or discouraged eventually, though some made names for themselves – names of dissent, of defiance, and of determination that remained usable only for a time until they had to be changed again.

Acknowledgements

This book assumed shape during a long voyage that began in 2001, when I embarked on a postdoctoral research project at the Centre for Modern Oriental Studies in Berlin on maritime labour in the Indian Ocean under British colonialism. At a time when many cultural and social historians echoed the public celebration of neoliberal 'globalization' by conjuring up counter-histories of 'subaltern globalization', my colleagues Katrin Bromber, Jan-Georg Deutsch, Friedhelm Hartwig, Brigitte Reinwald, and I examined the unevenness of the spaces produced by European imperialism in the Indian Ocean region: growing interconnectedness, we found, was accompanied by severe restrictions on movement and mobility. My project examined, in this context, labour relations of Indian merchant seamen (or so-called 'lascars') on British ships.

At that time, historical research on 'lascars' took a leap forward with Gopalan Balachandran's important work that had commenced several years earlier. My own studies, published in a series of articles between 2002 and 2008, focused on the question of how it was possible that European steamship companies succeeded in confining Indian shipworkers to a segment of the global maritime labour market defined by much lower pay and inferior rights over more than a century despite the unusually high mobility of that workforce and its potential access to more remunerative labour markets across the oceans.

Two discoveries then triggered a change in the trajectory of my research. Firstly, the unusually dense documentation of the shipping accident resulting in the loss of the S. S. *Egypt* permitted a glimpse of the generally unrecorded everyday practices of the ship work 'lascars' performed on British steamers. Secondly, I delved into the autobiographical writings of an Indian seafarer and communist activist, Amir Haider Khan, that had been edited and published by Hasan Gardezi in a labour of love. 'Dada' Amir Haider's memories of his seafaring life were unusual in many ways, but particularly because of their strong emphasis on the labour process on steamers.

A fellowship in 2011 at the International Research Centre 'Work and Human Life Cycle in Global History' (Re-Work) in Berlin gave me the opportunity to consider a reorientation of my research from the examination of segmented labour markets to the practices of racial management on British steamers operated by ethnically segmented crews. In my own research group at the Centre for Modern Indian Studies in Göttingen, the groundbreaking doctoral research of Anna Sailer on the organization of production in the colonial jute industry of Kolkata and its political consequences proved convincingly that historians are well advised to take the labour process more seriously.[1] Moreover, discussions with Nicole Mayer-Ahuja were particularly important for this shift towards the historicization of labour processes.

It would be disingenuous, however, if I pretended that this insight hit me out of the blue in my study. In my pre-academic life, highly (and to a large extent self-)educated workers like my typesetting instructor Hermann Schneider taught me to take industrial 'skills', those presumably minor forms of knowledge, very seriously; my works council chairman Klaus Fischer and many other working-class activists taught me that social domination nests concealed in technicalities of the labour process and can be challenged effectively only if these technicalities are well understood. They were good teachers and without them this book would not have been written.

A first result of this new emphasis in my work was published in 2013 in a book chapter.[2] The research could be deepened after 2012 when

1 The thesis was revised and published as Anna Sailer, *Workplace Relations in Colonial Bengal: The Jute Industry and Indian Labour, 1870s–1930s*, London: Bloomsbury, 2022.

2 'A Freedom Still Enmeshed in Servitude: The Unruly "Lascars" of the S.S. City of Manila or, a Micro-History of the "Free Labour" Problem', in R. Ahuja (ed.), *Working Lives and Worker Militancy: The Politics of Labour in Colonial India*, Delhi: Tulika, 2013, pp. 97–133.

Kamran Ali and Jaffer Ahmed enabled me to access original manuscripts of Amir Haider Khan's autobiographical writings in Karachi. I also acknowledge the support I received over the years from archivists and librarians in the British Library, the UK National Archive, the National Maritime Museum in London, and the National Archives of India in New Delhi. But then institutional obligations and different research commitments brought my work on this project to a standstill for about five years. I began to return to it in 2018, though it was only at a time of protracted illness in 2021 that I found the opportunity to draft a book manuscript. In completing the monograph, I received great support from many sides. I presented parts of it to various academic audiences in Bern, Delhi, Glasgow, Göttingen, Kolkata, Marburg, Trier, Zürich, and the University of Newfoundland. The questions and comments offered by the participants helped me to sharpen my argument. Some of the material used in chapters 8 to 10 was discussed and published in a condensed form in a volume edited by Nicole Mayer-Ahuja and Marcel van der Linden.[3] I am grateful for the comments I received from the editors and for the permission to reuse this material.

Large parts of the book manuscript were closely read by Valerie Burton, Leon Fink, Andreas Gestrich, Nicole Mayer-Ahuja, and Radhika Singha. I cannot thank these colleagues enough for the perceptive, critical, and encouraging comments they offered from the vantage points of their respective historical specializations. Student research assistants, namely Karl Müller-Bahlke, Maresa Emons, and Jan zum Mallen, helped me at various stages in finalizing the manuscript and in ascertaining and securing rights for the reproduction of images used in this book. I also wish to thank the editorial team of Verso, and especially Sebastian Budgen and Jeanne Tao, and copy editor Julie McCarroll for their professionalism and support. Finally, a word of thanks to James Jones, who designed an imaginative book cover that is much to the liking of the former typesetter that I am.

'Production by an individual outside society', wrote Marx, 'is as much of an absurdity as is the development of language without individuals

3 'Industrial "Cyclopes" and "Native" Stokers: British Steamshipping and the Attractions of "Racial Management" (c. 1880–1930)', in Marcel van der Linden and Nicole Mayer-Ahuja (eds): *Power at Work. Control and Resistance in Heteronomous Labour Relations*, Berlin: de Gruyter, 2023, pp. 211–37.

living together and talking to each other.'[4] This workpiece, too, is the result of overlapping and combined efforts, though I own up to the arguments, their occasionally unconciliatory presentation, and to all errors the text still may contain.

Ravi Ahuja, Göttingen, May 2024

4 Karl Marx, *Grundrisse. Foundations of the Critique of Political Economy (Rough Draft)*, London: Penguin, 1993, p. 48.

Index

Page numbers in *italic* indicate *figures*.

abolitionism, 53
Across the Red Sea (Billman), 130
Adam, Mohammed (Mahomed), 92, 96, 187
Adams, Caroline, 8n15, 211n11, 227n78
African American radical movements, 223–4, 231
'agenciology', 205, 219
'*ag wallahs*', 92, 117
alienation, 141, 203–4, 211, 213
Allen, Christopher James, 151n39
All-India Trade Union Congress (AITUC), 67–9
Alty, Thomas, 173
Amalgamated Marine Workers Union (Britain), 57, 69, 197
American Federation of Labor (AFL), 220
American Line, 178
'animality', 26–7, 141–3
anti-Asian
immigration restrictions, 181
resentment, 47
anticapitalism, 11, 145. *See also* capital/capitalist
Anti-Christ (Nietzsche), 54
Arabia (ship), 92
Asiatic Articles of Agreement (lascar articles), 94, 162–3, 168, 181, 216
Asiatic Strangers' Home (London), 116
Aspinall, Butler Cole, 23
Associated Press (news agency), 67
Azevedo, Phillip, 91–2

Balachandran, Gopalan, 8, 10n24, 56n59, 57n62, 65n19, 80n35, 163, 169n39
Bald, Vivek, 211n11, 214n24, 219n47, 221, 223n67, 224n69, 228n82
Baldwin, James, 221
Baldwin, Stanley, 68, 77–9

Baptista, Joseph, 64–6, 91, 109, 111
Barrett, James R., 213n18
Bass, Robert P., 152n44
Bateson, A. D., 75
Belgian colonialism, 3
belongingness, 140–1, 143, 213. *See also* alienation
Benga, Ota, 143
Bengal, 34, 68, 79, 83, 114, 170–1, 202
Benjamin, Walter, 4n7, 205
Berland, Oscar, 225n72
Beveridge, James, 62–3
Billman, Torsten, *Across the Red Sea*, 130, *131*, 132
'black gang', 126, 129–30, 137–8, 143, 146, 161, 165, 172, 186
Blume, Harvey, 143n11
Board of Trade (Britain), 23, 63, 68, 73, 83, 98, 101, 174, 195, 202
  inquiry, 22–4, 36, 58, 63, 68–71, 76, 78, 81, 90–113, 121, 184–99, 201
  Manning Committee (1896), 51, 157–8, 160
  president of, 36, 68, 71, 76, 78
  regulations, 184–5, 196
boat stations, 103–6, 117, 186, 199
  drills, 92, 102–3, 117, 184, 188, 195–6, 199–200, *200*
Boat Stations Bill, 183–5, 191
Bombay (Mumbai), 7, 10, 21–2, 34, 51–2, 56, 62–3, 65, 83, 88, 90, 92, 96–7, 101, 103, 109, 111, 114, 167, 177–8, 180, 184, 207, 210, 222–3
Bombay Chronicle (newspaper), 44, 62, 64, 69, 74, 91, 196
Bonné, Mirko, 14n28
Boyce, Gordon H., 17n5
Bradford, Phillips Verner, 143n11
Brassey, Thomas, 152
Brest, 28, *60*, 61–4, 90, 217, 231
Britain's Indian Empire, 160
British Consul,
  in Brest, 63, 201
  in Rio de Janeiro, 148
British imperial business monopolies, 78
British imperialism. *See* imperialism
British Indian Seamen's Institute (London), 72
British India Steam Navigation Company (BISN), 17–18, 47, 77, 112, 155, 170
British 'Jack tar', 25–6
British seamen for Royal Navy, 48
British shipping industry, 10, 16–21, 24, 47, 56, 87–8, 112, 123, 146–8, 151–3, 160, 170, 194, 204, 207
  annual employment, 153–4
British (Tramp) Shipping Assistance Act of 1935, 55
Broeze, Frank, 10, 43n8, 67n28, 77n27, 78n29
Bucknill, A. J., 69–70
bulk carrier, 5
Bullen, Frank T., 88n56, 128n29, 147n24, 149n30, 150, 151n37, 166n25
Bulwer-Lytton, Victor (Earl of Lytton), 79
Burgess, Douglas R., 122n2
Burnell, A. C., 7n11
Burton, Valerie, 129n32, 137n65, 138n67, 147n19, 147n22, 147n24, 165n22, 168n33–4, 169, 170n41, 171n48, 176n67, 178–9, 227n75

Cadwallader, F. J. J., 149n28
Calcutta (Kolkata), 10, 34, 56, 65, 79–80, 83, 92, 180
Cameron, Alexander, 110
Campling, Liam, 5n8, 16n1, 167n28
capital/capitalist, 5, 162
  accumulation, 12–13
  centralization of, 5, 17
  -intensive maritime technologies, 5–6, 11, 25, 123, 134, 166, 174
  -labour relationship, 145
  production, 3, 5
  rationality, 203
  regimes of exploitation, 205
  world economy, 85
Cardiff, 56, 175–6
Carr, Douglas Gerald, 74–5, 90, 97–9, 192, 203
Cartwright, Charles Walter, 66, 89, 101–2, 105, 110–11, 183, 185–7, 191, 196
caste, 84–7, 224–5
Cathery, Edmund, 48, 55
Challis, Abraham, 93, 95, 106
Chaudhuri, Kirti Narayan, 115n36
child labour, 92, 171, 177–8, 207
Chin, Aimee, 126n16
Chinese Exclusion Acts, 214
Chittagong, 34, 83, 114
'chivalry', 26, 30–1, 42, 75. *See also* gender: and shipping accidents
chote log, 211
Choudhury, Yousuf, 8n15, 171n47, 211n11–12, 227n78
Chura, Patrick J., 141n5
City and Ellerman Line, 200, 207
City Line, 180
City of Valencia (ship), 202
Clan Drummond (ship), 42
class
  anxieties of, 31
  behavioural patterns, 9, 26, 176
  conflict, 48
  divisions, 26, 138, 145, 192
  and human devastations, 212
  identity, 141
  ideologies of, 26, 85, 143, 176
  and race, 13, 41–57, 85, 87, 198, 210 (*see also* 'race'; 'racial')
  relations, 15, 24, 49, 140–1, 144
Clinton (ship), 148, 168
coal
  -burning steamers, 16, 20–2, 25, 117, 120–2, 151 (*see also* labour process)
  political economy of, 151–2
  transition in shipping from . . . to oil and diesel, 5–6, 117, 150–4, 218
Colás, Alejandro, 5n8, 16n1, 167n28
Collyer, Andrew, 21, 29, 66, 74–6, 88–9, 97, 101–2, 104, 110, 111–13, 188, 192, 196, 200
colonial
  anthropology, 84–5, 160
  empire, 17, 24, 151–2
  ideology, 2, 9
  labour regime, 12, 87, 154–5, 181
Coloured Alien Seamen's Order (1924), 55
commodified labour, 3, 14, 85, 229–30. *See also* labour power
communication, 137, 190–1
  collapse, 105–21
  direct, 165–6
  hierarchical, 104, 111
  lateral and personalized, 191
  in moment of crisis, 193

communication (*continued*)
  oral, 132
  unidirectional, 115
communism, 3, 39, 56, 212–13, 222–4, 231
Congo, 3, 143
Conrad, Joseph, *The Nigger of the 'Narcissus'*, 13, 14n28, 50–5, 85, 151n37
conservatism, 50–1, 54–5, 57, 183
container shipping, 5–6, 12
contract/contractual
  inferior . . . status, 2, 163
  labour relations, 12, 149, 170, 222
  (un)freedom, 163, 175, 181
  working conditions, 2
  See also 'race'; 'racial'
'coolie', 2, 41–5, 62, 84, 108, 160, 192, 202
Cotter, Joseph, 55, 57, 69, 80, 91–2, 197
counter-enlightenment, 52–3, 162
Court of Inquiry. *See* Board of Trade, inquiry
Cowling, Mary, 143n10
Coxe, J. C., 119n50
Crozier, Michel, 136n58
culturalism, 14, 162
Cummings, Thomas, 130, 132
Cunard Steamship Company, 152, 178, 199
Curtis, Lewis P., 143n10, 144n12
Cuthbert Laws, 148
cyclopean machines, 122–3

Daily Herald (newspaper), 38, 47, 66, 155, 198–9
Daily Mail (newspaper), 20, 30, 35–7, 42, 48, 60–1
Daily Mirror (newspaper), 60–1, *60–1*
Dalziel, James, 45
Daman, 92, 96
Darby, L. F. C., 73
Das, Rajani Kanta, 171n50
Daud, Mohammed, 67
Davis, Michael Shawn, 216n33
deck crew, 82, 91–2, 105, 108, 117, 120, 129, 137–8, 186–7
dehumanization of the worker, 142–4, 203
de Kerbrech, Richard P., 126, 128n25, 128n28, 132n42–3, 136n60, 138n68, 150n35, 154n51
Delap, Lucy, 27n32, 43n6, 75, 183n2
democracy at sea, denouncement of, 53, 183
depersonalization, 204, 211–12, 217, 223, 225
Desai, Dinkar D., 57n62, 80n35
desertion, 149, 166, 175, 214
  rates, 152–3, 163, 179
  See also jumping ship
De Silva, Antonio Phillip, 91
Detroit, 222–4
diesel, 5–6, 20, 117, 150–2; *see also* coal: transition in shipping from . . . to oil and diesel; oil
discharge books (or certificates), 124, 146, 148–9, 157
Dixon, Conrad, 8, 50n35, 120n54, 124n8, 129n32, 146n19, 149n28, 152n43, 168n33, 183n1, 195n43
'docility' (of Indian seafarers), 9, 13, 88, 146
Donkin, 51–3, 57
Douglas, Gavin, 129n31, 132n41
Dowling, Robert M., 140n1
Drury, Horace B., 152n44

Duff, Joseph, 35
Dundee Advertiser (newspaper), 113
Durand, William F., 136n58, 136n62

Ebert, Friedrich, 202
L'Éclaireur de Nice (newspaper), 30
Economist (magazine), 196
Edgerton, David, 19n11, 151n38
Egypt, Royal Mail Ship
composition of crew, 156–7
crew lists, 191
documentation of accident, 23–4
list of 'native' deck crew, *59*
press coverage of accident, 28–40
sinking, brief account of, 21–2
verdict, 195–8
Engels, Frederick, 142n6
engine-room crew, 92, 137–8, 156, 184. *See also* 'black gang'
Engine Room Practice (Liversidge), 44, 123n7, 125n14, 126n19, 127, 134n49, 136, 155–6, 161, 168n37, 176–7
engineer, ship, 12, 25, 44, 103, 117–18, 120, 123–5, 127–9, 136–8, 145–8, 150, 155–7, 165, 169, 175–6, 209, 214–16, 218–19, 222
An English and Hindoostanee Naval Dictionary (Roebuck), 44, 114–16, 119
Esch, Elizabeth, 3n6, 14n30, 86, 88, 159–60, 161n9
essentialism, 14, 162
ethnic/ethnicity, 44, 85, 190–1
categorization, 14, 83–4, 87, 162, 216, 230,
compartmentalization, 12–13, 45, 157, 159, 164–6, 193, 210, 217
diversity, 217
management-by-, 204
networks, 157–8
segmentation. *See* ethnic/ethnicity: compartmentalization
Evening News (newspaper), 35
Ewald, Janet, 9n19, 125n13, 137n65
exploitation, 4, 132–4, 145, 205, 211

Faqir, Musa (Moosa Fackeer), 92, 97–8, 187, 190–2
Fazuldin, Sabdin (Sabdeen Fazuldeen), 92, 96–7, 103, 106, 185–6
Featherstone, David, 10n24, 56n59
financial crisis of 2008, 10
Fink, Leon, 6n9, 54n54, 146n19, 152n44, 155n55
Finley, Moses, 52n43
Fire and Boat Stations Bill. *See* Boat Stations Bill
Fisher, Michael H., 7, 8n13, 9n21
Fletcher, Max E., 20n18, 150n33
Fox, Stephen, 122n2
Franklin, George Denne, 72
Frey, James W., 9n20
Friedberg, Erhard, 136n58
Frost, Diane, 56n60
Furuseth, Andrew, 38, 155, 214

Gardezi, Hasan N., 107n9, 133n47, 169n40, 206n2, 207n3, 213n19, 215n31, 223n63, 223n65, 225n72
Gardiner, Robert, 17n2
Gardner, Katy, 8n15, 227n78
Garvey, Marcus, 224
gender, 26, 31
and shipping accidents, 26–7, 31, 35–6, 64, 75–6, 81

gender (*continued*)
masculinity, maritime/'civilized', 13, 26–7, 30, 42, 150–1
See also chivalry
Gerstenberger, Heide, 7n10, 12, 114n35, 123, 124n9, 124n12, 126n17, 127n22, 128n25, 129n31, 133n44, 134n49, 135, 136n58, 136n60, 137n65, 146n18, 147n21, 162n11, 165n22, 166n27, 167n30, 175n62, 194n43
Ghadar Party, 220, 222
Ghosh, Amitav, 94n12, 114n34, 115
Ghosh, Deevlana, 9n19
Ghosh, Kaushik, 87n54
Gilbert, James, 78–9
Gillison & Chadwick (shipping company), 181
'globalization' narratives, 10
Goa, 24, 91, 170, 223
Goan stewards, 34, 62, 65–7, 91, 109, 157, 184
Golden Deeds of India (Turnbull and Turnbull), 37
Goodall, Heather, 9n19, 10n24
Gorky, Maksim, *My Childhood*, 212
Gramsci, Antonio, 135, 213
Great War. *See* World War: First
Green, Edwin, 20n16
Green, Nile, 115n40
Gujarat, 114, 170
Guthrie, John, 128n25, 136n60

Hadfield, Robert L., 1–2, 4
Haider, Gulam, 214
The Hairy Ape (O'Neill), 140–58, *144*, 181
Haji, S. N., 153
Hakim, Adi, 56n59
Hall Line, 180
Hamburg-Amerika-Linie (HAPAG), 201
Hanley, James, 178n77
Hansen, Betty, 35
Harcourt, Freda, 16n1, 17n5, 18n8, 174n61
Hardy, A. C., 150n34
Hardy, George, 2–3
Hariharan, K. V., 77n27
Harmsworth, Alfred (Viscount Northcliffe), 20, 35
Harrison, Norwood, *Manual of Lascari Hindustani*, 117–18
Hay, Douglas, 54n53
Haywood, Harry, 223n64, 224, 225n72
Headrick, Daniel R., 122n1
heat cramps, 118, 129–30
hegemony, ideological, 10, 48, 80. *See also* racism/racist: 'common sense'; racism/racist: as hegemonic ideology
Helbig, Karl, 126, *127*, 128, 137n64, 165n22, 167n30
Henderson, Henry, 50
Henry, James, 192–3
heroism, 29–30, *32*, 34, 37, 39, 46, 74
hierarchical communication, 104, 107, 110–11, 189–91
hierarchy, shipboard, 6–7, 12, 53, 117, 120–1, 123–5, 147–8, 155–7, 159, 162–3, 169, 174–5, 182–5, 193–5, 207
Hindustani
maritime (*see* 'lascari bat')
military, 115, 118
Hirachand, Walchand, 78
Hofstede, Geert, 14n29, 162n12

Holland, David, 8n15
Hollingdale, R. J., 54n51
Holt, Thomas, 37n32
Hood, William Hogg, 50n31, 139n69, 149n30, 157n60, 165, 168n35, 178n75, 179n80, 180n82, 183n2
Hoover, Herbert, 159–61
Hope, Ronald, 18n7, 25n29, 127n22
Horniman, Benjamin G., 69, 74, 77
'Horniman's law', 100, 110
Huebner, Erick, 202
Hughes, Patrick, 148–9, 168–9
Hyslop, Jonathan, 9n19, 54n53, 72n7, 125n16, 133n45, 135n55

Iberian maritime technology, 115
illegal arms trade to India, 72
imperialism, 3, 42
  age of, 13, 24, 45, 85
  anti-, 69, 220
  British, 1–2, 16, 84, 160, 220
  British shipping, 17–9, 24
  colonial, 24
  corporate, 19
  trade union, 57
imperial loyalism, 63–4
Inchcape, Earl of. *See* Mackay, James Lyle
India, government of, 22, 67–8, 70, 77, 84, 168, 197
Indian Army (British), 74–5, 115
Indian Chambers of Commerce, 76
Indian Educational Service, 36
Indian National Congress, 222
Indian Ocean
  maritime economy and culture, 9, 115
  seafaring, 7, 43–4, 93
  shipping, 11, 77, 114, 155
Indian seafarers
  age range of trimmers and stokers, 171–2
  deckhands, 43–4, 70, 93, 184 (see also *khalasi*)
  employed in British merchant ships, 49–50, 78, 118, 191–2
  employment of, 8–9, 24, 49–50, 56, 71, 78, 118, 153, 155, 157
  honour to, 79–80
  'iron plaques' for, 202
  lower wages and compensations, 2, 38–9, 56, 153, 162
  photographic representations of, 58–60, *60*
  regional origins, 10, 56, 83, 92, 170–1
  restrictions on employment of, 26, 47, 55, 65, 71, 76–8, 80, 108, 197
  terminology to refer to, 43–4
  See also 'lascar'; Goan stewards
Indian Seamen's Union (Calcutta), 66–7, 69, 80
Indian Seamen's Union Bombay, 65, 67, 80
India Office, 23, 34, 68–70, 110–11, 195, 197, 202
Industrial Workers of the World (IWW), 3, 141, 220, 222
insubordination, 49, 146–7, 149, 170, 176, 179–80, 210
internationalism, 10, 220, 222, 231
International Labour Organization (ILO), 6, 168, 171
Irish
  immigrants, 138–9, 143–4, 154, 162, 179
  'Liverpool-', 154, 162

Irish (*continued*)
racial discrimination of, 143–4, 154
seafarers, 53, 179, 216–7, 220
irrationality, structural, 13–14, 85, 162, 193, 203
Irrawaddy (ship), 116
Ismail, Musa (Moosa), 92, 96

Jaffer, Aaron, 9n21, 114n34
Jan, Svenja von, 72n7, 202n69, 228n81
Jasanoff, Maya, 51n39
Jilla, A. D., 44
jingoism, 26, 46, 70–1, 77, 87
John Bull (magazine), 197–8
Jones, Stephanie, 18n6, 18n9, 19n12, 19n14, 20n15, 20n19, 152n41
Juhn, Chinhui, 126n16
'jumping ship', 175, 211, 213–15, 225

kala admi (black man), 45, 98
Kamp, Jeanette, 175n63
Kennerley, Alston, 124n12, 126n17, 128n25, 128n29, 132n41–2, 133n45, 134n49, 136n60, 137n63–4, 138n68, 166n27, 167n30, 171n49
khalasi, 43–4, 82, 93–4, 96–7, 102–3, 109, 111–12, 187
'khalasi watch', 168–9, 181
Khan, Amir Haider, 106, 107n9, 133, 169–70, 177–8, 180, *206*, 206–31
kharwa, 44. See also *khalasi*
khulasee, 44. See also *khalasi*
Kilroy's Stoking Indicator, 132
Kipling, Rudyard, 2, 40
Kirkby, Diane, 10n24
Kolsky, Elizabeth, 97n25
'Kroo Boys', 55

labour market, 7, 164, 171, 220, 226–7
colonial, 155
competition, 26, 46–7, 54–5,
military, 86
racially segmented, 14, 85–6, 163, 228, 230
labour power, 17, 25
extraction of, 12, 164, 167
overexploitation of, 132–4
racial taxonomies of, 85, 229–30 (*see also* 'race')
labour process, 164, 231
division of labour on steamers, 123, 137, 155, 165–6, 218
internal labour reserve, 172–3, 180–1
labour-intensive, 25, 126, 133–5
maintenance tasks, 129, 166, 174, 177, 180
need for cooperation in, 124, 147, 165, 169–70, 182, 190, 193, 231
need for uninterrupted operation, 25, 132, 166, 175–81
racialized, 12, 14–15, 24, 85, 156–7, 161, 163–4, 226
removal of ashes, 128–30, 132, 148, 168, 174
in steamer stokeholds, 12, 25, 120–81
supervision of, 156, 165, 169, 170–2, 180
transformations of maritime, 6
zones of uncertainty in, 136, 147, 161–2, 165, 167, 172, 182
See also racial management and skills
Lahiri, Shompa, 7n12, 93n9–10
Lancet (journal), 130

Land, Isaac, 147n19–20
Lane, Tony, 124n8, 138n67, 152n43, 176, 211n12, 227
'language test' (for ship's officers), 107–8
lascar
  meanings, 1–2, 43–4, 84
  See also Indian seafarers; *khalasi*
lascar articles. *See* Asiatic Articles of Agreement
Lascar Hindustani for Ship-Surgeons (Parry), 118
'lascari bat', 112–18, 120, 168, 195
Lascari-Bât (Valentini), 116–17, 168
'Lascar money', 57
'Lascars at Boat Drill', *200*
'Lascar War Memorial' (Calcutta), 79
Leatherby, James Norman, 150n32
Le Barzic, Capitaine, 29
Lebowitz, Michael, 86n50
Leder, Wilhelm, 128n24
Leicester Chronicle (newspaper), 198
Lennervald, Dan, 131
liberalism, 13, 37–8, 46, 49, 55, 78f
Linebaugh, Peter, 11
liners, 6–7, 11, 17, 20, 22, 25, 28, 47, 56, 122, 147, 164, 167, 176–8
  companies, 17, 56, 151, 178, 199
  labour management models on, 178–81, 227
  schedules, 176–7, 179
  See also tramp shipping
Liverpool, 7, 56, 116, 138–9, 154, 175, 227
Liverpool Echo (newspaper), 198
Liverpool Shipowners' Association, 173
Liverpool Steamship Owners' Association, 178
Liversidge, John G., *Engine Room Practice*, 44, 123n7, 125n14, 126n19, 127, 134n49, 136, 155–6, 161, 168n37, 176–7
Lloyd, W. W., 130n38
London, 7–8, 46, 72, 90–1, 93, 95, 116, 164, 199, 207–8
Los Angeles Times (newspaper), 35
Losurdo, Domenico, 37n32
Lukács, Georg, 212n16, 229–30
Lyon Republicain (newspaper), 31, *33*

Macedonia (ship), 62–3, 191
Mackay, James Lyle (Lord Inchcape), 18–21, 71, 76, 78
Mackinnon, William, 18
MacMunn, George, 86n52
Malaya (ship), 66
Manchester Guardian (newspaper), 37–8, 42, 48
Manjrekar, Naina, 9n22, 147n23–4
Manual of Lascari Hindustani (Harrison), 117–18
marine engineering manuals, 44, 125–8, 134–7, 161, 176
The Mariner's Friend or Polyglot Indispensable (Ter Reehorst), 119
maritime dictionaries
  English–Hindustani ('lascari'), 44, 114–20, 125, 168
  for European languages, 118–20
maritime lingua franca, 107, 115, 157
maritime logistics, 5, 17
Maritime Session of the International Labour Conference in Genoa (1920), 62
Marseille, 7, 22

Marsh, Arthur, 38n33, 50n35, 54n54, 57n63
martial races, 86–7, 160. *See also* racial management
Marx, Karl, 122–3, 134–5, 142
masculinity. *See* gender
master and servant law, 54
Mauretania (ship), 199
Mazarello, A., 62, 65
McFee, William, 128, 132n41, 133–4, 145–6, 149–51
McKay, Claude, 227
McPherson, Kenneth, 67n28
Mead, Margaret, 221n58
Medina (ship), 66
Meerut Conspiracy Case, 222
Melville, Herman, 116, 158
Mercantile Marine Committee, 46, 49–50, 146, 148, 154, 157–8, 160–1, 173
Mercantile Marine Office
  Liverpool, 50, 132, 173–4, 177
  London, 95
Merry Mount (ship), 217–18
Miller, James J., 218
Minority Movement, 3, 56
Monk, Lee-Ann, 10n24
Monterey, Carlotta, *144*
Montgomery, David, 38n33
Morning Post (newspaper), 37, 198
Moscow, 222–4
Moss, Michael, 20n16
'motley crew', 10–12, 114, 116, 157, 164
Mulkane, Joseph, 220
multilingualism on board ship, 7, 12, 116
Munro, J. Forbes, 16n1, 18n10
Mustafa, Baram (Barrum Mustapha), 75, 92, 97–100, 103, 109–10, 186–7, 203
My Childhood (Gorky), 212

Nadri, Ghulam, 9n20
Napier, Christopher J., 151n40, 152n41
Napoleonic Wars, 8
Nashik Road Central Jail, 223–4
National Transport Workers' Federation, 199
National Union of Seamen (Britain), 46, 55–7
nationalism, 30
  Indian, 69–70, 77–8, 220
  Irish, 220
'native' (seafarer)
  meaning and connotations of, 13, 43–5
  namelessness of, 43, 58, 191, 203, 217
  representation of, 61–2, 70
Nautical Magazine, 148
Nelson, Bruce, 216n33
New York, 7, 140–1, 143, 213–15, 220, 222, 227–8
New York Times (newspaper), 28, 35, 39–40, 42
Nickel, John, 141n3, 145n13
Nietzsche, Friedrich, *Anti-Christ*, 54
The Nigger of the 'Narcissus' (Conrad), 13, 50–5
Northcliffe, Viscount. *See* Harmsworth, Alfred
Notley, Frank Bartlett Stewart, 80–1

occupational health, 129–30
Oceana (ship), 42, 47–8, 112

Odysseus, 52
oil (as fuel), 6, 20, 133, 150–1, 181, 217–19. *See also* coal: transition in shipping from . . . to oil and diesel; diesel
O'Neill, Eugene, *The Hairy Ape*, 140–5, 149, 155
Oscar, Alan, 183n2. *See also* Whall, W. B.
Ouessant (Ushant), 21

Paasch, Heinrich, 119
Palermo (ship), 91, 99, 103
Pall Mall Gazette (newspaper), 36, 41, 196
panic, 31, 38–9, 64–5, 74, 192
  on the part of 'lascars'/'natives', 34, 39–40, 42–3, 81–3, 106, 121, 195, 197–9
pan-Islam, 220
panjari wallah, 92
Pankhurst, Sylvia, 39
Parry, Shedden Chalmers, *Lascar Hindustani for Ship-Surgeons*, 118
Pashtuns ('Pathans'), 34, 83
Pels, Peter, 84n47
Peninsular and Oriental Steam Navigation Company (P&O), 17–24, 29, 34–6, 39, 42, 47–8, 55–6, 62–3, 71, 75–8, 80, 90–2, 95–102, 112–14, 116, 124, 145, 151–2, 155–6, 167–8, 170, 172, 179–81, 183–4, 187, 196–7, 200–1, 227
Perlin, Frank, 85n48
Le Petit Journal (newspaper), 28–32, *32*, 37
Pioneer (newspaper), 72
Piper, Frederick Southwell, 113–14
plantation economy, 87
Plimsoll, Samuel, 54–5
port cities, 7, 11, 46, 83, 175. *See also* Basra; Bombay; Brest; Calcutta; Cardiff; Liverpool; London; Marseille; New York; Southampton
port infrastructure, 5–6
Punjab, 92, 170, 206

Quinlan, Michael, 130, 146n19

'race'
  and assumed behavioural patterns, 36, 42, 73, 81–3
  and class, 13, 41–57, 85, 87, 198, 210. *See also* class
  as essential difference, 125, 145, 161–3
  imaginary 'bonds' of, 54–5, 192
'racial'
  dichotomy versus taxonomy, 87, 96
  discrimination, 93, 98, 141, 193, 223–4, 228–9
  dividend, 55, 197
  exclusion, campaigns for, 26, 37–8, 45–6, 55, 65, 76–7, 87–8, 125, 193, 197, 214, 220, 222
  hierarchy, 13, 24, 34, 53, 125, 155, 218–21, 228
  management, 3–4, 14–15, 85–7, 112, 157–82, 193, 196, 203
  radicalization of alienation, 203–4, 211
  segmentation, 45–6, 157–9, 164–6, 210, 217
  segregation, 47, 193, 210, 214, 216–17, 224

'racial' (*continued*)
subordination, 3, 13, 45, 85, 162, 192
superiority, assertions of, 230
taxonomies, 84–7, 159–61, 172, 181
racialized labour regulation, 3–4, 15, 24, 226
immigration laws, 163, 181, 226–7
work contract, 8, 162–3, 226–7
racism/racist, 13, 34, 45–6, 51
'common sense', 2, 24, 26, 38–9, 42, 228–9 (*see also* hegemony, ideological)
as hegemonic ideology, 13, 26, 38, 45, 192 (*see also* hegemony, ideological)
roots in commodification, 14, 85, 230
'scientific', 35, 85–7, 172
social causes of, 221
stigmatization, 40, 61, 87–8, 138–9, 143, 155, 162–3, 208, 210
terms of abuse for people of colour, 13–14, 38, 41, 45, 50–5, 88, 159, 192, 219, 221
Radcliffe, Henry, 154
Rasul, Abdul (Abdool Rasched [Rasool]), 92, 94, 100
Raza, Ali, 72n7
Rediker, Marcus, 11, 146n18, 175n63
Rees, J. D., 84
Reuters (news agency), 31, 62
Roberts, Stephen E., 133n46, 226n73
Roebuck, Thomas, *An English and Hindoostanee Naval Dictionary*, 44, 114–16, 119
Roediger, David R., 3n6, 14n30, 55n57, 86, 88, 141, 159–61
Roy Chowdhury, K. C., 67–8, 71–2
Royal Indian Marine, 125
Royal Mail Steam Navigation Company, 20
Royal Seamen's Pensions Fund, 57
Ryan, Victoria, 38n33, 50n35, 54n54, 57n63

Safadi, Alison, 115n40, 118
Sager, Eric W., 126n17, 135n57, 136n60, 146n18
Said, Edward, 14n28, 51
Salemink, Oscar, 84n47
Saluppo, Alessandro, 55n56
Samuel, Raphael, 123, 134
Schwerer, Admiral, 29, 31
Scindia Steam Navigation Company, 77–8
Scott, Harry, 73, 193
seamen
African, 3, 13, 54–5, 125, 138, 143, 157, 176 (*see also* 'Kroo Boys')
African American, 143, 216, 228–9
Arab (Yemeni), 24, 55, 125, 176
Chinese, 38, 47, 55, 125, 155
'coloured', 8, 13–14, 26, 55–6, 82, 87, 160, 214, 219, 221, 226
European, 2, 43, 47–9, 62, 65, 78, 81, 102, 125, 153, 156–7, 160–2, 168–9, 171–3, 178–9, 190–1
Filipino, 38
See also Indian seafarers
'sea lawyer', 50, 52, 143
'scientific management' (Taylorism), 86, 132, 135–6, 143. *See also* Frederick Taylor
segmentation of steamship crews. *See* ethnic/ethnicity: compartmentalization
Seine (ship), 21, 23, 28–9

serang (foreman), 91, 101, 103, 111–12, 114, 120, 124, 156, 165, 169–70, 172, 184–5, 187, 191, 195, 209, 227–8
Shaw, Alexander, 71, 76–7
Sherwood, Marika, 8n14, 26n31, 43n8, 46n19, 56n59, 108n12
shipboard conflict, 9, 148, 207, 217, 220, 228
shipmaster, 45, 49–50, 52, 79, 114, 137, 146, 148–9, 157, 169, 183, 188, 199, 214
shipping disasters, 1, 28, 55, 66, 182
  Arabia, 66, 92
  Clan Drummond, 42
  Hammonia, 201–2
  Oceana, 42, 47–8, 112
  Titanic, 22–3, 47
Shipping Federation (Britain), 55, 148
Shipping Subsidies Committee, 179
Singha, Radhika, 31n13, 87
skill, 124–5, 135–7
slavery, 3, 14, 45, 53, 86, 143
Small, George, 116
Smedley, Agnes, 220
smuggling of firearms, 72
Soderberg, Gunnar, 39
Southampton, 178–9, 199, 227
Southby, Enid Corbould, 72
Spry, A. E., 198
Stanziani, Alessandro, 181n86
steam engines, 25, 122, 126, 133, 157
stigmatized labour, 138–9, 141–5, 149, 154–55, 162–3, 181–2, 210
Streets, Heather, 86n52
Sturmey, S. G., 17n3–4, 20n17, 56n60, 167n28
subsidized mail services, 17–18, 48, 77, 179
Suez Canal, 179
suicides at sea, 132–3, 226
Sutherland, Thomas, 179–80
Sylhet, 170

Tabili, Laura, 8, 26n31, 27n32, 45–6, 49n29, 55n58, 56n59, 56n61, 57n62, 154n50, 163, 166n24, 176n67, 201n68
Taylor, Frederick Winslow, 135, 143. *See also* 'scientific management'
Ter Reehorst, Karel Pieter, *The Mariner's Friend or Polyglot Indispensable*, 119
Thakurdas, Purushottamdas, 68
Thiele, Reinhold, 130n38
Thomas, Robert, 36
Thompson, Peter, 126n16
Thorne, William, 78–9
Tilbury docks (London), 72, 100, 103, 183–4
The Times (newspaper), 20, 34–5, 37, 65, 83
Times of India (newspaper), 63–4, 83
tindal (deputy foreman), 82, 92, 1 20, 124, 156, 165, 169, 184–7, 191
Titanic (ship), 22–3, 47, 150. *See also* shipping disasters
Todd, John, 188n27
Todd, Lindi R., 9n19
Tomek, Beverly, 225n72
Toryism. *See* conservatism

trade unionism
British, 23, 37–8, 46–50, 54–7, 69, 87, 108, 153–5, 178, 197–8, 209
Indian, 65–70, 80, 222
US, 38, 141, 155, 214, 220, 222
See also specific unions
tramp shipping, 56, 130, 166–7, 175–6, 178–9, 226. *See also* liners
transfers (of crew), 90–1, 99, 103, 163–4, 184, 207, 209
Traven, B., 227
Tsandis, E. C., 171n50
Tupper, Edward, 46
Turnbull, Eleanor Lucia, 36–7
Golden Deeds of India, 37
Turnbull, Harold George Dalway, 36–7
Golden Deeds of India, 37

US merchant marine, 38, 216, 229
Ushant (Ouessant), 21

Valentini, A. I., *Lascari-Bât*, 116–17, 168
Van Rossum, Matthias, 9n20, 175n63
viceroyalty of India, 18–19
'victimologies', 205
Victoria docks (London), 72, 164
Villain-Gandossi, Christiane, 119n52
violence/violent
of colonial labour regime, 3
colonial 'shooting accidents', 97
corporal punishment, 146–7
counter-, 147–9
extrajudicial, 146, 149, 192–3
homicide, 149
Visram, Rozina, 7
'voicelessness', 53, 55, 62

'wage slavery', 208, 213, 227
Wait, Jim, 51–3, 57
Washington Post (newspaper), 34–5
Watts, Cedric, 50, 51n37–8, 54n50, 54n52
Weber, Max, 85n49
Weberian 'formal rationality', 85
Welke, Ulrich, 12, 114n35, 123, 124n9, 124n12, 126n17, 127n22, 128n25, 129n31, 133n44, 134n49, 135–6, 137n65, 147n21, 162n11, 165n22, 166n27, 167n30
West Hartlepool, 207, 210, 228–9
Whall, W. B. (Alan Oscar), 183n2, 188n27
White Line, 178
white supremacism, 172–3, 193
Whyte, Thomas, 111, 186
William Cory & Sons, 151
Williams, Robert, 199
Williams, Whiting, 46
Wilson, Horace Hayman, 44n10
Wilson, Joseph Havelock, 37, 38n33, 39, 46, 54–6, 153–4
Wolheim, Louis, 144, *144*
Workers' Dreadnought (newspaper), 39
'Workers' Welfare League of India', 69
working-class memoirs, 170, 207, 211–13
working hours, 129, 168–9, 181
World War
First, 6, 10, 16–18, 37, 67, 79, 87, 150, 160, 204, 216
Second, 5–6, 18, 151, 215

'Young Workers' League' in Madras, 223
Yule, Henry, 7n11